# anthony bourdain's

# LES HALLES COOKBOOK

**Strategies, Recipes, and Techniques of Classic Bistro Cooking**

WITH JOSÉ DE MEIRELLES & PHILIPPE LAJAUNIE

Photographs by Robert DiScalfani

BLOOMSBURY

Published by Bloomsbury, New York and London
Distributed to the trade by Holtzbrinck Publishers

All papers used by Bloomsbury are natural, recyclable products made from wood grown in well-managed forests. The manufacturing processes conform to the environmental regulations of the country of origin.

Library of Congress Cataloging-in-Publication Data

Bourdain, Anthony.
    Anthony Bourdain's Les Halles cookbook : strategies, recipes, and techniques of classic bistro cooking / Anthony Bourdain, José de Meirelles and Philippe Lajaunie.
        p. cm.
        Includes bibliographical references and index.
        ISBN 1-58234-180-X (hc)
1. Cookery, French. 2. Les Halles (Restaurant) I. Title: Les Halles cookbook.
II. Meirelles, José de. III. Lajaunie, Philippe. IV. Title.

TX719.B736 2004
641.5944--dc22

                                    2004002399

First U.S. Edition 2004
1 3 5 7 9 10 8 6 4 2

Designed by **Helicopter, New York**
Printed and bound in Italy by **Artegrafica S.p.A., Verona**

TO NANCY

# contents

A man who is rich in his adolescence is almost doomed to be a dilettante at the table. This is not because all millionaires are stupid but because they are not impelled to experiment.

—A. J. LIEBLING

# introduction

This is not a cookbook. Not really.

It will not teach you how to cook.

The recipes, for the most part, are old standards, versions of which you can find in scores of other books.

What's different about this volume is that the recipes are from Les Halles, the New York City restaurant where I have been, since 1998, the executive chef. Which is to say that they are the official recipes from the best goddamn brasserie/bistro in the country. These are the actual recipes—scaled down, of course, from the rather larger-volume requirements of our very busy restaurant.

There may be thousands of bistros just like Les Halles in France—many of them as good—but there is only *one* in America. (Okay, actually there are four. We have three other joints: another one in New York, one in D.C., and one in Coral Gables, Florida. My loyalty is understandably to the Mothership on Park Avenue South, where, for no small amount of time, I toiled regularly behind the stove.) Les Halles is authentic, as authentic as any place can be outside of France.

This book aims to be a field manual to strategy and tactics, which means that in the following pages, I will take you by the hand and walk you through the process in much the same way—and in the same caring, sensitive, diplomatic tone—as I would a new recruit in my restaurant kitchen.

Which means that if, from time to time, I refer to you as a "useless screwhead," I will expect you to understand—and to not take it personally. If you hang in there, do good work, show a little love and respect for the food, I'll probably buy you a beer later at the bar.

I will assume only that you can handle a knife with reasonable competence, without being a danger to yourself or others. That you like

food. That you will show up on time. And I will show you, to the best of my ability, how to organize those great metaphysicals, your time, your space, your state of mind, so as to most efficiently attack each task and each recipe. You will learn how to set up for meals like a professional, how to square away your "station" so that you will be able to work in a lean, mean, clean, and organized fashion without tripping over yourself like some useless grab-ass and ruining my food.

So listen up. You will not do too many things at once. You will not lose your head. You will not run your area of operations (i.e., your kitchen) into a chaotic train wreck. You will learn to prioritize tasks like a cold-blooded professional, breaking down recipes into manageable sections so that final assembly, or "pick-up," will not send you into gibbering paralysis (a.k.a. *dans la merde,* or "in the weeds").

Cassoulet, for instance. You can take a peek now. The recipe is on page 213. Looks like a pretty damn intimidating recipe, right? Jesus! Look at all those ingredients! Don't sweat it, amigo. No professional makes cassoulet from scratch all in one afternoon, or even all in one day. It's actually a relatively relaxing, drawn-out process, mostly conducted in one's leisure time. The dish is broken down into a series of small functions, all performed at a luxuriously relaxed pace, often while doing something else. It's actually one of the easiest recipes on the menu to drill out. Once prepared, final service—in the restaurant and at home—is a "gimme," a line cook's dream. Throw in pot, sprinkle with bread crumbs, toss in oven, and forget about it. This is the sort of dish professionals are happy to get an order for when cooking twelve other things at the same time.

If you can make a decent chili, you can make cassoulet. A lot of the same principles are at work. Don't let the French name fool you. Ever.

You should know that if you can already handle a knife and if you have a small, comfortable repertoire of American or ethnic household standards, then you are already *way* ahead of the vast majority of restaurant professionals when they first pick up a French knife and attempt *frisée aux lardons* on the salad station.

Still scared? Still feel uncomfortable with all those ingredients, all those unpronounceable French names? An early traumatic experience at the hands of a snooty French waiter get your shorts all twisted? What is your major malfunction, dipshit? This stuff is EASY!

At Les Halles, and let me repeat here, the *best,* the most authentic frog pond in the whole damn U.S. of A., almost every single cook in its thirteen-year history has been a rural Mexican with no previous cooking experience. Almost everyone lacks any kind of formal training and entered the business as a dishwasher or night porter. If you think that they spent their childhoods whipping up Mexican regional favorites and developed a natural affinity for food, you are dead wrong, my friend. Ask my *saucier* to make chicken mole and you'll get a blank stare and a middle finger. Back in the old country, Mom did that.

Now, of course, they are, pound for pound, some of the best cooks of *cuisine bourgeoise* in America. I would proudly put them up against any cheese-eating, long-lunch-taking, thirty-two-hour-a-week-working socialist clock-puncher from across the water. Any day. They'd mop the floor with them. This is less a testimonial to my training abilities than it is evidence of the triumph of persistence, hard work, pure hearts, and a sense of humor.

Anyone who says "cooking is in the blood" when talking about professionals is talking out of their ass. *Eating* well is in the blood. An appreciation of the glories of the table, of good ingredients well prepared, is in the blood. The enjoyment of a long lunch—at table with good friends, tearing into the good stuff made with love and pride—*that,* arguably, is in the blood, or at least in your cultural heritage. But you've got that already, right? Otherwise you wouldn't be here. You wouldn't have forked over thirty-five bucks to some publishing conglomerate for this book. Would you?

Well? Would you?

Speak up! I CAN'T HEAR YOU!!

The ability to make a good steak frites or sole meunière or cassoulet is a skill that any reasonably coordinated person with a good heart and an average work ethic can accomplish. We will assume, for the purposes of discussion, that you have both.

Granted, the ability to prepare these dishes a hundred times a night, at high speed, in coordination with twenty or so other tasks—while listening to Mexican rap and nursing a savage hangover—is not something everyone should attempt. That requires a special breed. But that's not what this book is about.

As these dishes are rooted in the history, traditions, and soil of France, you might assume that the "finest ingredients" are the basis of many of the preparations—and thus, in large part, unavailable to you. And it is

absolutely true that good ingredients in season are indeed fundamental to any great cooking. Certainly a recipe will taste a hell of a lot better when you use the very best. But it is a shameful lie when other books on French regional cooking imply that the lush, fire-engine-red, vine-ripened tomatoes, perfect white asparagus, prime beef, and tender, young, free-range chickens you see in their heavily styled, near pornographic photo inserts are necessary to a good final product. The implication that every French housewife and *traiteur* have always been able to slip on their Dockers and their Weejuns, hop in the SUV, and roar off to the organic greenmarket to pay some hippie twice the going rate is nonsense.

The kind of French cooking we're talking about here, the most beloved, old-school, typical, and representative cooking, the wellspring of all that came after, did *not* originate from cooks with a lot of money to throw around. Most of these preparations and recipes evolved from shrewd, enterprising, hard-pressed, dirt-poor people who, like all great cooks, in all great national cuisines, were simply making the very best of what they had. Which, in many cases, was sweet fuck-all.

We have always looked to France as the greatest of chef-driven (as opposed to ingredient-driven) cuisines because France had no other choice but to cook well. For much of its history, French cooks had to be good. Or they'd starve, or go broke. For the most part, good cooks were hungry, they were downtrodden, they had—until the revolution—to continue to please cruel, oppressive, and capricious masters. Every scrap, every root, every snail, every crust of bread was potential money or sustenance. The bedrock elements of a standard American "fancy" high-

end meal—a good steak, lobster, shrimp—were simply unattainable.

To this day, you will have a very hard time finding a piece of steak in France that approaches in tenderness and quality the fat-marbled, grain-fed, antibiotic-jacked sirloin they've got at your local supermarket. Bred for double duty as both meat and dairy, most French beef (with the exception of the extraordinary Charolais) frankly sucks. The "good cuts," meaning the rib eye, the sirloin, and the vastly overrated filet mignon, are still the province of the wealthy few. Leaving the nasty bits to the rest.

Thankfully, the French know what to do with the tough, bony, squiggly, and fatty stuff. And they've been doing it, and doing it well, for years. They are damn good at it. (God bless 'em. Let's give credit where credit is due here.) Short growing seasons, bad transportation, minimal refrigeration, and hard luck are the story behind nearly every great original cook. Make no mistake.

It is no accident that in just about every country you might want to visit, the good cooks seem always to hail from the most ass-backward and impoverished backwaters. Whether it's Minas Gerais in Brazil, Issan in Thailand, the Deep South in the United States, or some depressed, jerkwater burg in France, that's where the good cooks inevitably come from, the cooks "free," as A. J. Liebling put it, "of the crippling handicap of affluence."

Take a long look at the cover of Jacques Pépin's magnificent memoir, *The Apprentice.* Look at young Jacques, age thirteen and a half, standing there frightened but proud in his baggy *commis* outfit. That's old school. You think young Jacques was looking forward to an assured future of sports cars for graduation presents, spring break, frat parties, and a summer abroad when he first struggled into those clothes? No way.

As far as I'm concerned, there's no one more respected or authoritative or better qualified to talk on this subject than Pépin—and there's an episode in his book that's illustrative of this. When talking about the roots of his cooking, he describes his early travails at family bistros: a series of fly-by-night joints run on a razor-thin profit margin by his hardworking mother. Young Jacques and his mother would trawl the markets each morning: first a reconnaissance, followed by a last-minute swoop, grabbing up the very worst products—from the most highly motivated sellers—at the very lowest prices. They would then return to the kitchen to transform all that limp produce and second-best meat into something marketable, something nourishing, something good…something *magical.*

That's what cooking has always been about, at its very essence. Whether we're talking about a one-lung *boui-boui* or a three-star Michelin, it's all about *transformation,* about taking the ordinary and making it extraordinary. *That's* magic. And as any chef, speaking honestly, will tell you, you don't necessarily have to be a magician to make magic. What happens to a soup or stew overnight, completely independent of what cooks may or may not have done, is magic. What happens to bread in the oven is magic. Beef bourguignon and coq au vin, once the ingredients are thrown together in the pot, will become magic all by themselves—as long as you don't mess up the heat. Beloved old warhorse elements of French cuisine like duck or goose confit, which any conscientious cook can easily make, can have an unearthly power over the most cynical culinary professional. All you need is fat, some herbs, garlic, salt, and pepper.

Over the years, I have had the privilege of sittting down with a number of three-starred chefs and culinary gurus and knocking back a few glasses of wine while discussing such things. Asked what single dish they would choose given only a few hours to live, their choice for the last bite to cross their lips, they uniformly pick something homey and simple from their less than luxurious childhoods. The word "mom" or "mother" usually comes up, as do shy smiles and proud declarations, like the one from Le Manoir aux Quat' Saisons' Raymond Blanc: "I am a peasant!"

As a death-row meal, Pépin chose "a good piece of bread—and some good butter." Ferran Adrià has said he'd eat skillet-fried green asparagus, with olive oil and sea salt, and André Soltner is said to have eaten the same thing for lunch nearly every day of his working life at Lutèce: plain buttered fettuccine, with just the slightest bit of foie gras.

One of my favorite stories—and I dearly hope it's true—is about the recently departed and much-missed Jean-Louis Palladin. Asked by an enthusiastic journalist when and how he "decided" to become a chef, he avoided the usual chef spiel, which most of us are all too happy to foist on a credulous public: that we dreamed from childhood of briny sea urchins redolent of the Med; white truffles as big as your fist; big, knobby hunks of filet mignon swimming in *sauce périgourdine*. Palladin, a giant, a titan, a chef's chef, the mention of whose name still causes other chefs' eyes to mist over with affection and respect, looked witheringly at the inquiring journalist and replied, "Why did I decide? When did I decide? …Madame!! My parents sold me into *slavery*!"

Palladin, of course, was a genius. You ain't EVER gonna cook like him. And neither will I. But you do not have to be a genius to cook good French food. French chefs are very rarely even the best and brightest flowers of their far-flung regions of France. Traditionally, the smartest or eldest, the most promising kids, were the ones on whom scant financial resources would be dedicated. They'd be sent off to university. The rest of the kids got packed off to hotel school or an apprenticeship or were left to the tender mercies of Uncle Henri, the local butcher or *charcutier* or pâtissier, under whose tutelage they'd soon, at least, be making a little money.

So. Feel better now?

Having determined that you need be neither prodigy, nor genius, nor to the manor born, and that you do not have to live near a Dean & Deluca or be pals with Alice Waters to cook French food…what *do* you need?

You need the *will*.

You need the desire.

You need the determination to go on—even after you've scorched the first batch of stew, burned the sauce, mutilated the fish fillet, and lopped off a hunk of fingertip.

You need persistence, the ability to understand that with every mistake comes valuable information. I'll tell you what I tell every rookie cook in my kitchen, after he ruins a perfectly good consommé: "Throw it out.

Start over. Do you understand what you did wrong? Good. Now don't do it again." Know that you can *read* about breaking a butter sauce all you like; until you've actually broken it—just when you needed it—you won't understand it on an instinctive, cellular level. Screwups are good. Screwups—and bouncing back from screwups—help you conquer fear. And that's very important. Because some dishes *know* when you're afraid. They sense it, like horses, and will—as my friend Fergus Henderson will tell you—"misbehave."

Eventually, your hands, your palate, even your *ears* will learn, they will *know* when things are going right, and will sense in advance when things are in danger of going wrong.

Do not be afraid.

You will need a pure heart, and a soul, meaning you are cooking for the right reasons.

You don't collect and cook recipes, or compile dining experiences, like a butterfly collector. You must enjoy what you're doing. If there is any real sin in the culinary universe, it is the sin of snobbery. If you're afraid of a little grease on your chin or of eating with your hands, are squeamish about bones, fish heads, and guts, are ambivalent about garlic, are too precious with your food, then put this book down now (you probably didn't get any food on it yet) and return it. It's not for you. Buy another cookbook. One with lots of purty pictures.

You need passion, curiosity, a full spectrum of appetites. You need to *yearn* for things.

Chefs' appetites and enthusiasms, you may have noticed, rarely end with food. I am deeply suspicious of any cook who is less than enthusiastic as well about sex, music, movies, travel—and LIFE. A few years back, dining with friends at one of the "best" restaurants in the country, we sat back, after many courses of lovely but sterile, artfully arranged plates of food, curiously unsatisfied. I wondered aloud what was wrong. One of my companions suggested that the chef "cooked like someone who's never been properly fucked in his life."

You need love.

Hopefully it's love for the people you're cooking for, because the greatest and most memorable meals are as much about who you ate with as they are about what you ate. But love for what you're doing, and for the ingredients you're doing it with, will more than suffice. I suggested once to a maniacal barbecue professional that cooking well was not a profession, it was a calling. He laughed and went further: "It's an illness." I knew just what he meant. You must like cooking for other people, even if you neither know nor like them. You must enjoy the fact that you are nourishing them, pleasing them, giving the best you've got.

You must ultimately respect your ingredients, however lowly they might be. Just as you must respect your guests, however witless and unappreciative they might be. Ultimately, you are cooking for yourself.

—ANTHONY BOURDAIN
NEW YORK CITY, 2004

# les halles

## What the Hell Is It?

I came to Les Halles in 1998 after my previous venture, an absurd Ed Sullivan–themed restaurant-nightclub, finally shriveled up and died. I answered an ad in the *New York Times,* and after a midafternoon interview with José de Meirelles, I wasn't so sure I wanted to sign on. It was the interview hour, that dead zone between lunch and dinner, when restaurant dining rooms are at their very saddest and ugliest. The walls and ceilings, which have still never been painted, were nicotine-stained and spattered with wine from a thousand popped corks. A long butcher counter by the door, momentarily unattended by a butcher, was filled with roasts, sausages, tripe, and steaks. In the merciless late-afternoon light, with no one in the dining room, no mood lighting, and a bored-looking bartender pretending to work by repeatedly mopping the bar with a side towel, the room had the all-too-familiar look of a place where nothing was happening—or was likely to happen soon.

José was nice enough, but his accent threw me. I thought he was French, from some region of France with which I was unfamiliar. The Auvergne? Savoie? Could he be Corsican? I didn't know. (He is, in fact, a proud but extremely Francophile Portuguese.) He insisted on speaking French with me, and as Les Halles had traditionally liked a genuine Frenchman at the helm in the kitchen, he appeared eager to convince himself that the American with the French-sounding name was, in fact, French. At one point, he suggested that should I take the job, we could, for public consumption,

turn the inappropriate Anthony Michael into the more marketable Antoine-Michel. This did not, I thought at the time, bode well.

The kitchen looked small, dirty, and grim, like a Second World War–era submarine with bowed, carbon-encrusted pans and stoves that appeared prehistoric. Stains had spread across the acoustic tile ceiling like infected wounds, indicating leaks, and the downstairs prep areas were even less cheerful.

Dining-room tables were tiny and set with white paper and unimpressive glassware. Chairs, bar stools, and mirrors reflected years of neglect and abuse. In that light, and through the prism of my own unhappy circumstances, the restaurant looked doomed to failure. I was not charmed by the black-and-white photographs of meat-laden butchers on the walls, nor by the French bistro posters, and the French pop tunes on the sound system grated on the remainder of my hangover.

The interview concluded with José inviting my wife and me to dinner the following Tuesday to "see what it's all about."

I left that day determined to pass on both the dinner and the job. I'd picked up on a bad vibe (something I'm usually very good at), a vibe of something—sloppiness, informality, too much enthusiasm from the boss—all things I'd learned to be instinctively wary of after twenty-eight years in the business.

I had no idea, of course, that Les Halles'

patina of neglect was in fact a deliberate, fiendishly clever, calculated, and soon-to-be-trend-setting strategy.

"I'm not taking it," I told my wife.

But she wanted steak frites. She was thinking about onion soup. "What? Are you nuts? We're broke! I'm hungry. It's a free French meal! I want a good steak frites! Let's go! We'll eat. You don't have to take the job!"

So, because my wife wanted steak frites, we went. And we ate. And I fell in love with Les Halles.

Unlike my first visit, this time when we arrived, the place was packed to the rafters, absolutely jammed, with people lined up out into the street. The butcher counter was covered with the glasses of people waiting for tables, while waiters in white, one-shouldered aprons hurried around the small, dimly lit dining room, squeezing deftly between tables. It was dark. So dark we could barely read the menu. And it was loud. The clatter of a hundred or so very happy customers, all of them leaning into dishes, eating and talking with abandon, competed with yells from the kitchen, a warbling Edith Piaf on the stereo, the ring of the register. Something clicked. I knew, even before my food arrived, that I was going to love it.

There was stuff on the menu I hadn't seen since childhood summers in France: *rillettes de porc! boudin noir! merguez! pied de cochon!* I felt myself slipping into a blissful fugue state, caught up in the sheer Frenchness of it all. I ordered a crock of lovely, extravagantly fatty rillettes, followed by a dinosaur-era roast loin of pork with prunes. Nancy got

her soup and her steak. I was thrilled to see that the place served the defiantly nonbogus *rumsteck,* as opposed to the cowardly sirloin obligatory in most faux brasseries. The frites were served with a chipped crock of deliciously heart-clogging béarnaise. My pork was old school, with a heavily reduced brown jus and roasted potatoes. It was perfect. The real deal. After years of wandering the culinary margins, messing about with metal rings and avocados, I was home.

A bottle or two of Gigondas, a *tarte aux pommes,* and an as-it-should-be *crème brûlée* later, I decided I would take the job.

I've never regretted it.

I should point out here, by the way, that I am in no way responsible for the creation of Les Halles. They've been making steak frites and steak tartare and most of their menu dishes the same way for years. They were successful before I arrived and will, no doubt, be successful long after I jump the shark and join Rocco DiSpirito on *Hollywood Squares.* The restaurant opened in 1990, the creative issue of José and his business partner Philippe Lajaunie—who'd been sous-chef and waiter, respectively, at Park Bistro—and Park Bistro chef Jean-Michel Diot (now the owner of San Diego's Tapenade). Apparently, they'd been thinking about meat. The conventional wisdom of the late 1980s dictated that relatively fat-free fish and grilled chicken were what the dining public craved. The dining public wanted infused sauces that had never seen bones, fat, or flour. They wanted vegetables.

But Philippe had been reading Emile Zola's foodie classic *The Belly of Paris* and had been thinking about all those bistros around the old nineteenth-century central marketplace (*les Halles*) in Paris. The bistros were places where a market worker in a bloodstained apron could kick back after work, buy a glass of *gros rouge,* and, if he had some tripe or a hunk of shank pilfered from the market, could have it cooked for him. Philippe had been further inspired by a recent trip to Ecuador, where he'd visited a steakhouse with a long meat display counter by the door where one could select one's *asado* and have it cooked to order.

José and Jean-Michel had been thinking about a place where they could get some hand-ground fresh steak tartare, made the old-school way (raw, fresh, and mixed tableside), or a good steak frites. A bold, unfashionable, and carnivore-friendly concept began to take shape.

At the time, there was little evidence that the New York dining public shared the trio's enthusiasm for slabs of French-cut meat, raw beef, high-fat charcuterie, and organ meat. More than one prospective partner declined, recoiling in horror at the absurdity of it all. But when the doors opened, Les Halles was immediately besieged. Displaced Frenchmen, nostalgic New Yorkers looking to relive happy moments, fashion models taking a break from dietary regimes, reactionaries, meat-eaters, mobs of people who were simply sick to death of the little-food-big-plate-candy-ass-low-fat creations of the day—they all recognized Les Halles as a place where you could dress down, cut loose, gnaw bones, suck marrow, talk loudly, drink a little too much wine, and have a good time.

The restaurant has stayed busy nearly every day since then—lunch, dinner, weekends, holidays, and national disasters.

The brasserie craze of a few years back brought a lot of competition. For a while, every idiot with a string of overpriced rug-joints or fusion lounges seemed to be busily distressing chairs, deliberately cracking mirrors, and covertly photographing our genuinely nicotine-stained ceiling in order to get that "authentic" tobacco shade. (Apparently, a mix of India ink and tea works well.) A lot of these places opened up, the kind of places that keep a few orders of tripe in the freezer just so they can write *tripes* on the "real French" signs out front. Generally, their waiters are too good-looking (and pronounce *vichyssoise* as "veeshy-swah" and *niçoise* as "nee-swah"). Their onion soup is watery, their steaks boring sirloins, and their frites suck, the same frozen Simplot Classics (or painstakingly ruined imitation of same) as at every other TGI McFunsters. Specials are too modern, the cheese is unripe (Brie, of course), their prices too high, and if they're popular, like one place in the Meatpacking District, they treat you like a steaming loaf of dung if you're not a hot young actor on OxyContin.

At Les Halles, we treat everybody the same. If you're beautiful or famous, we'd *like* to be extra nice to you. We really would. But you're still waiting for your table. You're still gonna be packed in cheek by jowl with the other customers—and at the same time—and the waiters are still going to talk to you like you're a brother-in-law. We're just too busy. And we've been around too long to care who you are. You're smart enough to have found your way to us. That's qualification enough. You've made it past the meat counter. Presumably, you really like meat. You like our kind of French food. You're one of us.

# general principles

While you may, for very good reasons, not wish to be one of us, you would do well to emulate professional cooks in certain aspects of your efforts at home. You should, whenever and to whatever degree possible, begin to think like a chef.

The absolute foundation of professional cooking, and the most useful thing I can teach you, is the concept of *mise en place*. As a cook, your "meez" is your first principle, your belief system, your religion, your Tao. All else springs from this basic relationship with your food and your environment. Literally speaking, *mise en place* means "put in place," but it is so much more than that.

For the professional, one's meez is an obsession, one's sword and shield, the only thing standing between you and chaos. If you have your meez right, it means you have your head together, you are "set up," stocked, organized, ready with everything you need and are likely to need for the tasks at hand.

You know where everything is. You know how much you have. (The right amount, of course.) As a result, your mind is similarly arranged, rested, and ready to cook—a perfect mirror of your work area.

In less metaphysical terms, having your meez together means that you have cleaned and cleared your work area in advance and have assembled every item of food and every utensil and tool you will require, and put them in accessible, comfortable locations, ready for use. You have already thought out what you are going to do, meaning you have read the recipe, broken it down into its constituent parts, and formed a coherent plan of attack. You have everything. *Everything* you will need is at the ready, including side towel, oven mitt, hot water for quick cleaning, trash receptacle, favorite music. EVERYTHING. Once you've got food on the stove you do *not* want to have to break away chasing after a garbage bin or a towel or even a sprig of parsley. You need parsley? You will *know* where it is. Because you pre-positioned it there just a little while ago.

Try this when preparing for your next meal: Put everything in a heap in front of you. Every ingredient. Every tool. Then think. Think about the stages to follow. As you reflect on what you are going to do, and when, and where you're gonna put all this, a plan will emerge:

"Well…I won't be needing the cream until later, so I'll put that in the fridge. Someplace I can grab it quickly when I need it…The butter…Hmmm. It would be nice if it were soft when I use it. I'll leave that out." And so on. THINK! Generally speaking, any recipe has three distinct stages, often separated by considerable periods of downtime. This is good. This will mean that even with the more complicated dishes, you will often have time for a drink or a nap.

## THE THREE STAGES OF WISDOM

### DEEP PREP

This refers to all the time-consuming, unglamorous tasks like peeling and chopping garlic, washing vegetables, peeling shallots, making stock, preparing the more durable "mother" sauces, basic scraping, boning, tying, chopping, and scrubbing. In a restaurant situation, dishwashers and rookie cooks usually perform these tasks. So even you should have no problem. All you need is time, patience, and ruthless attention to detail.

### PREP

This is where you prepare all your basic ingredients, measured in the amounts you will need. They will be chopped, blanched, pre-seared, softened—in every way brought as far along as you can bring them without compromising (too much) the quality of the finished product. For example: risotto. If you're making risotto for your guests and only begin cooking when they're sitting at the table,

drinking your liquor, then I admire you as a person of principle. But as a host you are a disaster. While you're in the kitchen, stirring away over low heat like some smug, self-satisfied prima donna, your guests are getting impatient and ugly drunk and are spilling your best single malt on your couch. They're rifling your medicine cabinet. And they're talking about you behind your back. Restaurants generally half cook their risotto and spread it out, still pellet hard, to cool on sheet pans. When they get an order, they finish it, taking it the rest of the way in half the time. Does this impact the quality of the finished product? Well…yes. A bit. But one must constantly make value judgments like this. Which is better? Perfect risotto (which your by-now hammered guests will probably be blissfully unaware of) or happy, well-fed guests? You decide. Presumably, you know your friends.

Generally speaking, during the prep period, prior to the arrival of your victims, you will bring your ingredients to the next-to-last stage, then arrange them, like an artist's palette, at the ready, using cute little crocks or packets of plastic wrap—whatever works for you. You do not want to be measuring out ingredients when showtime comes. Unless you're talking about salt, pepper, a pinch of this, a pinch of that, you want it to be measured, ready, and easy to grab. Your butter for finishing a sauce will be ready and on station. It will be fucking SOFT. You will *not* be staggering around the kitchen like a headless chicken later, looking for a knob of butter, frantically warming it in your filthy hands. Flour needed for dredging? It's right there, next to the fish fillet you were planning on rolling around in it. Beaten eggs? Unless you're talking about making an omelette (last minute, please), they're there, good to go. Diced vegetables? Ready. Tomato *concassé*? Check. You will, during the prep phase, do everything you can to get ready for final assembly.

Prep, by the way, should be fun. In fact, many

professionals, I among them, find prepping to be much more enjoyable—even deeply satisfying—than the actual *à la minute* cooking of the finished dish. There is something really great about transforming a big heap of raw ingredients into an organized array of useful foodstuffs. Putting an old Curtis Mayfield soundtrack on the sound system, working at one's own pace, one attains a relaxing, almost Zen-like state of calm. From chaos, one slowly but surely creates order. And when the work is done, and the music's over, there is no more beautiful moment than when one takes stock of the fruits of one's labors, everything in its place, one's meez complete, a moment of true beauty, certainty, and nearly limitless possibilities.

## FINAL ASSEMBLY

Your meez is complete, all ingredients are taken to the next-to-last stage, everything is conveniently at hand. If, for example, duck confit or demi-glace is required, you have it right there, staring at you. Hell, you finished *that* yesterday. All your garnishes, dry ingredients, herbs, *everything* is sitting out, in appropriate amounts, in your own, hopefully hyperarranged, fashion. READY TO USE.

Your guests arrived (or imminently arriving), you approach the work area, having determined way ahead of time the sequence of events to follow. You look at the clock, take a deep breath, and you begin.

You have already, long ago, made some important decisions about exactly how far along you have taken each dish. Once the appetizer is served, you don't want to be hopping out of your chair to tend to the next course. Cooking for a date, you do not want to leave the object of your affection alone and shuddering with

desire at the table, while you struggle with a last-minute *beurre rouge* in the kitchen. Many dishes are fragile. They sense desperation. If you're racing and sweating to finish up a hollandaise before the mood is lost, your sauce will know it—and will break every time. Food respects confidence, and abhors uncertainty. Unless you are one cool, calm, cocky son of a bitch who wants to dazzle guests with his talent in the kitchen—to make them marvel at your grace under fire as you peel the sizzling hot outer fat off a veal shank at the very last minute and chop fresh herbs to order—then don't overreach. The culinary theater you had in mind might well end with second-degree burns and the sight of you hopping around the kitchen, dribbling sauce down your shirtfront.

Ask yourself always: How far can I take this dish? Can I sear the roast, or the duck breasts, ahead of time? Then just pop them in the oven to finish when the guests arrive? Will that béarnaise sauce hold up in a thermos without poisoning my loved ones? Or should I attempt a last-minute emulsion under their bemused gaze?

Don't sneer.

It's what we do every day in restaurants. The age-old question of durability versus quality. The quest for the perfect balance between what's good, and what's serviceable.

Prioritize.

Most questions that arise are easy to answer. If you're asking yourself whether you should dress the green salad before the guests arrive, the answer is always, *always,* "No." But for thornier questions like "Should I blanch the penne (very al dente, of course), then spread it, unrinsed, moistened with a little olive oil, on a sheet pan, and then give it a dip before finishing it in sauce at the last minute?" you will have to look deeper into your heart and the hearts of your guests. (If it's dry penne, I'd say blanch, by all means. Fresh penne? No. But then you shouldn't be using fresh penne anyway.)

Some of the more delicate and fragile flowers of the classic brasserie repertoire, such as sole meunière, anything souffléed, and most sauté dishes, absolutely require constant attention, from beginning to end. They have to be cooked at the last minute, then served piping hot and damn fast. Unless you're cooking for close, close friends—people who've seen you naked, and for whom sitting around the table, in the kitchen, watching you cook is a pleasure—then these are bad choices for home entertaining.

If you are unsure of your abilities or your skill at timing courses, or are in a situation where you absolutely MUST NOT fail (boss over for dinner, girl/boy of dreams giving you one shot to get them in the sack), then think like a country club or banquet chef when selecting your menu. Think *durable*. Think food with a wide margin of acceptability. Dishes that can take a beating, absorb a few tiny errors without noticeable effect: Braised dishes. Stews. Roasts. Reheatable dishes, without any bright colors that might fade or turn to sludge. When company shows? Just reheat, garnish, and serve.

Just like the pros.

When guests arrive, you get to linger over drinks with them and seat them in an unhurried manner, and then, with a few final flourishes, you crank up the heat, arrange on the plate, jam a few sprigs of chervil or rosemary on top—and you look like a freaking prodigy, seemingly effortlessly whipping out a dish that actually took hours, or even days, to prepare. You are now free to join your friends at the table for an evening of carefree conversation and savage drinking, happily sucking up all that well-deserved praise. You might even be able to enjoy your own food.

# [ Part A ]
# scoring
# the good stuff

I'm a list fanatic. Write it down on a list, I believe, and there is far less chance that you will ever find yourself beginning a sentence with the pathetic excuse, "Sorry… I forgot to…"

The very process of writing a list clarifies and focuses the mind. Write enough of them and you will begin to think in lists, automatically prioritizing. While this can leach into your personal relationships and be hell on your friends and loved ones, it makes for crisper and more efficient cooking.

Before you go to the market to shop for supplies, it is a very good idea to have a shopping list. While your shopping list should be a fairly free-flowing document, your prep list, once written, should be a rigid, inflexible manifesto, tyrannical and unwavering in its requirements. On both lists, every task, every item, should be written in neat, legible fashion, to be ticked off as it is accomplished.

This is an exercise in behavior modification as much as anything else.

Once completed, it is a very good idea, I've found over the years, to allow yourself at least one evening—and a full night—to think about your lists, to dream about your meal plans. After choosing what you plan to prepare, reviewing the recipes, making general shopping plans and a plan of attack—even drafts of shopping and prep lists—it is beneficial in the extreme to allow your mind to wander freely, returning of its own volition to the job to come. Surprising ideas, stratagems, changes, and improvisations will come to you. Second thoughts will win out over initial brainstorms and excessive zeal. A full evening only partially occupied with the imminent meal, and a night's sleep, are often followed by concentrated hours of inspired and creative productivity.

No matter how well you've planned,

conceptualized, and considered, however, once you set to market, plans change. You *must* react to what you find (or don't find), adjusting your plans according to quality, availability, and seasonality, and the best advice of people smarter and more knowledgeable than you. Chances are, your fishmonger knows more about lobster than you. If he rolls his eyes, sighs, and suggests that maybe now is not the best time for lobster, he's almost inevitably right. You would be well advised to listen.

You may have thought you wanted to make strawberry tart when you headed out to the market, your head filled with visions of the brightly colored *fraises des bois* set on a picnic table in France you saw in a magazine or cookbook. But this is not France—and chances are, strawberries aren't in season, and the Californian or Mexican ones, sitting in neat rows at the supermarket, are woody, watery, flavorless, and unripe.

Time for a change of plans.

You thought you wanted mussels, but the ones you find at the market seem to be gasping their last. Half of them are open…and there's a distinct whiff of low tide. Maybe today's not the day for mussels.

Much of the time you're screwed before you even arrive at the market. These days, show up at a supermarket butcher counter looking to score some pork belly or *onglet* or even a beef shank, and you're likely to get a blank stare from the well-pimpled neophyte "butcher" sawing sirloins on a band saw near the back. Try to find a really fresh piece of codfish in, say, Omaha, and you will very

likely be disappointed. Fresh crawfish, decent scallops, Dover sole? Good luck.

I feel your pain. I really do.

But what did I tell you about thinking? And planning, numbnuts!?

America is not France. In fact, France, if you listen to agro-activists there, is increasingly becoming not France. Not the France, certainly, of those pornographic cookbooks you've been beating your meat to.

## RECONNAISSANCE

Before you even pick out a recipe, you should familiarize yourself with what's on the market. You don't even have to buy anything. Just look. Make yourself aware. Talk to people who know. Armed with real information, you can then return to this book, for instance, secure in the knowledge that "Hey, those carrots looked good! And the butcher says he's always got some nice beef shoulder. Maybe (daube of beef) is a good idea!" You think that our role model, Madame Dupont, in some tiny town in the Gironde can just wander over to the fish market and say, "Donnez-moi a nice piece a freakin' cod—and make it snappy"? No way.

First of all, Madame, being French, would never be so foolish as to plan a meal around a fish she has no reasonable expectation of finding on the day of the event. Second, cod is a very, very perishable item. Even if the fish guy has cod, it might very well not be up to Madame's rigorous standards.

Simply put: If you're going to put all the time and work and thought into preparing a nice meal for your friends, you'd better be damn sure you're actually going to have all the ingredients you need. You would be particularly foolish to go out and buy nearly everything you need for bouillabaisse, only to find that the central ingredients are unavailable. There are plenty of things you can substitute. Farm-raised supermarket salmon for monkfish or striped bass is not one of them.

You can swap a good-quality, freshly killed kosher chicken for *poulet de Bresse*—at least as far as our needs are concerned. But you can NOT substitute kielbasa for *boudin noir*.

What to do? What to do?

Good cooks do not exist in a vacuum. They are at the very end of a long supply train that begins, in our fortunate case, all over the world. You need friends to navigate. You need connections. You need to be a citizen of the world—or, at least, of your local markets.

Think of food like drugs. If you were a druggie, and you moved to a new and unfamiliar town, chances are you wouldn't know where to score your drug of choice. First thing you'd do is seek out other drug users. You'd pick out an obvious spot, like the parking lot of a methadone clinic, a bad part of town, a pawnshop, a Phish concert, and you'd make "friends" with fellow travelers of similar interests. Soon, no doubt after a few bad experiences, some trial and error, you would find what you need.

Same thing with food. Kind of.

The acquiring of food is, or should be, a series of personal relationships, involving, over time,

continuing business transactions and no small amount of trust. Ideally, your butcher knows what you like and where to get it, and trusts you to show up on the appointed day and pay for what he has "fronted" money to get for you. You, in turn, trust your butcher to supply what he said he would, and *when* he said he would. You trust that the quality will be good, that you will be charged a reasonable price for it—and that he has not been grinding dead zoo animals into your pâté mix.

This kind of relationship takes time; but as with any great relationship, it will hopefully endure. It takes shrewdness and people skills to be a good shopper. In a sense, what you are looking to engage in is what the Central Intelligence Agency, in their training materials, refers to as "agent recruitment and development."

First, you need to find a butcher. This, sadly, is no small task in our increasingly homogenized, standardized, sanitized übermarket-choked country. The guy behind the counter at Costco is unlikely to have veal foot or pig's feet or tripe festering in his cooler all year, waiting for you to show up and buy them.

So the first task is to find a butcher (and a fishmonger and a produce guy and a specialty purveyor) who recognizes what kind of lunatic cook you are and is willing to work with you. In a perfect world, you should have two or three of each. This will take time, persistence, and patience. But you said you loved to cook, right? Were you lying? Stop whining. Don't put the book down and head for the Chee•tos. This part should be fun. Go to the Yellow Pages. Search online. Find the culinary societies, foodie groups, professional suppliers, and food nerds in your area. There always are some. Pump the chefs at your favorite restaurants for information on their suppliers, advice, introductions, telephone numbers. If you're a good, regular customer, you might well be able to score some items directly off them. If you're generous enough to regularly send drinks back to the kitchen, there's no telling how helpful a well-disposed professional can be.

When looking for a butcher, for example, you are looking for an independent operator, someone not answerable to some corporate behemoth in some industrial park in another state. You want a guy who owns his own store and doesn't mind placing special orders for good customers. It is entirely likely that such a person would be happy to have a customer for the occasional shank or shoulder or kidney, as this is often stuff that would otherwise end up in the grinder—or the trash. If he can sell that breast of veal, it means he can pay less himself for the whole primal section when he buys for his veal chop and roast customers. As he knows better than anyone, every time his wholesaler puts a knife to the meat he buys, he pays more per pound. If he has a few regulars he can count on when he's planning to make a buy for veal chops, people he can call and say "Hey! I'm getting some beautiful milk-fed veal in on Friday. I'll have some kidneys, some lovely kidney fat to cook fries in, and some nice shoulder for blanquette," then that's a beautiful thing. That's exactly the kind of relationship you're looking for.

If you buy all your meat from him and, of course, loudly and actively recruit all your friends to do the same, you can perhaps go in

on a case of *onglet* now and again. You can buy a trunkful of veal bones for next to nothing, have a stock-making party, and your whole foodie circle can load up their freezers with veal stock and demi-glace. Even if you have no friends, as a regular customer you can surely convince your butcher to order you something special. He knows where to get it.

There is the added advantage that many longtime butchers and fishmongers like a lot of the esoteric stuff themselves, so they might well be pleased to have a customer who's actually interested in what they knew all along to be good. Tell a fishmonger to keep an eye out for some nice-looking trash fish, fish heads, fish racks or roes—and show a willingness to pay him for it—and you will make him very happy. You might even score some bones for fumet for free.

A good butcher or fishmonger is a thing of beauty. He will cut the product the way you want it. Make suggestions how to cook it. Unfortunately, they are also a vanishing breed. So when you find one, bring that person into your circle of acquaintances and don't let go.

But let us assume the worst. There is no independent butcher or fishmonger in your sorry-ass corner of suburban sprawl, only strip mall after strip mall filled with shrink-wrapped sirloin steaks and graying chopped meat. Here's another strategy.

One of the great things about America, if not the greatest thing, is that so many people not from America live here now. Large numbers of South and Central Americans, Europeans, and Asians have spread through even the formerly most Wonder-bread spaces of our vast interior, building communities, opening restaurants—and, best of all, starting up their own supply trains. All over the unjustly maligned Midwest and in Texas, for instance, there are significant Vietnamese and Laotian neighborhoods of varying size, and these people like to eat like they did back home. Thank God they do. Because they are often the saving grace in towns where there would otherwise be nothing but Outback and Chili's and the Colonel and the freakin' Cheesecake Factory.

You want fresh black cod, or feathered tripe, or pig's feet, or fresh-killed chicken or blood or uncured pork belly? Find where they're getting theirs in the Asian community, friend. Fresh fish is a religion in much of Asia. If there's a Chinatown or an Asian market near your area, you can almost always find the good stuff. Need esoteric pork products? If the Asians don't have it, the Mexican or Latino market will. Duck? I believe the Chinese know a thing or two about that particular animal, yes? Eastern European Jews certainly know about chicken. When you can't find any hippie-raised free-range stuff, there's always kosher. If you're lucky enough to have Hasidim in any number around, there is every likelihood of fresh-killed poultry. If you need lamb that was saying "baaa-baaa" yesterday, a Muslim halal butcher shop is the place to go. In all likelihood, there's someone in your family who is not from these shores who likes it the old way. Maybe it's time to pump Granny for information on where she used to get her pig knuckles and real sauerkraut back in the old days. Who knows, the store might still be there.

Above all, do not be a snob. It's the worst sin there is for a cook. Always entertain the possibility that something, no matter how

squiggly and scary looking, might just be good. Veal feet are some of the nastiest-looking objects ever to appear in a shop window, but once you've made a stew or stock with those bad boys (all that lovely natural gelatin and flavor), I guarantee you'll change your opinion. The cute little bunnies hanging upside down in the window of the Chinese butcher shop might make your children cry, but they will sure taste good braised. A butcher who displays poultry with heads still on is just the kind of guy you're looking for. He could well turn out to be your best friend.

There will be some ingredients that you are simply not going to find easily where you live. The Tarbais beans you are advised to use in the cassoulet recipe (page 212), for instance, are going to be very tough to locate. I have thoughtfully provided information on some suppliers (page 288) who will be all too happy to send the stuff by mail. Most of these guys require minimum orders, so I suggest you get a catalog and shop around. Load up on nonperishable hard-to-find goodies. If the same company sells Tarbais beans and boudin noir, buy some boudin too, and toss it in the freezer. Sexy dried mushrooms, high-quality vanilla beans, white anchovies, imported canned tuna like you've never had, all sorts of cute oils and vinegars, legumes, foie gras, sea salt, spices, and the like will last forever. Buy lots and your larder will always be at the ready. You will be the envy of your friends.

As painful as it might be, it's also a good idea to suck up a little at the overpriced "gourmet specialty shop." You know the one. The guy selling tiny, ridiculously expensive bottles of white vinegar with sprigs of thyme in them, at postapocalyptic prices. Even if he stocks nothing more interesting than expensive canned tomatoes, he very likely knows, or at least has an idea, where to get what you need. He's on the mailing lists. He's inundated with catalogs every week.

Produce is tough. Produce is perishable. Asparagus, if not in season or available near you, may well be in season somewhere else—usually for a lot of money. With produce it is advisable to use what is good and fresh and prime locally, but if you must have Cavaillon melons from France, so be it. However, if you need only two melons, and your produce guy doesn't stock them (and why should he?), he is unlikely to order them for you unless you go for a whole case. Wholesale produce is sold by the case—and what's he going to do with the rest after he's taken care of you? He's stuck watching his profits rot. Alternatively, what are *you* going to do with a whole case of very expensive melons?

So unless you can go in with some friends, form an impromptu food co-op, the smart thing to do is choose something else.

Always scout produce markets early before making hard-and-fast plans. There may be nothing better than a fresh cèpe mushroom in season, but there are few things sadder than a dirty, woody, and old one. If there is no reason to expect beautiful wild mushrooms in the market, and you can't get them by mail order, then scratch the mushrooms already. Adapt. Ask yourself instead, "What is good now?" and proceed accordingly.

A fresh peach tart can be a revelation. But if you think you're making one in January, you are dangerously deluded. Sure, you can likely get some peaches off a plane—at twice the price—but why would you? In winter, you should be thinking about turnips and parsnips and cabbages and beautiful little spuds, not about tomato salad.

Same goes for fish. Check with the fish guy first. Call him. Ask, "What's good? What will be good tomorrow? Do you have any reason to expect softshell crabs in February?" Fuck no!

Which will often be followed by "but I've got some really nice…"

Some unscrupulous merchants will be all too happy to accommodate even your most egregious imaginative folly. Fish Guy reaches into the cooler and pulls out what are clearly frozen last-season leatherback softshell crabs, you have to ask yourself if maybe you should wait until spring. Unless you want your softshell crab sauté amandine to suck, then you know the answer.

Nothing illustrates the chronic, delusionally determined drive toward mediocrity better than the tomato. Walk into any middle-of-the-road Italian restaurant and you will surely find the inevitable "mozzarella and tomato caprice." Most of the year, if you're foolish enough to order it, you will receive a few shamefully unripe slices of red-colored cardboard. The owner thinks the dish is "authentic." He thinks this is what people want. He thinks they want it year-round. "It's an Italian restaurant! You have to have tomato and mozzarella! Always!" Few customers, it appears, ask themselves the question: "Why the fuck am I eating this?"

Of course, no self-respecting "authentic" Italian would be caught dead eating crap tomatoes—or foisting them on their loved ones. Italians wait for fresh tomatoes. And when they have them, they exult in them, enjoy them to the fullest, knowing they will soon be gone. They plan ahead, canning and sun-drying tomatoes while they're still good, preparing to enjoy those tomatoes in appropriate but different forms year-round.

A final word on greenmarkets and the Slow Food movement. Whether you fully share the views of the Slow Food sustainable agriculture organics posse or not, it is well worth making their acquaintance. Locate the Slow Food chapter in your area and reach out to them for information. If there is even a nascent greenmarket near you, it is wise to cultivate a relationship with as many growers, farmers, vendors, and even activists as possible. Eventually, as this movement gains strength and influence, you can tap into whole networks of production and supply—whether they achieve their goals of agrarian wonderland or not. You may feel, as I do, "I don't care if it makes me glow in the dark, or causes the occasional tumor in lab rats, as long as it tastes really really good," but it is hard to argue with the proposition that slow food is more often than not good food; and within this wild, ungainly, and rapidly growing movement you will find all sorts of fascinating characters: renegade cheesemakers, artisanal bread bakers, exotic mushroom wranglers (and poachers), raisers of boutique pigs, and a worldwide network of obsessive foodies—all with varying agendas, and all of whom, like

you, are interested in the good stuff. You don't have to switch to Birkenstocks, or save Flipper, or buy into the philosophy. You can just buy their cheese. Anyone who has abandoned a career as a Wall Street lawyer to dedicate his or her life to the production of artisanal sausage or goat cheese—regardless of what kind of wacky conspiracy theories he might believe in, or her taste in music—is probably well worth knowing. More and more, there's good stuff everywhere, often right under your nose. Your local greenmarket vendors may currently offer only fingerling potatoes and bran muffins, but if you patronize them, encourage them, and support them, others will follow. Who knows? You might someday get those wild strawberries you wanted.

# [ Part B ]
# the knife

A sharp knife is a must.

A dull knife, as any line cook knows, leaves a bigger, nastier wound—and worst of all, does a lousy job. If there is one investment that you absolutely *cannot* live without, one thing you need above all else, it is a decent knife—along with a sharpening stone so as to treat it with the care and respect it deserves, and a diamond steel for honing. Do I need to belabor this point? I will anyway.

Your knife, more than any other piece of equipment in the kitchen, is an extension of the self, an expression of your skills, ability, experience, dreams, and desires. It can also be the most direct and glaring expression of your complete ineptness and uselessness as a cook.

You must therefore first purchase a knife of good quality and reputation—a size comfortable to your hand and also capable of doing the job. Henckels, Wüsthof, and Global all make excellent chef knives of varying sizes and weights. Pick one. And then, for God's sake, maintain your fine piece of German or Japanese cutlery. If you're springing one hundred twenty bucks for a knife, only to leave it unloved and unsharpened, bouncing around in a drawer full of old Ginsus and other kitchen crap you've accumulated over the years, you will richly deserve the deep,

jagged finger wound you will undoubtedly inflict on yourself next time you try to julienne a pepper in a hurry. As you mash vainly at your food, with the now dull and useless blade—growing increasingly frustrated at the clumsy, ugly result—you might just as well be using a rusted medieval meat ax. If you are incapable of demonstrating pride in your tools, you are incapable as well of making food you can be proud of. It's that simple. You sin against the Kitchen Gods. In a perfect world, cooks who abuse fine cutlery would be locked in a pillory and pelted with McNuggets. The world would soon become a better place.

It does not take much to give your knife a few careful passes on a water-lubricated sharpening stone, followed by a few swipes on the steel. Since you are very likely handing over some serious lucre when you buy your knife, insist that a salesman show you *precisely* how to do it. If he can't? Wait until you can find a salesman who will. For the timorous and feebleminded among you—and for any howler monkeys in the tertiary stages of syphilis who might be reading this—some manufacturers now sell a clever little device that clips to the back of the blade and rolls your knife at exactly the right angle on the sharpening stone—thus obviating the skill almost entirely.

# [ Part C ]
# stock: the source

What's missing in your home cooking? Why doesn't that dish you painfully re-created from the chef's recipe taste like it does in the restaurant? What's wrong with your soup, your sauces, your stews? The answer is almost certainly "stock." Restaurants make their own stocks. It's a constant process. All day long, somewhere in the restaurant, there are stocks simmering, demi-glace reducing, bones roasting, and scraps of vegetables being collected. Stock is the foundation, the basis for much of French cuisine. It would be unthinkable to live without it in a professional situation.

So what's *your* problem? Well…*space,* for one thing. Making stock takes up a lot of room. Making a good demi-glace, or reduced sauce, requires even more. Once done, you've got a storage problem: where to *put* all that stuff? And how to use it before it goes sour? Most cookbooks will disingenuously suggest that "broth" or bouillon or some canned product will suffice as substitute for a good dark veal or chicken stock. That is just not so.

You can cheat on *light* chicken stock (substituting canned chicken broth). You can cheat, *sometimes,* on fish stock (using a good powdered or paste base). But bouillon cubes don't make it. They taste like…well…salty bouillon cubes. Canned beef broth or watery bouillon will not reduce into the kind of rich, full-bodied mother sauce you're looking for. For some things, you *need* to do it right.

Below are a few basic formulas for restaurant-quality—or, I guess I should say, bistro-quality—stocks and demi-glace. If you're planning on working at the French Laundry or with Ducasse, these products will not live up to the chef's standards. The method and style of these preparations is rough, crude, far from classic—and perfectly workable in most restaurant situations. Thomas Keller might fire your ass for a lot of what I'm about to tell you to do, as this method will provide a less refined, provincial-quality result that would be unacceptable in a multistarred joint. But you will have a huge edge over most home cooks and will be able to crank out a decent, useful product by most restaurant standards.

Let's do dark stock first. You want dark stock when the finished product needs color, needs rich, caramelized flavors—when making a red-wine meat sauce, for instance, or a beef stew. Veal stock is the basis for the most important sauce you'll need, which is demi-glace. Now, classically, demi-glace was a reduction of equal parts reduced veal stock and sauce espagnole. No one makes espagnole anymore. What most restaurants refer to as "demi" is simply a strong, dark, highly reduced veal stock that has been strained and reduced again with red wine and shallots. I'll walk you through it.

Take as many veal bones as you can fit into your largest heavy-bottomed pot or pots, wash them in cold water, and dry them. Lay them out in a lightly oiled roasting pan, no more than two layers deep. If you want to cheat, as many of us do, throw a wad of tomato paste on top of the bones, sprinkle a handful of flour over them, and mix through.

Place the roasting pan in a preheated 350°F/180°C oven. Roast the bones, turning occasionally to work the tomato paste and flour through the grease. Avoid scorching. You do *not* want any black color. While the bones are roasting, assemble the following vegetables in an amount totaling no more than one third the volume of the bones: 50 percent white onion, 25 percent carrot, and 25 percent celery. *Peel* the carrots and onions. Remove the celery leaves. Make sure there are no stems, greens, roots, or dirt to cloud up your already workmanlike stock recipe. Roughly chop the vegetables into large chunks. Put the vegetables in *another* oiled roasting pan, and roast them, stirring frequently, until evenly browned and caramelized.

Dump the bones and vegetables into the pot or pots, and fill nearly to the top with *cold* water. Add a few sprigs of thyme, some whole black peppercorns, and a couple of bay leaves. Bring up nearly to a boil—BUT NEVER BOIL—then reduce the heat to a simmer. Simmer slowly for eight to ten hours, occasionally skimming foam, scum, and oil from the top. When done, lift out the bones and strain the liquid through a fine strainer or chinois—or better yet, through cheesecloth draped in a strainer. Do it as many times as you can stand. The more the better.

You now have a basic brown veal stock. I suggest that at this point you reserve some, cool it down in an ice bath to room temperature, then store it in the refrigerator, or in the freezer in small meal-size batches for future use. It's always nice to have some veal stock kicking around. The greater part of

your dark veal stock, we're going to make ersatz demi with. This is the good and truly useful stuff you want for sauces. It takes a *lot* of stock to make a relatively small amount of demi, so make as much as you can. You're not going to want to do this again for a while.

In a heavy-bottomed stockpot, dump in red wine equal in amount to about one fourth of the volume of stock. Add a few peeled chopped shallots. Begin reducing the red wine over high heat. When about half the wine has cooked away, add your stock, bring to a near boil, and then reduce the heat to a gentle simmer. Let me stress again: DO NOT EVER BOIL YOUR STOCK! Gently simmer and simmer and simmer and reduce, reduce, reduce until you have a lush, dark, intensely flavored brown sauce. It should be reasonably thick, but not candy-sticky. Not yet. If you like sticky, shiny, highly reduced sauces (and I do, now and again), wait until later. This stuff you just made is the mother, the source for all other sauces down the line. You can bring it down more later, infuse flavors, add garnishes, all sorts of crafty business. For now? When your demi looks good, simply repeat the straining process (if anything, even more carefully), cool in batches in an ice bath, and store.

Storage: You can freeze this stuff in batches, large or small. I like the Julia Child idea of filling ice cube trays with the stuff, so that you can later pop out a cube at a time for small meals or for jacking anemic sauces or stews with flavor, color, and texture.

Of course the preferred option when making a duck dish requiring stock—or a duck sauce— is that one use duck stock. Lamb sauce or a lamb stew, naturally, would be better with lamb stock. And so on. At Les Halles, we have three or four gigantic stockpots filled with various bones simmering away on a specially dedicated stovetop at all times.

If you have followed my suggestion and loaded your freezer with nice, dark veal stock, you may not want to repeat this whole process—with lamb or duck or pork bones—every time you need a different meat sauce. So cheat. Once you have a good batch of veal demi and veal stock socked away, anything is possible. Let's say you're making gigot (leg of lamb) and you want a good, hearty brown lamb sauce. No prob. Yank a little demi out of the freezer and into a pot. Maybe splash in a little stock if it gets too strong or too thick. Add a few roasted lamb bones, some seared lamb scraps, a few cloves of garlic, and a sprig of rosemary, and simmer together for an hour or so on low heat. Then, of course, strain, strain, reduce. Do not add salt to anything until reduction is nearly complete; when you reduce, the sauce or stock will get saltier and saltier. Voilà! Perfectly useful lamb sauce. You can do the same thing with duck (sans garlic and rosemary) or pork. We'll be doing all sorts of sauces with this basic principle later on.

Chicken is another matter. A lot of chefs, in fact, have turned completely away from dark veal stocks and use only dark, highly reduced chicken stock. Generally speaking, it *is* preferable to use dark, reduced chicken stock when making a sauce for game birds. But know that a lot of the hotshots these days use it very successfully for everything. The process is the same: Roast your chicken bones and vegetables. Toss in pot. Cook. Treat as above.

White stocks are different. You don't *want* color. Here, you roast nothing. Simply put the fresh, washed bones straight into the pot with the veggies and the herbs and simmer for six to eight hours. No tomato, nothing that might color the end product. White stocks are essential for many, if not most, soups. If making a *blanquette de veau,* which is all about the color white, or a white cream sauce, you would definitely want to use a white veal stock.

Fish stock (fumet) is treated like white chicken stock, unless you're looking for an intensely flavored, darkish stock for soup (as with *soupe de poisson*, or bisque). For fish stock, you generally want to use the bones of white, nonoily fish. Salmon or, God forbid, mackerel or bluefish, will not do. You want the "racks," meaning the spine and bones, and if you care to waste a perfectly good one, you can add the head with gills removed. No guts, please. Remember to wash the bones thoroughly in cold water before use.

Some cute improvisations on fish stock, useful for those dark bisques and soups and shellfish soups, would be to use roasted shrimp or lobster shells instead of bones. Just don't burn the damn things. They get godawful bitter.

Do try to make stock and demi. It's easy; it's relaxing. You can train a chimp to do it, and it'll make your house smell nice. If you're lucky enough to have a chest freezer in the garage or cellar, or have a lot of freezer space, throw out all those toaster waffles, frozen dinners, and microwave egg rolls and *make room*. You have more important things to store there.

Stocks are almost always the most time-consuming part of a recipe. If you already have enough on hand, you've got your "meez" together, and everything that follows will be much, much easier. And your food will be much, much better.

# soups

# soupe au pistou

**A French vegetable soup similar to minestrone. Pistou is similar to pesto.**

## INGREDIENTS

**1 cup/225 g white beans** (pinto, great
  northern, or Tarbais are all good)
**2 ounces/28 ml olive oil**
**2 garlic cloves,**
  thinly sliced—as in *Goodfellas*
**1 medium onion,** diced small
**1 lb/450 g seeded, chopped,
  fresh, ripe tomato**
**2 leeks,** washed thoroughly and
  cut into $^1/_4$-inch/6-mm slices
**2 small zucchini (courgettes),**
  diced small (Remember to use only
  the outer parts of the zucchini and
  the yellow squash: do *not* use the
  seed cavities. Throw them out.)
**2 small yellow squash,** diced small
**1 fennel bulb,** diced small
**4 cups/900 ml light chicken stock or broth**
**1 bouquet garni** (see Glossary)
**3 ounces/75 g elbow macaroni**
**salt and pepper**

## PISTOU INGREDIENTS

**1 bunch of fresh basil leaves,** picked
  from stems, washed and dried
**6 garlic cloves**
**$^1/_2$ cup extra-virgin olive oil**
**4 ounces/112 g grated Parmesan cheese**
**salt and pepper**

## EQUIPMENT

large, heavy-bottomed pot
wooden spoon
ladle
mortar and pestle
  (or food processor, if you're criminally lazy)

**SERVES 6**

**FIRST**

The day *before* you make the soup, soak the beans in plenty of cold water for 24 hours. Since you have time, you might consider making your own chicken stock at this point.

**NEXT DAY**

Put on some music. Drain and rinse the beans, then cook in either water or chicken stock until *nearly* done—meaning still a little hard in the middle. Do not cook the beans to mush, please. When ready, drain and rinse in cold water to arrest cooking. Put aside. You'll need them later. Do all your knife work, meaning the dicing, slicing, and so on.

Now we are ready to begin the actual cooking. Right? You've got everything? Assemble your prepped ingredients in an organized fashion. You've got your "meez" together? Let's go…

In the large, heavy-bottomed pot, heat the olive oil. When the oil is hot, add the garlic and onion and sauté on low heat for a few moments to release the flavors. When the onion begins to clear and become translucent, add the rest of the vegetables and continue to sauté on low heat (sweating them) until slightly soft. Add the chicken stock or broth and the bouquet garni and bring to a quick boil on high heat, then immediately reduce the heat until you have a nice, gentle simmer. Add the elbow macaroni and continue simmering until it's nearly cooked through. Drop in the beans. Simmer, stirring occasionally, remembering to skim, skim, skim with the ladle to remove scum and foam.

Most soups get better the next day. This is not one of them. Anytime you've got pasta, zucchini, or squash incorporated in a soup, it's going to get ugly the next day. Ditto basil paste. This lovely, colorful, fresh-tasting soup will turn a nasty, army fatigue color by tomorrow. And the pistou will take over the soup. So eat it all now.

While the soup is simmering, make the pistou. In the mortar and pestle, grind and pound the basil and garlic together until it becomes a sludgelike paste. With a fork, slowly incorporate the olive oil a little at a time. Fold in the Parmesan at the end. Season with salt and pepper. You can, I suppose, cheat and use a food processor for this; plenty of, if not most, restaurants probably do. But that would be wrong.

After about 30 minutes, when the soup is ready (meaning the macaroni and the beans are cooked through but *not* mushy or overcooked, still maintaining their structural integrity), whisk in your pistou, salt and pepper to taste, and serve immediately.

# onion soup les halles

**INGREDIENTS**

**6 ounces/168 g butter**
**8 large onions (or 12 small onions),**
 thinly sliced
**2 ounces/56 ml port**
**2 ounces/56 ml balsamic vinegar**
**2 quarts/2.2 liters dark chicken stock**
**4 ounces/112 g slab bacon,**
 cut in ¹/₂-inch/1-cm cubes
**1 bouquet garni** (see Glossary)
**salt and pepper**
**16 baguette croutons** (sliced and
 toasted in the oven with a little olive oil)
**12 ounces/340 g grated Gruyère cheese**
 (real, imported Gruyère!)

**EQUIPMENT**

large, heavy-bottomed pot
wooden spoon
ladle
8 ovenproof soup crocks
 (Restaurant supply shops sell these by
 the hundreds. Be sure to use ovenproof.)
propane torch (optional)

**SERVES 8**

The better and more
intense your stock,
the better the soup's
going to be. This soup,
in particular, is a very
good argument for
making your own.

**PREPARE THE BROTH**

In the large pot, heat the butter over medium heat until it is melted
and begins to brown. Add the onions and cook over medium heat,
stirring occasionally, until they are soft and browned (about 20
minutes). Onion soup, unsurprisingly, is *all about the onions.* Make
damn sure the onions are a nice, dark, even brown color.

Increase the heat to medium high and stir in the port and the vinegar,
scraping all that brown goodness from the bottom of the pot into the
liquid. Add the chicken stock. Add the bacon and bouquet garni and
bring to a boil.

Reduce to a simmer, season with salt and pepper, and cook for 45
minutes to an hour, skimming any foam off the top with the ladle.
Remove the bouquet garni.

## THE CROUTONS AND CHEESE

When the soup is finished cooking, ladle it into the individual crocks. Float two croutons side by side on top of each. Spread a generous, even heaping amount of cheese over the top of the soup. You *want* some extra to hang over the edges, as the crispy, near-burnt stuff that sticks to the outer sides of the crocks once it comes out from under the heat is often the best part.

Place each crock under a *preheated,* rip-roaring broiler until the cheese melts, bubbles, browns, and even scorches slightly in spots. The finished cheese should be a panorama of molten brown hues ranging from golden brown to dark brown to a few black spots where the cheese blistered and burned. Serve immediately—and *carefully*. You don't know pain until you've spilled one of these things in your lap.

If your broiler is too small or too weak to pull this off, you can try it in a preheated 425°F/220°C oven until melted. A nice optional move: Once the mound of grated cheese starts to flatten out in the oven, remove each crock and, with a propane torch, blast the cheese until you get the colors you want.

## HALF-ASSED ALTERNATIVE

Your broiler sucks. Your oven isn't much better. Can't find those ovenproof crocks anywhere. And you ain't ponying up for a damn propane torch, 'cause your kid's got pyromaniac tendencies. You can simply toast cheese over the croutons on a sheet pan, and float them as garnish on the soup. Not exactly classic—but still good.

## NOTE ON THE PROPANE TORCH

This is a very handy-dandy piece of equipment, especially if your stove is not the greatest. Nearly all professional kitchens have them; they're not very expensive and they can be used for a variety of sneaky tasks, such as easily caramelizing the top of crème brûlée or toasting meringues.

# mushroom soup

This is a ridiculously easy soup to make. It's tasty and durable, and it gets even better overnight.

## INGREDIENTS

6 tbsp/75 g butter
1 small onion, thinly sliced
12 ounces/340 g button mushrooms
4 cups/900 ml light chicken stock
   or broth
1 sprig of flat parsley
salt and pepper

2 ounces/56 ml high-quality sherry
   (don't use the cheap grocery-store
   variety; it's salty and unappetizing and will
   ruin your soup)

## EQUIPMENT
medium saucepan
wooden spoon
blender

**SERVES 4**

## METHOD

In the medium saucepan, melt 2 tablespoons/28 g of the butter over medium heat and add the onion. Cook until the onion is soft and translucent, then add the mushrooms and the remaining butter. Let the mixture sweat for about 8 minutes, taking care that the onion doesn't take on any brown color. Stir in the chicken stock and the parsley and bring to a boil. Immediately reduce the heat and simmer for about an hour.

After an hour, remove the parsley and discard. Let the soup cool for a few minutes, then transfer to the blender and *carefully* blend at high speed until smooth. Do I have to remind you to do this in stages, with the blender's lid firmly held *down,* and with the weight of your body keeping that thing from flying off and allowing boiling hot mushroom purée to erupt all over your kitchen?

When blended, return the mix to the pot, season with salt and pepper, and bring up to a simmer again. Add the sherry, mix well, and serve immediately.

## IMPROVISATION

To astound your guests with a Wild Mushroom Soup, simply replace some of those button mushrooms with a few dried cèpes or morels, which have been soaked until soft, drained, and squeezed. Not too many; the dried mushrooms will have a much stronger taste, and you don't want to overwhelm the soup. Pan sear, on high heat, a single small, pretty, fresh chanterelle or morel for each portion, and then slice into a cute fan and float on top in each bowl.

And if you really want to ratchet your soup into pretentious (but delicious), drizzle a few tiny drops of truffle oil over the surface just before serving. Why the hell not? Everybody else is doing it.

# fennel and tomato soup

**INGREDIENTS**
4 tbsp/56 ml extra-virgin olive oil
2 **fennel bulbs,** cored and thinly sliced
1 **small onion,** finely chopped
1 **small potato,** cut into $1/4$-inch/6-mm cubes
1 **8-ounce/225-ml can plum tomatoes**
6 **cups/1.35 liters light chicken stock or broth**
**salt and freshly ground black pepper**

**EQUIPMENT**
large pot
wooden spoon
blender

**SERVES 6**

**METHOD**

In the large pot, heat the oil over medium-high heat and add the fennel, onion, and potato. Reduce the heat to medium low and let the vegetables sweat for 10 minutes, taking care to not let them brown. Add the tomatoes and cook for 10 minutes more. Stir in the chicken stock; bring the mixture to a boil. Reduce to a simmer and cook for 1 hour.

Remove the pot from the heat and let the soup cool for a few minutes. Transfer the mix to the blender and, working in batches to avoid accidents, purée until smooth. Return to the pot, bring to a boil, lower to a simmer, and season with salt and pepper.

**IMPROVISATION**

You can boost the flavor elements by adding a few slices of garlic with the vegetables at the beginning and a few drops of Pernod at the very end. You can also get cute by garnishing each bowl with a few bits of diced tomato and a drop or two of basil or parsley oil (see page 261).

# soupe au vin

**INGREDIENTS**
**1 bottle/1 liter of red Bordeaux wine**
**2 tbsp/28 g butter**
**1 cup/225 g slab bacon,** cut into
  $^1/_2$-inch/12-mm cubes
**5 leeks,** washed and cut into
  $^1/_4$-inch/6-mm dice
**1 small onion,** finely chopped
**2 tbsp/28 g flour**
**3 cups/675 ml light or dark chicken
  stock or broth**
**1 bouquet garni** (see Glossary)
**salt and pepper**

**EQUIPMENT**
2 large pots
wooden spoon
whisk

**SERVES 6**

**Don't substitute cheap
cut-rate red wine; it
will taste like cheap
cut-rate soup.**

Bring the wine (except for a single splash, which you should hold in reserve) to a boil in a large pot. After 5 minutes of rolling boil, remove it from the heat and set aside. In the other large pot, heat the butter over medium heat and once it has melted, add the bacon and sweat it for about 5 minutes. Stir the leeks and the onion right in there and let them cook over low heat for another 10 minutes, or until the onion is soft and translucent.

Stir in the flour and cook for 2 minutes more, then whisk in the wine and chicken stock and add the bouquet garni. Bring to a boil, reduce to a simmer, and cook for 45 minutes. Season with salt and pepper, remove the bouquet garni, then serve, topped with the remaining splash of raw wine.

# vichyssoise

**INGREDIENTS**
4 **tbsp/56 g butter**
8 **leeks,** white part only,
  cleaned and thinly sliced
2 **medium potatoes,** cut into small cubes
4 **cups/900 ml light chicken stock**
  **or broth**
2 **cups/450 ml heavy cream**
1 **pinch of nutmeg**
**salt and pepper**
4 **fresh chives,** finely chopped

**EQUIPMENT**
large, heavy-bottomed pot
wooden spoon
blender
medium mixing bowl
large bowl, filled with ice water

**SERVES 6**

In the large, heavy-bottomed pot, melt the butter over medium-low heat. Once the butter is melted, add the leeks and sweat for 5 minutes, making sure that they do *not* take on any color. Add the potatoes and cook for a minute or two, stirring a few times. Stir in the chicken stock and bring to a boil. Reduce to a simmer. Cook on low heat, gently simmering, for 35 minutes, or until the leeks and potatoes are very soft. Allow to cool for a few minutes.

Okay, the next part is tricky. Slowly, and in *small* batches, purée the soup at high speed in the blender. Do this bit by bit, *never* filling the blender up too high (over halfway up). Make sure the blender's lid is on, and that you're leaning on the damn thing when you turn it on. You do *not* want a face full of boiling starchy, sticky hot potato–leek purée. Trust me. It hurts like a motherfucker. This is one of the more frequent kitchen accidents—even in professional kitchens. So be careful.

When everything is blended, return the soup to the cooking pot and whisk in the cream and nutmeg. Season with salt and pepper. Return to a boil, reduce to a simmer, and continue cooking for 5 minutes. You can thin out the soup with a little additional stock at this point, if needed.

Transfer the soup to the mixing bowl and chill over the ice bath, stirring occasionally. When the soup is at room temperature—and only when it's at room temperature—cover it in plastic wrap and put it in the refrigerator overnight, or until cool.

When ready to go, check the seasoning, sprinkle with freshly cut chives, and serve in chilled bowls.

This is a soup that *does* get better over time. But keep it covered with plastic (not foil) in the refrigerator, as it will pick up other tastes. And *never* put it in the refrigerator while still hot.

# soupe
# de poisson

## INGREDIENTS

6 tbsp/75 ml olive oil
4 garlic cloves
2 small onions, thinly sliced
2 leeks, whites only, washed and
   thinly sliced
1 fennel bulb, thinly sliced
1 18-ounce/500-g can
   plum tomatoes, chopped
2 lb/900 g tiny whole fish (like porgies
   or whiting), gutted but heads intact, or
   4 lb/1.8 kg fish bones and heads
1 bouquet garni (see Glossary)
zest of 1 orange
3 strands of saffron

salt and pepper
1 ounce/28 ml Pernod
rouille (see page 260)
grated Parmesan

## EQUIPMENT

large, heavy-bottomed pot
wooden spoon
large bowl
mallet (or heavy object)
fine strainer

**SERVES 8**

In the large, heavy-bottomed pot, heat the olive oil over medium heat. Add the garlic, onions, leeks, and fennel and let them sweat for about 5 minutes, stirring occasionally with the wooden spoon. Add the tomatoes and cook for another 4 to 5 minutes, then add the small fish or the bones. Cook for about 15 minutes, stirring occasionally. Add water to cover, as well as the bouquet garni and orange zest. Stir well; add the saffron, salt and pepper, and Pernod. Lower the heat and simmer for about an hour.

Remove the pot from the heat and let the soup cool slightly. Taking

care not to splatter or scald yourself, strain the liquid into the large bowl. In the pot, crush the heads, bones, and vegetables as much as possible, then transfer that to the strainer. Push and squeeze every bit of liquid and solid goodness through with the mallet or heavy wooden spoon. Return to the pot.

Bring the soup back up to heat and serve with croutons, rouille, and some grated Parmesan on the side. The idea is to smear a little rouille on the croutons, float them in the soup as garnish, and allow guests to sprinkle cheese as they wish.

# lobster bisque

## INGREDIENTS

3 2-lb/900-g lobsters, in their shells,
  cut into 2 pieces (see **NOTE**)
3 tbsp/42 ml olive oil
2 onions, finely chopped
4 garlic cloves, sliced
2 leeks, white part only, finely chopped
2 celery stalks, finely chopped
1 tbsp/14 g tomato paste
$^1/_4$ cup/56 ml Cognac
6 cups/1.35 liters water
1 bouquet garni (see Glossary)
salt and pepper
2 cups/450 ml heavy cream
juice of $^1/_2$ lemon
2 tbsp/28 g chopped fresh chives

## EQUIPMENT

cleaver or knife
towel
large pot
wooden spoon
spider or large slotted spoon
heavy-duty food processor
  (any doubts about yours?
  move on to another recipe)
strainer
medium pot

NOTE: Live, 2-pound/900-gram lobsters are expensive. There is no reason to fork over big money for lobster when you intend to use them for soup. What you want are what's called in industry parlance "stiffs," meaning sleepy, limp, or recently deceased lobsters. If your fish guy sells lobsters, chances are he has a few of these lying around and will be happy to sell them to you at a vastly reduced price. If not? Just wait. He will. Express your interest in acquiring stiffs at a good price, and have him gather what you need over time, socking the dead ones away in the freezer until he has the amount you need.

**SERVES 6**

## MAKE THE SOUP

First, cut the lobsters into pieces. There are several points on a lobster's body where cuts can be made, with the cleaver or knife, without messing up your blade. Basically, between all joints. Lobster tail should be wrapped in the towel and whacked with the knife's blunt end.

Then, heat the oil in the large pot, and when nice and hot, add the chunks of lobster (still in the shell). Cook over high heat for 5 to 6 minutes or until the shells are bright red all over. Do *not* scorch. Add the vegetables (*and* garlic) and cook until soft and translucent, then stir in the tomato paste and mix well. After another 2 minutes of cooking and stirring, remove the pot from the heat and stir in the Cognac (unless you *like* setting your hair on fire, and enjoy the taste of burnt, brackish lobster shells). With the spoon, scrape the bottom of the pot to dislodge all those tasty brown bits. Return the pot carefully to the fire, add the water and the bouquet garni, and season with salt and pepper. Bring to a boil, then reduce the heat and simmer. Let the soup simmer over low heat for about 45 minutes.

Using the spider or slotted spoon, remove the lobster pieces and transfer to the food processor. Pulse the lobster until it is broken down into small pieces. This will probably make an atrocious noise as the shells go spinning around and crunch into a shell-flecked but delicious sludge. Hopefully your food processor can handle it. Hopefully you will not burn out the motor. If it's a good, strong machine—and you don't smell the troubling odor of overheated machine parts or burning wire—then you're good to go. Pulsing a little at a time, rather than running the machine into overdrive, is probably the smart way to go. Pulse. Let it rest. Pulse again. Repeat. Return the lobster to the pot, stir in the cream, and bring the mixture to a boil. Reduce to a simmer and cook for another 30 minutes. Strain the soup into the medium pot, pushing *hard* on the solids to extract *every little bit* of liquid possible. Make final seasoning adjustments with salt and pepper.

## SERVE

Bring the soup to a boil, adjust the seasoning, stir in the lemon juice and chives, and serve immediately.

# salads

# salade niçoise

## INGREDIENTS

2 **tbsp/28 g salt** (*plus* more to taste)
6 **ounces/168 g haricots verts**
  (skinny French green beans), trimmed
4 **small red bliss potatoes,** scrubbed
1 **garlic clove,** peeled and slightly crushed
6 **tbsp/84 ml extra-virgin olive oil**
3 **tbsp/42 ml red wine vinegar**
**black pepper**
1 **head Boston or Bibb lettuce,** washed,
  dried, outer leaves discarded, inner leaves
  torn in half
1 **green bell pepper,** cored and cut into
  $1/_8$-inch/3-mm slices
8 **anchovy fillets** (the expensive white
  ones would be best), drained, rinsed,
  patted dry (4 cut into quarters)
1/4 **lb/112 g niçoise olives,** pitted

4 **ripe plum tomatoes,**
  cut lengthwise into quarters
**12-ounce/340-g can high-quality
  tuna in olive oil**
4 **hard-boiled eggs,** peeled and cut
  lengthwise into quarters

## EQUIPMENT

medium pot
slotted spoon (spider)
medium bowl, filled with ice water
fork
wooden salad bowl

**SERVES 4**

In general, don't let
blanched vegetables sit
in water for too long; and
pat them dry when
removing from water.

### PREP

Fill the medium pot three-quarters full with water and add the
2 tablespoons/28 g of salt. Bring to a roaring boil and add the beans.
Anytime you blanch a green vegetable, the more water and the more
room, the better. You don't want to jam the beans into a small pot, or to
bring the water temperature down when you add them. They need plenty
of room to swim around. Cook the beans for 6 minutes, then remove them
with the slotted spoon and plunge them immediately into the ice bath.
As soon as the beans are cold, remove from the ice bath and set aside.

Fill the medium pot with cold water. Add the potatoes and bring to a
boil over high heat. Cook for 20 minutes, or until the potatoes are easily
pierced with a paring knife or fork. Remove the potatoes from the
boiling water and cool them in the ice bath. Once cool, remove from the
water and reserve. (Cut lengthwise into quarters at the last minute.)

Impale the garlic clove on the fork and use it to rub the inside of the salad bowl. Add 4 tablespoons/56 ml of the olive oil and the red wine vinegar and whisk well with your garlic-studded fork. Season with salt and pepper.

Core and wash the lettuce in cold water and spin (if you have a salad spinner) or shake gently dry.

### SERVE
Place the haricots verts, potatoes, lettuce, bell pepper slices, quartered anchovies, olives, and tomatoes in the salad bowl and toss well to coat the vegetables. Divide the mix among 4 chilled plates. Drizzle each with some of the remaining olive oil and finish each plate with tuna, hard-boiled egg, and a whole anchovy fillet. Serve immediately.

# frisée
# aux lardons

## INGREDIENTS

1 lb/450 g slab bacon, cut into
   1-inch/2.5-cm cubes
1/2 baguette, cut into 1/2-inch/1-cm slices
drizzle of olive oil
3/4 cup/170 g chicken liver
   vinaigrette (see page 255)
2 heads of frisée, washed and
   torn into pieces
1 shallot, thinly sliced
salt and freshly ground black pepper

6 ounces/168 g Roquefort (that's
   *real* Roquefort, knucklehead!), at
   room emperature

## EQUIPMENT

medium saucepan
strainer
sauté pan
salad bowl

SERVES 6

### PREP

Prepare the bacon by placing the cubes in the saucepan, covering them with water, and bringing to a quick boil. When the water boils, drain the bacon, discarding the water.

Toast the baguette slices in the oven with a drizzle of olive oil. Make sure you have your vinaigrette ready to go.

### COOK

Place the sauté pan on high heat for 2 minutes, or until sizzling hot. Add the bacon and cook until crispy and brown. Place the cooked bacon in the salad bowl and discard all but 2 tablespoons/28 ml of the bacon fat. Over medium-high heat, add the chicken liver vinaigrette to the now empty but still hot pan and bring to a boil. Remove from the heat.

### SERVE

Place the frisée in the salad bowl with the bacon and add the shallot. Toss the salad with the vinaigrette and season with salt and pepper.

Spread some Roquefort on each of the slices of toasted baguette. Divide the salad among six serving bowls, top each with two cheese-smeared toasts, and serve.

# asparagus & haricots verts salad

Again, if the asparagus at the market is over the hill, woody at the base, or nasty looking, wait until you find some good stuff. You're looking for thin, brightly colored, tender (all the way down) asparagus, with its florets still tightly coiled.

## INGREDIENTS
salt
1 bunch of asparagus, trimmed, stem peeled, and bound together with kitchen string (all spears facing in the same direction)
6 ounces/168 g haricots verts, trimmed
3 tbsp/42 ml extra-virgin olive oil
juice of 1/2 lemon
white pepper
1 navel orange, segmented

## EQUIPMENT
large pot
slotted spoon
large bowl, filled with ice water
small bowl
fork
salad bowl

SERVES 4

### PREP
Fill the large pot with water, add a few tablespoons of salt, and bring to a boil. Add the asparagus and cook for 5 minutes, or until bright green and tender. Remove from the boiling water with the slotted spoon and place in the ice bath. *Be gentle!* Once cold, remove the asparagus from the water, discard the string, and set aside.

Bring the same water in the same pot back up to a rolling boil and cook the beans for 5 minutes, then remove with the slotted spoon and drop into the ice bath. When cold, remove and set aside.

In the small bowl, combine the olive oil and the lemon juice and mix well with the fork. Season with salt and white pepper.

### SERVE
Pat the vegetables dry with paper towels. Combine the vegetables in the salad bowl. Add the vinaigrette and toss gently to coat. Add the orange segments and serve immediately.

# leeks vinaigrette

**INGREDIENTS**
**8 leeks**
**salt**
**sauce gribiche** (see page 251)

**EQUIPMENT**
kitchen string
large pot
large bowl, filled with ice water
tongs
serving platter

**SERVES 4**

**PREP**

Cut the leeks just where the color turns from white to green. Trim off the roots, as close to the ends as possible. Cut each leek down the middle (the long way) almost to the root. Float the leeks in cold water and rinse well to remove all grit and dirt. Now do it again.

**COOK**

Make two bunches of four leeks each and tie them into a bundle with kitchen string. In the large pot, bring water to a boil and add a good handful of salt. Boil the leeks for 10 to 12 minutes, or until they are tender. (Do *not* cover the pot!) Remove the leeks from the boiling water and plunge into the bowl of ice water. When cool, remove them with tongs, drain them, and pat them dry with a kitchen towel.

**SERVE**

Arrange the leeks on the serving platter and spoon a generous hit of sauce gribiche over each leek.

# tomato salad

This dish, you will be astonished to hear, is all about the tomatoes. If you can't get a good tomato, don't make the damn dish. If the tomatoes are unripe, or flavorless greenhouse jobs, or simply *not* tomatoes of noble birth, then wait until you find some good ones.

## INGREDIENTS

2 lb/900 g heirloom tomatoes,
  cored and cut into wedges
coarse sea salt and freshly ground
  black pepper
1 red onion, thinly sliced
1 garlic clove, slightly crushed
$1/4$ cup/56 ml extra-virgin olive oil

2 tbsp/28 ml balsamic vinegar
1 sprig of fresh basil, leaves only

## EQUIPMENT

2 colanders
fork
wooden salad bowl

**SERVES 6**

**PREP**

Degorge the tomatoes by placing them, already cut into wedges, into a colander and sprinkling them with $1/2$ tablespoon/7 ml of sea salt and $1/2$ tablespoon/7 ml of black pepper. Let sit for 30 minutes, then brush off and remove the seeds.

Place the sliced onion into a separate colander and sprinkle with sea salt. Let sit for 30 minutes, then brush off the salt and squeeze out any excess water.

**SERVE**

The whole thing breaks down after 2 hours, so if making ahead, don't dress the salad until just before serving. Better yet, don't make this ahead of time.

Prick the garlic with the fork and rub the clove inside the salad bowl. Add the olive oil and the vinegar and whisk. Season with salt and a little pepper. Add the tomatoes, the onion, and the basil leaves. Toss with the vinaigrette. Arrange on plates and sprinkle a little fresh black pepper over the top.

**IMPROVISATION**

My Tante Jeanne made this dish differently but deliciously. She used *red* wine vinegar instead of the balsamic, sliced *shallots* instead of the red onion, and sprinkled a mound of freshly chopped *parsley* over the top at the very end. Personally, I prefer her version to our house model. You might try both and pick your favorite.

# appetizers

# celery rémoulade

**INGREDIENTS**
1 lb/450 g celery root (celeriac), peeled
juice of 1 lemon
$^1/_4$ cup/56 g good-quality mayonnaise
  (homemade is preferred, but
  not necessary)
2 tbsp/28 g Dijon mustard
1 tbsp/14 ml walnut oil
$^1/_2$ cup/110 g chopped walnuts
salt and freshly ground black pepper

**EQUIPMENT**
sharp knife or mandoline
  (vertical slicer)
cutting board
large bowl
small bowl
whisk
wooden spoon

**SERVES 6 TO 8**

**JULIENNE THE CELERY ROOT**
Cut the peeled celery root into thin slices. Stack a few slices one on top of the other and cut them into very thin strips. (A cheap, Japanese-style vertical slicer or an old-style European mandoline can be very helpful here. You just run the whole celery root against the blade and badabing! If you don't have a mandoline, letting the celery root sit in the refrigerator will help soften it up for slicing with a knife.)

As soon as you have the strips, cover them with lemon juice to prevent oxidation—they'll quickly get dark and nasty-looking without the lemon juice—and place in the large bowl. Repeat this process until all the celery root is julienned.

A couple of nice inner leaves of Bibb lettuce can serve as a decorative cup for a more picturesque presentation. And though it totally breaks with tradition, and I don't necessarily condone it, some people like to add a little chopped parsley for color.

**MAKE THE SALAD**
In the small bowl, combine the mayonnaise, mustard, and walnut oil and whisk well. Pour this mixture over the celery root. Toss in the walnut pieces, season with salt and pepper—adding more lemon juice if you like—and heap on the plate.

# oeufs périgourdins

## INGREDIENTS
4 eggs *plus* 1 egg white
2 tbsp/28 g **Parma ham**, finely chopped
2 tbsp/28 g **black truffles**, finely chopped
1 tsp/5 ml **truffle oil**
1 sprig of **flat parsley**, finely chopped
**salt and pepper**
2 cups/450 g *plus* 1$^1/_2$ tbsp/21 g **duck fat**
(see Suppliers)

## EQUIPMENT
small pot
2 mixing bowls
2 forks
wooden spoon
heavy-bottomed pan
slotted spoon

### HOW TO HARD-BOIL A FREAKING EGG
Put your eggs gently into a small pot filled with cold water. Bring the water to a rapid boil. As soon as the water is boiling, shut off the heat and put a lid on top. After 10 minutes, remove the eggs and slide them carefully into ice water to cool. When cool? Peel. Here's how you know if you've done it right: If the egg is cooked through, the shell peels off cleanly, and the yolk is not surrounded by an unsightly gray ring. Gray ring? Try again.

**SERVES 4**

### PREP
Boil the eggs as above. When cooled and peeled, cut in half lengthwise, and neatly remove the cooked yolks from the cooked whites (as for deviled eggs). Now make your stuffing mixture: In a mixing bowl, combine the cooked yolks, ham, truffles, truffle oil, chopped parsley, salt and pepper, and the 1$^1/_2$ tablespoons/21 g of duck fat and crush together with a fork. Stuff the cooked egg-white halves with this mixture.

### SERVICE
Place the remaining 2 cups/450 g of duck fat into the heavy-bottomed pan and heat until sizzling hot (about 350°F/180°C).

**Don't get lazy; if the white isn't beaten to peaks, the fried result tastes awful.**

Beat the extra egg white in the second mixing bowl until it is frothy and begins to hold a peak, like a soft meringue. Using the slotted spoon, dip each stuffed egg into the egg white, then lay it into the hot duck fat and cook until crisp—about 45 seconds on each side. Serve immediately.

# brandade de morue

## INGREDIENTS
$^1/_2$ **lb/115 g salt cod**
$^1/_2$ **cup/110 ml heavy cream**
**1 bouquet garni** (see Glossary)
**4 garlic cloves,** crushed
$^1/_2$ **cup/110 ml extra-virgin olive oil**
**salt and pepper** (careful with
 the salt, buckaroo)
**2 sprigs of flat parsley,** chopped
**2 tbsp/28 g bread crumbs**

## EQUIPMENT
2 large mixing bowls
large pot
slotted spoon
wooden spoon
gratin dish

**SERVES 4**

You want the best-quality
salt cod you can get. If
you know *anyone* of
Portuguese or Spanish
heritage in your area,
they're a good bet to know
where you can score the
good stuff. Alternatively,
Scandinavians might be
able to help you out. As
a fallback, a Caribbean
market or grocery is
likely to have good salt
fish as well.

### PREP
Place the cod in one of the large bowls and cover to the top with cold water. The cod should soak for at least 24 hours to rehydrate, and you should change the water several times: once every hour for the first few hours, and then every few hours after that.

After 24 hours, remove the fish from the water and pat dry with a towel. (If your fish is too salty—you got lazy, you didn't change the water enough—boil a few potatoes, chunk them up, and toss them into the mix.)

### COOK
In the large pot, combine the cream, bouquet garni, and garlic and bring to a boil. Once the mixture is boiling, add the fish and reduce to a simmer. Cook for about 6 minutes, then remove the fish with the slotted spoon and place in a clean mixing bowl.

Bring the cream to a boil again and reduce slowly for about 10 minutes. Don't worry if the cream doesn't cover the fish—and *do not* add more liquid, or you will get the wrong consistency at the end. Remove from the heat and discard the garlic and bouquet garni. Stir in the olive oil and set aside.

**SERVE**
Preheat the oven to broil. Use your fingers to shred the cod very fine. Once it is thoroughly shredded, slowly introduce the cream and oil mixture, mixing well with the wooden spoon. After all the liquid has been added, adjust the seasoning and add the parsley. Transfer the mixture to the gratin dish and top with the bread crumbs. Cook under the broiler until a nice, golden-brown crust forms over the top—then serve, hot, with garlic toast.

# escargots

I could lie to you. I could tell you to use fresh snails, implying that we, of course, use only fresh ones at the restaurant. The truth? I don't know any restaurant, have never in twenty-eight years seen any U.S. restaurant—no matter how good or prestigious—use fresh snails. Oh, a lot of them have snail shells, but they stuff them with snails out of a can. I'm sure someone uses fresh. Somewhere. But let's face it, even if you could get fresh snails (and I would have no idea where to send you), by the time you've had a good look at the things in their living, natural glory, by the time you've dug them out of their shells for the first time…you're likely not going to want to eat them.

So do as the pros do: Find the best, priciest, preferably French canned snails (though the Taiwanese ones have been fooling the French chefs for years) and use those.

WARNING ON SNAILS
It is a peculiar feature of snails that occasionally they like to explode, spitting a boiling-hot, napalmlike mixture of snail fluid and molten butter at your face and genital region while cooking—and often in the moments after cooking. If you are accustomed to cooking while naked, I would strongly suggest covering strategic areas with an apron and keeping your face out of the way during the crucial time periods.

## INGREDIENTS

**24 snails**
**1 shallot,** thinly sliced
**$^1/_2$ cup/110 ml white wine**
**1 head of garlic,** peeled and separated
**1 ounce/28 g flat parsley leaves**
**4 ounces/112 g butter**
**salt and pepper**
**12 slices of baguette**

## EQUIPMENT

small sauté pan
strainer
food processor
baking dish (if you've got shells)
another sauté pan (if you
    haven't got shells)

**SERVES 4**

### PREP

In the small sauté pan, combine the snails, shallot, and white wine and bring to a simmer. Cook for 15 minutes, then drain and set the snails aside. I know, I know—they're ugly. But they're good. Hang in there.

In the food processor, combine the garlic and parsley and pulse until finely chopped. Add the butter and process until the mixture is a smooth, green paste. Season with salt and pepper.

If you have snail shells, place a snail in each shell and then stuff the remaining space inside with the parsley butter.

### SERVE

If you have the snails in shells, ready to go, simply preheat the oven to broil, place the snails in a baking dish, and broil until the butter is sizzling. Serve immediately with the bread.

If you have no shells, you can line a clean sauté pan with the baguette slices, add the parsley butter, and melt over high heat. When the butter is liquefied, add the snails. As soon as the butter is sizzling, remove from the heat and serve immediately.

# escargots aux noix

**INGREDIENTS**
salt
**5 ounces/140 g fresh spinach,**
  picked over and washed
**24 snails**
**1 cup/225 ml white wine**
**2 ounces/56 g shelled walnuts**
**2 ounces/56 g bread crumbs**
**3 ounces/84 g slab bacon,**
  cut into small cubes
**2 garlic cloves,** thinly sliced
**2 cups/450 ml white chicken stock or broth**
**2 Swiss chard leaves,**
  thinly sliced as for slaw
**6 fresh sorrel leaves**
**freshly ground black pepper**
**2 tbsp/28 ml walnut oil**

**EQUIPMENT**
large pot
tongs or slotted spoon
large bowl, filled with ice water
2 medium saucepans
strainer
food processor

**SERVES 4**

## PREP

Fill the large pot with water and bring to a boil. Add a few tablespoons/grams of salt, drop in the spinach, and cook for about a minute. Remove the spinach from the boiling water and, using the tongs or slotted spoon, drop it immediately into the ice-water bath. Once the spinach is cool, remove from the ice bath and squeeze dry. Chop well and set aside.

In a medium saucepan, combine the snails and white wine. Bring to a simmer and cook for about 15 minutes. Then remove from the heat, drain the snails, and chuck out the wine. Set the snails aside.

Place the walnuts in the food processor with the blade attachment and pulse until they are finely chopped. Add the bread crumbs and pulse for a few seconds more. Remove and set aside.

You can do all the above hours in advance (as long as you keep the spinach and snails refrigerated). Have a drink. Relax. Dress for company. Smoke a joint. Your work is practically done here.

## SERVE

Place the bacon in a clean saucepan and cook over medium-low heat until the fat has been rendered from the meat and the meat is slightly brown and crispy. Not too brown and crispy, though! Add the snails, crank up the heat a bit, and cook over moderate heat for about 5 minutes. Add the garlic and the chicken stock and simmer (do not boil!) for about 20 minutes.

Stir in the spinach and the Swiss chard. Cook over low heat for 5 minutes, until the chard has wilted; then add the sorrel. Continue to cook for a minute, then stir in the walnut and bread crumb mixture. Season with salt and pepper, drizzle with walnut oil, and serve.

# MOULES

I know, I know...I have famously frightened away hundreds of people from eating mussels. But you'll be handling and cooking these mussels yourselves, and presumably you'll be more conscientious than some college student with a part-time cook's job at a sports bar.

Mussels are beautiful. Mussels are delicious. Mussels are easy as hell to cook. Just make sure you buy nice, fresh, still-living mussels (cultivated or wild, as you wish). Wash them carefully in cold water, store them—if you are storing them—in the refrigerator, in a raised slotted pan or colander so they can be separated from whatever may drain out of them, and before beginning to cook, make sure that they are all closed. If there are open ones, tap them lightly and see if they then begin to close. If a few stay open and don't respond? Throw those out.

Mussels should feel heavy and alive. If a mussel feels suspiciously light and hollow, even if closed, throw it out. If they smell like anything other than cold deep seawater, don't buy them. Fresh mussels look black and shiny, the vast majority still tightly closed, and they smell good. Wild mussels often have "beards," little hairy projections sticking out of the side of the shell. Tear these off by hand just prior to cooking (and no earlier). Most mussels you'll find are cultivated anyway, so it's unlikely you'll have that problem.

All of the above being said, be assured that it is ridiculously easy to cook mussels. The "bang for your buck" factor with the following dishes is very, very high: Dump stuff in a pot, cook for a few seconds, and drop into a bowl

and you've got a great, good-looking comfort meal, perfect for summer afternoons or late-night, eat-with-your-hands wine-drinking marathons.

But let's say the boss is coming over for dinner, or a photographic team from *Gourmet* magazine is on its way to chronicle your swinging lifestyle. You might want to get artsy—and burn your fingers: When you yank your mussels off the fire, instead of just dumping them into a bowl—or eating them right out of the pot (both perfectly acceptable, fun ways to go)—you can stick your tender paws into the pot and *quickly* pick the mussels out and arrange them in a shallow, heated serving bowl. Spreading each shell open slightly and resting each mussel upright in a sort of tight floral or concentric pattern, starting with the outer layer and working inward and upward, you can (if you don't burn your fingers too badly) make a cookbook-ready money shot of a presentation that will have your guests thinking you do this all the time.

Just do it *quickly*. And give the sauce left in the pot a good shot of heat before pouring it over your erotically gaping mussels. If you do this in a restaurant, you can whack the customer another $2.50 for the same dish. So it might be worth a try.

# moules normandes

## INGREDIENTS

$^1/_4$ lb/112 g slab bacon,
  cut into $^1/_2$-inch/1-cm cubes
4 tbsp/56 g butter
1 shallot, thinly sliced
6 small white mushrooms, thinly sliced
$^1/_2$ apple, cored, peeled, and cut into
  small dice or chunks
3 ounces/75 ml good Calvados
1 cup/225 ml heavy cream

salt and pepper
6 lb/2.7 kg mussels,
  scrubbed and debearded
  (just before cooking)

## EQUIPMENT

small pot
large pot with lid
wooden spoon

**SERVES 4**

In the small pot, cook the bacon over medium-high heat until the meat is brown and the fat has been rendered, about 10 minutes, stirring occasionally to avoid sticking. Discard the fat and reserve the meat.

In the large pot, heat the butter until it foams. Add the shallot and cook until soft, about 3 minutes. Add the mushrooms and the apple and cook for 5 minutes, then stir in the Calvados, scraping the bottom of the pot with the wooden spoon to dislodge any good brown stuff that might be clinging there. Stir in the cream and season with salt and pepper.

Once the mixture has come to a boil, add the mussels and cover. Cook for 10 minutes, or until all of the mussels have opened. Shake. Cook for another minute. Shake again. Serve immediately.

# moules
# à la portugaise

**I had to include this. My boss is Portuguese.**

## INGREDIENTS

$^1/_4$ **cup/56 ml olive oil**
$^1/_2$ **onion,** thinly sliced
**6 garlic cloves,** thinly sliced
**1 ounce/28 g chorizo sausage,**
  thinly sliced (see **NOTE**)
**1 cup/225 ml white wine**
**salt and pepper**
**6 lb/2.7 kg mussels,** scrubbed and
  debearded (just before cooking)

**1 bunch of cilantro,** leaves only
**4 sprigs of flat parsley,** finely
  chopped

## EQUIPMENT
large pot with a lid

**SERVES 4**

In the large pot, heat the oil, add the onion, and cook until soft and beginning to brown, about 6 minutes. Add the garlic and the chorizo and cook for another 2 minutes. Stir in the wine. Season with salt and pepper.

Add the mussels and cook with the lid on until all the mussels are open, 8 to 10 minutes. Shake. Add the cilantro and parsley. (If you want, boost with a knob of softened butter.) Shake again.

Serve with Portuguese country bread on the side, or with a thick-crusted Italian or French *boule*.

**NOTE:** Now, José, being Portuguese, would probably prefer that you use the dark, very dry, more artisanal chorizo sausage you see covered with white mold, hanging from the rack in Portuguese specialty shops. As an ex-Provincetown cook, I came to love the still-red, undried fresh stuff you can usually find more easily. The fiery red, cumin-scented grease that comes out of these bad boys when you sauté them with the garlic is a beautiful thing—and they do magical things to shellfish when cooked together. Either way, you're covered.

# moules marinières

**INGREDIENTS**
4 ounces/112 g butter
2 shallots, thinly sliced
2 cups/450 ml dry white wine
salt and pepper
6 lb/2.7 kg mussels, scrubbed and
debearded (just before cooking)
4 sprigs of flat parsley, finely chopped

**EQUIPMENT**
large pot with lid
warmed serving bowl

**SERVES 4**

Heat the butter in the large pot over medium-high heat. Once melted, add the shallots. Cook for 2 minutes, until the shallots are soft and just beginning to brown. Add the wine and bring to a boil (cranking up the heat all the way). Season with salt and pepper.

Some nice country bread is a good thing to have on the table, for you and your guests to tear at and use for mopping up the sauce.

Dump the mussels into the pot, and slap on the lid. Cook just until all the mussels are open all the way (about 10 minutes, no more). Shake the pot, keeping the lid firmly pressed on top, then add the parsley and shake again. (You can toss in an additional knob of softened butter at this point, swirling it into the sauce for a nice, emulsified, enriching boost.) Pour the whole glorious mess into the warmed serving bowl and serve.

# moules à la basquaise

**The hardest part of this dish is roasting the peppers—and that ain't hard. If you're a total chicken-head, you can simply substitute jarred pequillo peppers...but then no one will respect you in the morning.**

## INGREDIENTS
**1 red bell pepper**
**1 green bell pepper**
**$^1/_3$ cup/75 ml olive oil**
**1 small onion,** thinly sliced
**2 garlic cloves,** sliced
**2 cups/450 ml dry white wine**
**salt and pepper**
**6 lb/2.7 kg mussels,** scrubbed
  and debearded (just before cooking)
**4 sprigs of parsley,** finely chopped

## EQUIPMENT
baking sheet (for roasting the peppers)
tongs
large bowl and some plastic wrap
  (for peeling the peppers)
large pot with lid
warmed serving bowl

**SERVES 4**

## PREP
Roast the peppers! So easy. So useful a skill. Simply preheat your oven to a screaming 500°F/250°C. Place the peppers on the baking sheet and roast in the oven until the skin blisters and blackens. (Turn occasionally to make sure the whole skin blisters, or you'll have a hell of a time

peeling them.) This should take about 30 minutes. Now, here's a very useful trick: When the peppers are cooked, remove from the baking sheet (using the tongs) and immediately put into the large bowl and cover tightly with plastic wrap. After about 10 minutes, remove the plastic wrap and allow the peppers to cool a bit so you don't scald your sensitive fingers.

Now slip off the skins. Tear off the stems. Gently remove the seeds. Then slice the peppers into strips and set aside.

### COOK

In the large pot, heat the olive oil over medium-high heat and add the onion. Cook until soft and just beginning to brown (does this sound familiar?). Add the peppers and garlic and cook for 1 minute, then stir in the white wine and the salt and pepper to taste. Bring the mixture to a boil.

Dump in your mussels and slap on the lid. Cook over medium-high heat for about 10 minutes, until the mussels are open. Shake while keeping the lid clamped down. Add the parsley (and a small knob of butter if you're like me) and shake again. Upend into the warmed bowl and serve.

A nice (Spanish) touch would be to serve this with some sliced (lengthwise) pieces of baguette which you have lightly toasted and rubbed with garlic and fresh plum tomato pulp. Good stuff.

# moules à la grecque

This one's a nice departure from the summer-style mussel recipes so far, a dish more suited to fall and winter, or post–Labor Day New England. You know, fluffy sweater and shorts, tourists all gone…that crisp, cool Cape Cod light. Okay, I don't live that way either. But it sounds good, right?

INGREDIENTS
$^1/_4$ cup/56 ml olive oil
1 fennel bulb, cored and thinly sliced
2 shallots, sliced thin
4 garlic cloves, crushed
1 cup/225 ml white wine
juice of 1 lemon
1 tsp/5 g coriander seeds
1 tsp/5 g fennel seeds
salt and pepper
6 lb/2.7 kg mussels, scrubbed and
   debearded (just before cooking)

EQUIPMENT
large pot with lid

SERVES 4

Heat the olive oil in the pot. Add the fennel, shallots, and garlic and cook, stirring occasionally, until soft. Stir in the white wine, lemon juice, coriander and fennel seeds, and salt and pepper and bring to a boil. Add the mussels. Slap on the lid. Cook until done. Shake. Cook for another minute. Shake again. Serve.

# tartiflette

**Here's more evidence that you can never have too much cheese, bacon, or starch.**

### INGREDIENTS
2¹/₂ lb/1.1 kg potatoes, peeled
2 tbsp/28 g vegetable oil
1 medium onion, thinly sliced
¹/₂ lb/225 g slab bacon,
  cut into small dice
³/₄ cup/170 ml white wine
salt and pepper
1 lb/450 g Reblochon cheese

### EQUIPMENT
large pot
paring knife
strainer
large sauté pan
wooden spoon
round, ovenproof dish

**SERVES 6**

Preheat the oven to 350°F/175°C. Place the potatoes in the large pot, cover with water, and bring to a boil. Cook for about 20 minutes, or until the potatoes are easily pierced with the paring knife. Remove from the heat, drain, and let sit until they are cool enough to handle. Cut the potatoes into a small dice and set aside.

In the large sauté pan, heat the oil over high heat and add the onion. Cook over high heat for about 5 minutes, until golden brown, then add the bacon and cook for another 5 minutes, stirring occasionally. Add the potatoes and wine and season with salt and pepper. Cook for 10 minutes over medium heat, stirring occasionally.

Remove the mixture from the heat and place half of it in the round, ovenproof dish. Spread half the Reblochon atop the potato mixture. Cover this with the other half of the potato mixture. Top with the remainder of the cheese. Bake in the oven for 20 minutes, or until golden brown and bubbling. Serve hot.

# rillettes

Rillettes is about as old-school a dish as you can get—and a tragically hard-to-find one. Seeing it on the menu at Les Halles, when I first applied to work there, was like finding an old friend. It gets right to the heart of what's good: pork, pork fat, salt, and pepper. Easy and cheap to make, it's one of the great casual starters of all time. Just shape into an attractive round or square, comb the top with a fork, and dig in. Smeared on toasted baguette croutons and enjoyed with cocktails, or served as an appetizer, it sets the tone for an enjoyable, eat-with-your-hands-and-have-a-good-time kind of evening. Kick off a meal with rillettes and you don't have to wipe the plate rims, garnish the entree, or remember to keep your elbows off the table. Rillettes is something you serve friends—and people you already know you like.

## INGREDIENTS
**2 lb/900 g pork belly,** cut into
   2-in/5-cm cubes
**1 lb/450 g pork shoulder,** cut into
   2-in/5-cm cubes
**4 cups/900 ml water**
**1 bouquet garni** (see Glossary)
**1 tsp/5 g salt**
**pinch of black pepper**
**1 lb/450 g pork fat,** cut into thin slices

## EQUIPMENT
large, heavy-bottomed pot
mixing bowl
2 forks
several small plastic or glass containers
plastic wrap

**SERVES A LOT—
AND FOR A LONG TIME**

**COOK**

Place the pork belly and shoulder in the heavy-bottomed pot. Add the water and the bouquet garni and cook over low heat, stirring occasionally. After 6 hours, stir in the salt and pepper and remove from the heat. Discard the bouquet garni.

Once the meat is cool enough to handle, transfer it to the mixing bowl and, using the forks, shred the meat, taking care to preserve the natural filament—meaning you want shreds, *not* mush. Feel free to shovel a little still-warm pork into your face. C'mon. You know you want it.

Next, divide the mixture among several small containers. Top each portion with a slice or two of pork fat to completely cover it, fold the mixture together a bit, then wrap each container in plastic wrap. Place in the refrigerator and let them sit for 3 days before serving. This is the hardest part of the recipe because it's *real* good. Just know that it only gets better as those flavors marry up in the fridge.

**Jesus, this dish is easy.
Don't tell your friends.
Let them think you're
a genius, a master
*charcutier,* while they're
busy cooing and gaping.**

**SERVE**

Scoop some out, form it into a vaguely artful shape (with a metal ring for instance), and garnish with toasted baguette rounds and cornichons. Left covered, rillettes will keep in the refrigerator for up to a month.

# foie gras
# aux pruneaux

Dumb-ass men's magazines—you know the ones: cars, clothes, B-list actresses in bikinis—are always asking me to do insipid articles on dishes "guaranteed to get you laid" or about "the food of seduction." I can't guarantee it as an aphrodisiac, but I would think that a man (or woman) who knows how to appreciate and cook foie gras would, in the simple act of searing a slice of luxuriously fattened goose liver, be exhibiting in one task both a delicate sensibility and an enticing cruel streak. Anyone not in PETA, with a profound love of the pleasures of the flesh, should be bowled over. Give it a try. Let me know how things turn out.

**INGREDIENTS**
**8 prunes**
**1 cup/225 ml port**
**2$^1/_2$ ounces/70 g fresh foie gras,**
   cut into 4 slices (see Suppliers)
**salt and pepper**

EQUIPMENT
small bowl
heavy-bottomed sauté pan,
   preferably cast-iron
slotted metal spatula or fish turner
serving platter
wooden spatula

**SERVES 4
(WHAT THE HELL—
MAKE IT FOR 2 AND
PIG OUT)**

### PREP

Place the prunes in the small bowl, cover with the port, and soak for at least 2 hours before cooking the foie gras.

### COOK

Season the foie gras with salt and pepper. Heat the sauté pan over high heat until very hot. Sear the foie gras in the pan (no butter or oil needed) for about 45 seconds per side. The foie gras will shrivel and shrink and kick out lots of fat. The idea is to sear it quickly on each side until nicely caramelized and brown, without melting the whole thing away. It's almost impossible to cook this dish too rare, so concern yourself with the external color. If it's brown on both sides, lift it out of the pan with the slotted spatula and transfer to a serving platter.

Quickly discard about half the fat that issued so enticingly from the foie, then add the soaked prunes. Using the wooden spatula, stir in a little of the soaking liquid to dislodge (deglaze) any browned bits in the pan. Cook for 2 minutes, reducing the sauce, then pour it all over the foie gras and serve.

### SERVE

**This is a last-minute dish. Foie gras is not something that should sit around. You want your guests to watch you cooking this.**

This dish is very nice served with a few thin slices of brioche toast to mop up the sauce. If you want to really look like a hotshot, you can also (much earlier in the day) reduce some balsamic vinegar to a thick syrup and then drizzle a tiny bit of it over the foie gras and the platter in decorative Jackson Pollock patterns as a sweet-sour garnish.

# pâté de campagne

You've made meat loaf, right? You've eaten cold meat loaf, yes? Then you're halfway to being an ass-kicking, name-taking *charcutier.* "Ooooh...pâté, I don't know." Please. *Campagne* means "country" in French—which means even your country-ass can make it.

Caul fat is the lacelike intestinal lining that you are going to use to line your terrine mold. It's one of those things you want to have ordered from your butcher way in advance, so that it's there, fresh and ready to go, when your other meat arrives. Caul fat is great, multipurpose stuff. Your butcher has probably heard the tales of his fellow butchers binding wounds with it. You can wrap forcemeats in it (as we will do), fish, or roasts. It helps keep shape and retain moisture, and it adds flavor. And it looks really cool and professional. It has the added benefit of being easy to work with.

## INGREDIENTS
$^1/_2$ **lb/225 g pork liver,**
   cut into chunks just small enough
   to fit into the meat grinder
$^1/_2$ **lb/225 g pork fat,**
   cut into chunks just small enough
   to fit into the meat grinder
**1 lb/450 g pork shoulder,**
   cut into chunks just small enough
   to fit into the meat grinder
$^1/_2$ **tbsp/7 g black pepper**
**scant pinch of allspice** (careful!)
**5 garlic cloves**
**2 shallots,** thinly sliced
**3 ounces/75 ml Cognac**
**3 ounces/75 ml white wine**
**4 sprigs of flat parsley**
**1 tbsp/14 g salt**
**1 egg**
**caul fat to wrap**
   (purchase from your butcher)
**1 cup/225 g duck fat** (see Suppliers)

## EQUIPMENT
large bowl
good strong meat grinder
   (unless you have the butcher
   do it for you)
terrine mold
aluminum foil
bain-marie (a big roasting pan with water
   in it, which you're going to put the terrine
   mold into)
meat thermometer
5-lb/2-kg weight

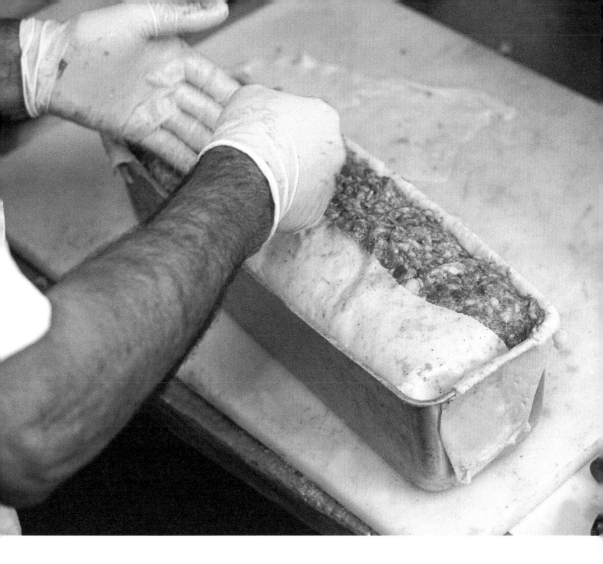

**MAKES A
2¹/₂-POUND/1.5-KG
TERRINE**

**PREP**
In the large bowl, combine the liver, pork fat, pork shoulder, pepper,
allspice, garlic, shallots, Cognac, white wine, and parsley and cover.
Refrigerate overnight. That was easy.

**CONSTRUCTION**
The next day, remove the mixture from the refrigerator, add the salt,
and pass everything through the strong meat grinder which you have
fitted with a medium blade. The grind size should *not* be too small
(paste) nor too large (chunks). Basically, you're looking for a grind size
about that of meat loaf. If you don't have a durable meat grinder, suck
up to your friendly neighborhood butcher and take your mix down to
him. He should like you by now; he doesn't get a lot of calls for pork

liver and pork fat. (If that's also not an option, trim off as much sinew as possible, cut the pork into small dice, and hope for the best.) When your meat and other ingredients are ground up, add the egg and mix through by hand. Preheat the oven to 325°F/170°C.

Next, line the terrine mold with one big piece of caul fat (or overlapping pieces, if you must) so that plenty of extra flops over the edge—enough to cover the top of the pâté when you fill the mold. Fill the terrine with the ground mixture, packing it tightly. Lift the terrine and firmly drop it onto the work surface (easy, don't go nuts) a few times, to knock out any air pockets. Fold over the remaining caul fat to neatly cover the pâté, trimming and tucking until it looks nice. Now cover the whole megillah with foil.

### COOK

Set up a bain-marie inside the preheated oven. Put the filled terrine in the center. *Obviously* you do not want the water level to be so high that the water leaks into the terrine mold. You want just enough water so that it comes up below the rim. Cook the terrine in the water bath in the oven for about $2^1/_2$ hours, or until the internal temperature is 160°F/70°C (this is where your meat thermometer comes in). When done, remove from the oven and allow to cool. Place the weight on top of the terrine (still in foil) and refrigerate overnight.

The next day, remove the weight, remove the foil, melt down the duck fat in a small saucepan, and pour it carefully over the pâté. Then refrigerate again for a few hours. The pâté will keep in the refrigerator for at least 5 days.

### SERVE

Serve with cornichons and maybe a tiny salad. If you did everything right, the pâté, when sliced, should be firm and moist, not dry or crumbly. The color should be uniform, not pink at the bottom and gray on the top. It should be cooked through, and the slices should have structural integrity, meaning they don't break when you cut them.

**If this recipe worked out for you, you can apply your newfound skills to all sorts of variations, including Pâté de Lapin on page 094.**

# pâté de lapin

**INGREDIENTS**

3¹/₂ lb/1.575 kg rabbit meat,
  cut into 1-inch/2.5-cm chunks
1¹/₄ lb/560 g pork fat,
  cut into 1-inch/2.5-cm chunks
³/₄ lb/340 g chicken livers
5 ounces/150 ml Calvados
3 ounces/90 ml apple cider
1 sprig of fresh thyme
  (leaves only, stem discarded)
4 garlic cloves, crushed
1 shallot, finely chopped
³/₄ lb/340 g foie gras
1 tsp salt
pinch/5 g of kosher salt
pinch/5 g of pink sea salt
  (*sel rose;* see Suppliers)
pinch/5 g of *quatre-épices* (a mixture of
  four spices; see Suppliers)
pinch/5 g of white pepper
2 eggs
¹/₂ cup/110 ml heavy cream
4 to 6 slices of thinly sliced fatback
  (or caul fat; see page 009)
1 cup/225 g rendered pork fat

**EQUIPMENT**

2 mixing bowls
meat grinder
spatula or wooden spoon
terrine mold
aluminum foil
bain-marie (a big roasting
  pan with water in it)
meat thermometer
5-lb/2-kg weight

### PREP

In a mixing bowl, combine the rabbit, pork fat, chicken livers, Calvados, cider, thyme, garlic, and shallot and mix well. Cover and refrigerate for 24 hours.

Remove the mix and the foie gras from the refrigerator and pass through the meat grinder. Place the forcemeat into a clean bowl and add the salt and spices. Mix well, then add the eggs and mix well again. Stir in the cream and mix yet again.

### CONSTRUCTION

I don't want to throw you a ringer here, but if you're confident in your abilities, there is a variation you might want to consider. You can, for instance, *not* grind some of the rabbit meat, pork fat, and foie gras. Instead you can hold them back, dice them, and add them to the mix at the last minute, when you're mixing it all up. This will add an artful sprinkle of center garnish scattered through the meat—attractive to look at when sliced—and a nice textural note. Just think of it as the French equivalent of putting a hard-boiled egg in the center of a meat loaf. (Not something I approve of, by the way—the egg, I mean.) In time, you can mess with your pâté in all sorts of bold new ways, adding diced ham, pistachios, black truffles—even layering carefully. For the time being, though, just grind your ingredients and jam the mixture into the terrine or terrines which you have lined with sliced fatback or caul fat. Bang out air pockets, pour in pork fat, and cover tightly with foil.

### COOK

Toss into a preheated 325°F/170°C oven—in the water bath—and cook until the internal temperature is 160°F/70°C, about 2$^1/_2$ hours. Remove from the oven. Allow to cool to room temperature, then place in the refrigerator with the weight on top for a few hours before slicing and serving.

# petatou

(from Jean-Michel Diot)

## INGREDIENTS

**2 lb/900 g red bliss potatoes,**
   cut in half, skin on
**salt**
**¹/₂ lb/225 g niçoise olives,**
   pitted and chopped
**1 tbsp/14 g fresh thyme leaves,** chopped
**¹/₄ cup/56 ml** *plus* **2 tbsp/28 ml**
   **extra-virgin olive oil**
**2 tbsp/28 ml balsamic vinegar**
**pepper**
**1 cup/225 ml heavy cream**
**1 egg yolk**
**2 tbsp/28 g flat parsley leaves,** chopped
**4 ounces/112 g soft goat cheese,**
   cut into 4 equally sized portions

## EQUIPMENT

medium pot
strainer
paring knife
3 mixing bowls
small pot
whisk
3-inch ring mold (an oiled casserole
   will work, in a pinch)
baking dish
spatula

**SERVES 4**

### PREP THE POTATOES

Place the potatoes in the medium pot and add water to cover. Add about 2 tablespoons of salt and bring to a boil. Cook for 20 minutes, then remove from the heat and drain off the hot water. Let the potatoes cool under running water. When they are cool enough to handle but still warm, remove and discard their skins. Cut the potatoes into small cubes with the paring knife and place in a mixing bowl. Add the olives, thyme, ¹/₄ cup/56 ml of the olive oil, and the balsamic vinegar. Season with salt and pepper and toss gently. *Gently,* okay? You're not making mashed potatoes. Set the mixture aside.

### PREP THE GLAZE

In the small pot, bring the heavy cream to a boil. Let it reduce by half, taking care to not let it scorch or boil over onto your stovetop. If it looks

like this is going to happen, just reduce the heat a little. While the
cream is cooking, place the egg yolk in another mixing bowl and beat
lightly with the whisk. When the cream is reduced, remove from the
heat and, whisking constantly, add the hot cream to the yolk. Add
most of this mixture to the cooked potato mix, holding back about
4 tablespoons/64 g.

### PREP THE DRESSING
In the third mixing bowl, combine the parsley and remaining olive oil
and mix well. Season with salt and pepper and set aside.

### FINAL ASSEMBLY
Preheat the broiler. Using a 3-inch/7-cm metal ring (or a cut-down
section of 3-inch/7-cm PVC pipe), shape the potato mixture into 4
cylinders in the center of the baking dish. Top each with a medallion
of goat cheese. Spoon 1 tablespoon/14 g of the remaining heavy cream
mixture atop each medallion. Place the baking dish under the broiler
and cook until the glaze is nicely browned. With the spatula, carefully
remove the finished *petatous* to individual plates. Spoon the parsley
dressing around each plate and serve.

# fish & shellfish

# skate grenobloise

Long thought of as a "trash fish," skate is one of the truly great seafood items: tender, sweet, well-textured—and cheap. Which is why many chefs are evangelical about running it as a special. As it becomes more popular it will no doubt become more and more expensive. Cleaning it, meaning removing the delicate fillets from the cartilage (though it's perfectly fine to cook it with cartilage intact) and the thick, rubbery skin (which *must* be removed), is tricky, so have your fishmonger do the work. Note also that skate, like other more delicate and subtle white-fleshed fishes, is very perishable. You want to buy it and cook it on the day it came in.

## INGREDIENTS
$^1/_4$ cup/56 g flour
salt and finely ground white pepper
2 skate wings, skinned and boned out
4 tbsp/56 g butter
1 tbsp/14 g capers
$^1/_2$ cup/112 g croutons
juice of 1 lemon
1 sprig of flat parsley, finely chopped
peeled, seeded segments of 1 lemon
  (optional)

## EQUIPMENT
shallow bowl
sauté pan
fish turner or slotted spatula
serving platter

SERVES 2

### PREP
Put the flour in the shallow bowl and season it with salt and pepper. Dredge the fish in the flour and shake off the excess. Re-season the fish with salt and pepper.

### COOK
In the sauté pan, heat 1 tablespoon/14 g of the butter over medium-high heat. When the butter has foamed and subsided, add the fish and

cook over high heat for 2 minutes. Add 1 more tablespoon/14 g of butter and turn the fish, cooking the other side for 2 minutes. Transfer the fish to the serving platter.

### FINISH
Discard the butter from the pan and then add the remaining 2 tablespoons/28 g of butter. Cook over high heat until it foams and subsides, then add the capers and croutons. Cook for 30 seconds, then add the lemon juice and parsley. (You can add the lemon segments at this point as well.) Remove from the heat and spoon the sauce over the fish.

# whole roasted fish basquaise

How many times, and in how many ways, can I say it? Fish tastes better *on the bone!* As every cook from every serious food culture from every generation knows, *the head—and the meat right behind it—is the best-tasting fish there is.* You know the old saw about the closer to the bone, the sweeter the meat? That ain't no lie. So please, free yourself up! Throw off your shackles and get right with the grand sweep of recorded culinary history. Start with this recipe.

## INGREDIENTS

2 Yukon Gold potatoes
salt
4 tbsp/56 ml olive oil
1 onion, thinly sliced
1 red bell pepper, cored, seeded, and cut into thin strips
1 green bell pepper, cored, seeded, and cut into thin strips
4 garlic cloves, crushed
2 sprigs of thyme, leaves only
$^1/_2$ cup/110 ml white wine
1 cup/225 ml chicken broth or light chicken stock
1 red snapper, about 2 lb/900 g, scales removed, gills removed, fins clipped, guts removed, but otherwise intact
pepper
juice of 1 lemon
4 sprigs of flat parsley

## EQUIPMENT

small pot
roasting pan
wooden spoon
bulb-type baster
baking sheet
serving platter

## STAGE ONE

Preheat the oven to 400°F/200°C. Place the potatoes in the small pot and cover them with water. Add salt to taste and bring to a boil. Cook for 10 minutes. The potatoes should still be firm. Remove them from the water and reserve.

## STAGE TWO

On the stovetop, heat the olive oil in the roasting pan until it almost sizzles. Add the onions and peppers and cook over medium heat until the vegetables are soft and browned. Add the garlic and thyme and cook for another 2 to 3 minutes. Stir in the white wine, scraping the bottom of the pan with the wooden spoon to dislodge all that good stuff. Stir in the chicken broth and bring the mixture to a boil.

Season the fish with salt and pepper inside and out. After the broth and vegetables have been boiling for 5 minutes, place the fish in the pan, add the potatoes, and toss the whole thing into the oven. Cook for about 30 minutes, basting the fish with the pan juices 2 or 3 times during cooking.

## STAGE THREE

Change the oven's setting to broil, remove the pan from the oven, and remove the fish from the roasting pan. Place the fish on the baking sheet and put it under the broiler for 3 to 5 minutes, or until the skin turns brown and crispy. Keep an eye on it: You *do not* want to scorch the thing. Transfer the fish to the serving platter. Add the lemon juice to the bell pepper and potato mixture, and season with salt and pepper. After a quick shot of heat and a stir or two, spoon the mixture over and around the fish. Garnish with the parsley and serve immediately.

*Do not* **neglect the cheeks, the meat at the collar, or the flaky bits between the bones. Feel free to eat with your hands.**

Now think of all the ways you can improvise on this dish.

# friture

This is one of my very favorite things on earth. You don't even really need a recipe, it's so simple. What you *do* need is a pile of very fresh, very small whitebait or smelts. By small, I mean no more than $1^1/_2$ inches long. The smaller and thinner, the better. Have your fish guy keep an eye out for them, and if and when available, pounce!

**INGREDIENTS**
**whitebait or smelts**
**soy or corn oil**
**seasoned flour**
**lemon wedges**
**extra-virgin olive oil** (optional)
**garlic,** chopped (optional)
**flat parsley,** chopped (optional)

**EQUIPMENT**
large pot

**SERVES AS MANY AS YOU LIKE**

Wash the fish in cold water. Grabbing each one, pinch the belly, and squeeze until the guts rush right out of the wazoo. Sure it's a little gross, but I promise you it'll be worth it. Rinse in cold water.

Heat a big pot of soy or corn oil until the temperature reaches 375°F/190°C. Quickly toss your fish in a light dusting of seasoned flour (salt and pepper, as well as cayenne, or nutmeg, or garlic powder…you get the idea), shake off the excess, and then drop them into the hot oil. Fry them until they're crispy and golden brown. Remove from the oil, and either serve with lemon or toss them with a little extra-virgin olive oil, some chopped fresh garlic, and some chopped parsley until lightly coated. Then eat with your fingers.

*Friture* should have the consistency of an ethereal French fry.

# coquilles saint-jacques with champagne

This recipe calls for sea scallops. Sea scallops are *not* those horrible little pencil erasers (a.k.a. calico scallops), nor the scallops that come in a plastic tub, marinating in some mysterious liquid. What you want are what's called, in the industry, "dry" sea scallops. Tell your fish guy. If he doesn't have them, tell him you're willing to wait. What you are looking for will be a fairly sizable, dry, almost sticky, sweet-smelling thing—decidedly *not* waterlogged. They're pricey. But worth it. Obviously, expensive Champagne is better here, but this dish still tastes good with $10 domestic brut.

**INGREDIENTS**
**2 tbsp/28 g butter,** softened
**1 shallot,** thinly sliced
**1 cup/225 ml fish fumet** (stock)
**1/2 cup/110 ml heavy cream**
**salt and freshly ground black pepper**
**16 sea scallops**
**2 tbsp/28 g clarified butter** (see Glossary)
**1/2 cup/110 ml Champagne**
**juice of 1/2 lemon**
**4 chives,** finely chopped

**EQUIPMENT**
small saucepan
strainer
sauté pan
tongs or fish spatula
wooden spoon
serving platter

**BEGIN THE SAUCE**

In a small saucepan, melt 1 tablespoon/14 g of the butter, then add the shallot. Let them cook over medium-low heat until soft but not browned, about 3 minutes. Add the fish fumet and bring to a boil. Cook over medium-high heat until it is reduced by half, then add the cream. Bring the mixture to a boil, reduce to a simmer, and cook for 15 minutes. Strain the sauce, season with salt and pepper, and keep warm.

As you may have already noticed, you're only going to need a half cup of that Champagne, and since you've had to crack a whole bottle, and it's going flat anyway, you may as well start drinking. That's what's called "the chef's prerogative."

**COOK THE SCALLOPS**

Pat the scallops dry (if necessary) and season with salt and pepper. Heat the clarified butter over high heat in a sauté pan and, once the butter is hot, add the scallops. Cook on one side for about 3 minutes, then turn them with tongs or a fish spatula to cook on the other side for about 3 minutes. You want a golden-brown crust on each round surface. Remove the scallops from the pan and set aside.

**FINISH THE SAUCE AND SERVE**

Discard the excess fat in the sauté pan. Return the pan to the heat and stir in the Champagne, scraping with a wooden spoon to incorporate the brown stuff. Reduce the Champagne over medium-high heat until it is thick enough to coat the back of a spoon, then whisk in the reserved cream sauce. Bring to a boil and whisk in the remaining tablespoon of softened butter. Remove the mixture from the heat and stir in the lemon juice and chives. Arrange the scallops on a serving platter and pour the sauce around.

**Take a big hit of the remaining Champagne and stagger to the table.**

# blanquette de homard

## INGREDIENTS

$2^{1}/_{2}$ lb/225 g haricots verts
  (skinny French green beans)
salt
12 pearl onions
6 tbsp/75 g butter, softened
pinch of sugar
2 2-lb/900-g lobsters
1 shallot, peeled and sliced very thin
1 leek, white part only, washed
  and sliced very thin
$^{1}/_{4}$ cup/56 ml white wine
1 cup/225 ml light chicken stock
  or broth
2 cups/450 ml heavy cream
white pepper
juice of 1 lemon
1 bunch of fresh chives, chopped
  small (that's *fresh*—not that freeze-dried
  garbage, okay?)
a few sprigs of flat parsley or chervil,
  for garnish

## EQUIPMENT

large pot
large bowl, filled with ice water
paring knife
small saucepan
big-ass knife, with a heavy-duty blade
wide *sautoir* (a large sauté pan with
  perpendicular edges) with lid, or
  with foil to cover
wooden spoon
tongs or slotted spoon
warmed serving platter
whisk

**SERVES 4**

**PREP**

First, the haricots verts. In the large pot, bring 4 cups/900 ml of water to a rolling boil. Add a large pinch of salt. Cook the beans until tender, but still bright green and slightly crunchy, about 7 minutes. Do *not* add the beans to the water until the water is roiling!! If your beans look army-green colored and limp, you've screwed up. Do it again. When the beans are properly cooked, remove from the boiling water and plunge them immediately into the ice water to shock them and arrest the cooking. When cooled, set them aside.

Okay. Take a breath. Relax. Next, the pearl onions. Peeling these little fuckers is a pain, I know. Just get it over with. When peeled, place the pearl onions and 2 tablespoons/28 g of the butter, a pinch of salt, and a pinch of sugar in the small saucepan and cover with water. The onions should peek out above the surface. Cook over medium heat for about 10 minutes, or until all the water evaporates. Make sure the onions don't take on any color. That would be bad. If they look like they're starting to get brown, or you think you need to add a little more water, do it. Just make sure you don't cook them too much; you do *not* want mush. You want tender, distinctive little onions that have retained their shape but are cooked through. Remove from the heat and set aside.

**Some delicate people like to "kill" the lobster before cutting it up, by putting the tip of the knife between its eyes and cutting open the head lengthwise. You can do it that way, but it's really not that much help; the lobster is still going to move long after it's dead.**

All right. That's done. Here comes the ugly part. You might need a drink for this: Cut the still wriggling, flopping, and protesting lobsters' tails into 4 pieces each, crunching right through the shells and leaving the meat intact. Don't worry. Lobsters are essentially big fucking bugs; they're too stupid to know they're dead. And if it makes you feel any better, they do much worse things to one another. Tear off the claws and crack them, meaning give them a good wallop on top, behind the hinge of the claws with the heel of your knife. Hopefully you're using an impressive hunk of German steel so you're not going to screw up the blade. When the blade goes in, cutting through the shell but *not* the meat, you can wobble or rock the blade a little, prying open a fissure in the shell with a resounding CRACK! Reserve the unused parts of the lobster—the knuckles and heads. That's *gold,* baby. Freeze them and use them some other time for lobster stock or lobster butter or bisque.

## COOK

In the wide *sautoir,* and over medium heat, heat 2 tablespoons/28 g of the butter until foaming and hot (but *not* brown) and add the shallot and leek. Reduce the heat to low and cover the pot with its lid or foil. Cook for 10 minutes, stirring occasionally. Remove the lid and crank up the heat again, deglazing by adding the white wine and scraping up all the good stuff from the bottom of the pan. When the white wine has nearly cooked away, add the chicken stock, bring to a boil, and reduce by half. Add the heavy cream, reduce heat again, and simmer. Add the lobster claws and tail pieces. Cover and cook for about 8 minutes over low heat. Remove the cover and throw in the precooked pearl onions and haricots verts. Add white pepper to taste. Simmer for another 2 minutes *with the lid off*.

## SERVE

Remove the lobster pieces and the vegetables from the pot and arrange artfully on the warmed platter. Quickly fire up the heat to maximum, bringing the sauce to a boil. Whisk in the remaining 2 tablespoons/28 g of butter, the lemon juice, and your no doubt impeccably chopped chives. Adjust the seasoning. Hopefully the sauce will be reasonably thick (but not gluey—just thick enough to coat the lobster). Pour it over the lobster and vegetables and garnish with parsley or chervil.

# quenelles de brochet

A quenelle is like a dumpling. This is basically a French version of gefilte fish. But better. *Brochet* is French for pike.

## INGREDIENTS

FOR THE QUENELLES
salt
4 ounces/110 ml milk
2 ounces/56 g butter
2 ounces/56 g flour
2 eggs, separated (yolks and whites)
5 lb/2.2 kg pike, bones and skin removed
4 ounces/110 ml heavy cream
pepper

FOR THE SAUCE
2 tbsp/28 ml salad oil
1 lb/450 g crawfish
1 small onion, thinly sliced
2 ounces/56 g tomato paste
1 tbsp/14 g flour
1 ounce/28 ml Cognac
4 ounces/110 ml white wine
4 ounces/110 ml water
salt and pepper

## EQUIPMENT
2 medium pots
wooden spoon
food processor
large mixing bowl
rubber spatula
2 large spoons
ovenproof casserole
large saucepan
strainer

**SERVES 6 TO 8**

This can be a tricky recipe, but it's well worth it. Just take it slow. One thing at a time. Get your *mise en place* together at your own pace, and the service part will be fun and easy.

### STAGE ONE
*The quenelles.* Preheat the oven to 375°F/190°C. On the stovetop, fill a medium pot with heavily salted water and bring to a boil. In another medium pot, combine the milk and butter and bring to a boil.

Immediately dump in the flour and stir vigorously with the wooden spoon until the mixture is smooth and does not stick to the spoon. Remove the pot from the heat, let cool slightly, then add the egg yolks, one at a time, stirring well each time you add a yolk. Good so far? Set the mixture aside. In the food processor, combine the fish, the egg whites, cream, and salt and pepper to taste, and purée until the mix is smooth and light. Put the mixture into the large mixing bowl and, using the rubber spatula, fold in the flour mixture that you set aside. That work out for you? No problems? Then let us proceed...

Using the two large spoons, form the cooled mixture into quenelles. When you've got a nice shape on your quenelles, lower the heat on your boiling water to a simmer and lower the quenelles carefully in with a spoon. Cook them for 10 minutes, then remove from the water and place in the ovenproof casserole. A good strategy here is to place the quenelles right into the water *as you make them*—one by one, in a clockwise pattern. Remove them accordingly. Sounds harder than it is. Confused? Frustrated? Just reread above. Remember, there's still no rush. Take as long as you like.

**What you're looking for is a formed dumpling, shaped like a swollen football. Fat in the middle, pointy on the ends. Take your time. If it doesn't work out at first, just re-form and try again.**

### STAGE TWO

*The sauce.* Let's assume you can't find whole, live crawfish. So cheat. Remember those lobster bits, the heads and knuckles you've got kicking around in your freezer? Chop them up and use them exactly as the recipe calls for you to use the crawfish. Just as good. And if you *really* want to do something sneaky and wonderful, you can buy frozen crawfish tailmeat. Just make the sauce using your lobster shells and scraps and then, at the very end—*after* you've strained the sauce—float some of the cute little bits of crawfish tail meat in the heating sauce until cooked through. Looks pretty impressive. Tastes delicious. You can pull the same gag using bits of lobster meat if you like.

Anyhoo...the sauce. In the large saucepan, heat the oil over medium-high heat and add the crawfish (or lobster chunks). Cook until browned. Then add the onion. Cook over medium heat, then add the tomato paste and flour, mixing well. Let cook for 2 minutes. Add the Cognac, which will flame—so watch out. When the flame subsides, add the wine and scrape the bottom of the pan with your wooden spoon to dislodge and deglaze. After about 5 minutes over medium-high heat, add the water and reduce the heat to a simmer. Let cook for about 25 minutes, then season with salt and pepper to taste. Strain the sauce over the quenelles, right into the casserole. If you've decided you want chunks of crawfish meat or lobster floating in the sauce, strain into another bowl first, then add the meat, *then* pour over the quenelles. Toss the casserole in the oven and bake for 30 minutes. Serve immediately.

# bourride

## INGREDIENTS

3 tbsp/42 ml olive oil

1 lb/450 g fish bones and trimmings (snapper, striped bass, grouper, or other white fish)

1 small onion, finely chopped

1 small carrot, finely chopped

$^1/_4$ bulb of fennel, finely chopped

1 leek, white part only, finely chopped

4 garlic cloves

1 large tomato, finely chopped

salt and pepper

2 cups/450 ml water

1 bouquet garni (see Glossary)

$^1/_4$ cup/56 ml heavy cream

4 6- to 8-ounce/170- to 225-g monkfish tails, cleaned and skinned

1 cup/225 g aïoli (see page 257)

## EQUIPMENT

large pot

wooden spoon

food mill

large bowl

serving bowl

medium bowl

ladle

whisk

**SERVES 4**

A pinch of salt over the tomato when it first goes into the pan helps to break it down.

## PREP

Over medium-high heat, warm the olive oil in the large pot and add the fish bones and trimmings. Reduce the heat to medium-low and let the ingredients sweat for 5 minutes. Add the onion, carrot, fennel, leek, and garlic and sweat for another 5 minutes, then add the tomato. Stir well and cook over medium heat for another 5 minutes. Add the bouquet garni and the water, season with salt and pepper to taste, and bring to a boil.

Once the mixture boils, lower to a simmer and cook for 30 minutes. Remove the bouquet garni and discard. Pass the whole mess through the food mill into the large bowl, then return it to the pot. Bring it

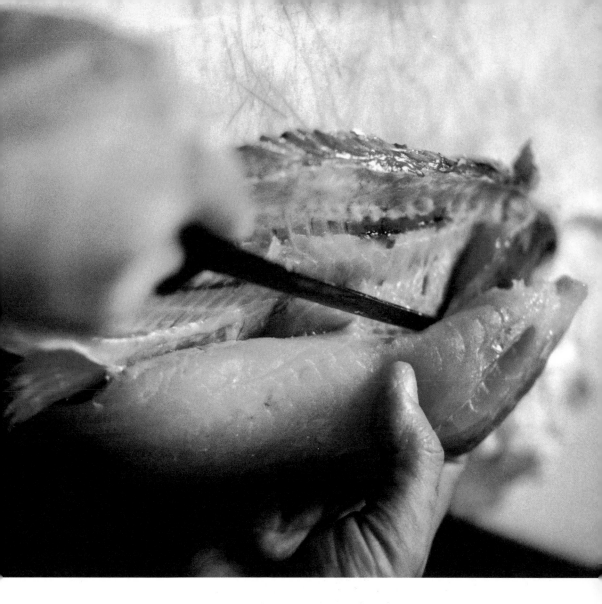

back to a boil, add the cream, and cook over high heat for 10 minutes, or until the liquid has reduced. Lower the boiling broth to a simmer and add the monkfish tails. Cook over low heat for about 10 minutes, making sure the liquid does *not* boil.

### SERVE
Transfer the cooked tails to the serving bowl and then bring the liquid back to a boil. Place the aïoli sauce in the mixing bowl and ladle 1 cup of the cooking liquid over it, whisking vigorously and constantly. Adjust the seasoning if necessary, then pour the sauce immediately over the cooked monkfish and serve right away.

# beef

# BEEF

**The French cut meat differently than you and I.**

**Actually, they cut meat differently than *you* do. At Les Halles, we have a French butcher and a French *charcutier* who do it the old-school way, cutting and preparing it in the fiendishly creative French style. (Unlike the French, we also have the luxury of American beef, which is, generally speaking, far superior.)**

So as not to drive your butcher to despair, however, I have done my very best to include recipes for only those French cuts that you are likely to find or be able to have prepared for you. Though there are all sorts of tiny, wonderful boutique cuts available from genuine French butchers, I'll describe only those for which there are analogous terms in English. If your butcher says he can't get any of these, he's either lying or lazy.

Now, while I won't bore and confuse you with esoterica and lavish descriptions of seldom-seen cuts like "the spider" or "the pear," there are some things you should know and appreciate about French butchering—and meat—in general.

Simply put, French butchering grew up around a very different system of distribution and economics than ours, so wily French butchers have, for generations, been tunneling after every little bit of goodness on the animal, in order to merchandise every single part. Whether you're talking about beef, lamb, veal, or pork, French cooking directly reflects this frugal attitude—and the necessity of dealing with the whole animal. As a result, "beef" is not the uniform concept it has too often become here. To the French, a side of beef is a magical mosaic of delicious possibilities. Each cut, each little bit, is viewed for its unique characteristics and best method of expression. Cooking meat in France, especially beef, requires transformation, the mission, more often than not, being to turn the lean and the tough into the tender and sublime.

Strangely, for a nation that gleefully ages just about everything else (game, cheese, wine, bad pop musicians), the French have no tradition of dry-aging beef. Generally speaking, French beef is fresh and relatively fat-free compared with its American counterparts—and trimmed down to its very essence. The French "faux-filet," for instance, compared with our "sirloin" or loin end "rib eye," is whittled down to only the lean, the outer layer of fat completely removed. There is no such thing as a porterhouse or a T-bone, as bones are generally avoided. And while American butchers usually work along the natural seams and lines of connective tissue, the French "cut" more.

Because French butchering grew up around largely rural situations—each community at one time had its own abattoir—a limited amount of beef was available to a particular village at a single time. The challenge was always to make use of what was left after the pricy sirloin, rib eye, and filet were sold. The French butcher learned where to find relatively small steaks off the shoulder, leg, and flank that were still suitable for grilling and searing, and how to get money for them. Better than most, they came to understand the constant balance and trade-offs between flavor and texture, fat and lean. They're an older country. They've given the matter a lot of thought.

In America, we tend to think that the most tender (and therefore expensive) piece of meat is necessarily the "best" and most desirable. Nothing could be further from the truth. Each cut has its own virtues—as well as drawbacks—and depending on intended use, one must always make decisions. Filet mignon may be the most tender steak on the animal. But while tender, it's also relatively flavorless—which is why it so often appears with sauce. Know this: Just because you can cut a steak with a fork does *not* mean it's good. You might also be interested to know

that while sirloins, ribs, and porterhouses for restaurant use are commonly delivered after being carefully hung and aged, tenderloins for filet mignon usually arrive vacuum sealed in Cryovac plastic, drowning in their own watery blood.

Here are some of the more useful cuts of beef you will find in this book.

*Rumsteck,* or rump steak: This is what we use for steak frites at Les Halles, distinguishing us from the rest of the herd, who favor sirloin. It is not the most tender cut of beef by a long shot, but it has a wonderful flavor and a pleasingly chewy texture that's just right with our famously ethereal fries. Cut into fairly thin 8- to 10-ounce slices, then given a few whacks with a mallet, it makes a delightful and authentic steak for grilling. I would not recommend it for well done, but then I never recommend you cook *anything* well done. It's a sin. *Rumsteck,* when ground fresh, makes a wonderful steak tartare due to its beefy flavor and relative leanness (though filet can be useful here, too).

*Onglet,* or hanger steak, an ever more popular cut with a ropy texture and a slight kidneyish flavor, is absolutely terrific for pan-searing or grilling. It takes marinade like a champion. Once known to Americans as "the butcher's tenderloin," it was usually taken home by the in-the-know butcher for personal use. Now you can sample its many pleasures. Your butcher *can and will* order this stuff for you.

The *entrecôte,* or rib eye, and its big bone-in brother, the *côte de boeuf,* have perhaps the perfect balance of fat, lean, and marbling—the best mix of flavor and texture. Dismayingly, all too many restaurant customers complain

that it's "too fatty," as they are just too dumb to appreciate the best steak on the steer. They should probably stick to the leaner but very flavorful sirloin, which is what their dumb asses were probably thinking of when they put in their order.

The *paleron,* or "chicken steak," is a shoulder cut perfect for braising or stewing, and if the beef is of top quality, you can even get a few steaks off of the *paleron.* For slow-cooked stews and braises, shoulder, neck, shank, short ribs (*travers*), and the awesome cheeks will always make a better product than the leaner stuff.

Leftover braised meat, by the way, should never be discarded. Smashed up and covered with mashed potatoes it becomes another classic of frugality, the tasty *hachis parmentier*—the French version of shepherd's pie.

*Bavette,* or flank steak, is a many-splendored thing in France, comprising a multitude of mini-steaks; but generally speaking, it's great for grilling, particularly over an open fire of dried grape vines or some good wood.

I urge you to buy the cheapest, toughest—but best quality—beef you can get. Then challenge yourself to make something delightful out of it. Experiment. Try. Fail. Try again. Stewing and braising and slow simmering will take you to far more interesting worlds, and are a lot more fun, than simply slapping a steak on the grill.

# boeuf à la ficelle

This dish, literally "beef on a string," doesn't really need a string. (The string was traditionally used to lower the meat into the broth and then retrieve it.) It's an easy, relatively light departure from the usual steak or roast—a more luxurious version of pot-au-feu—and it's pretty as hell. It does well accompanied by horseradish or horseradish sauce. (Just make a béchamel sauce, page 252, and load it up with grated horseradish to taste.)

## INGREDIENTS

8 **baby carrots,** peeled
8 **baby turnips,** peeled
2 **leeks, white part only,** washed and
  cut in half lengthwise
$^1/_2$ **onion,** studded with cloves
1 **bouquet garni** (see Glossary)
**salt and pepper**
2 **lb/900 g beef tenderloin**
**rock sea salt**
$^1/_2$ **cup/112 g cornichons**
$^1/_2$ **cup/112 g Dijon mustard**

## EQUIPMENT

large pot
tongs
platter
ladle
serving platter
fine strainer

**SERVES 4**

Put all the vegetables in the large pot. Cover with water and add the bouquet garni. Add salt and pepper. Over high heat, bring the water to a boil. When boiling, add the beef tenderloin and leave it for 20 minutes. I urge you to cook it no longer than this (medium rare). Use the tongs to remove the beef to the platter and let it rest for about 15 minutes.

Meanwhile, bring the boiling liquid down to a gentle simmer and carefully skim off any foam or scum with the ladle. Slice the beef in $^1/_2$-inch/1-cm slices and arrange them on the serving platter. Position the vegetables around them. Try to keep similarly colored vegetables separate, going always for maximum contrast. Bring the broth back to a boil and strain well. Ladle some broth over the meat and the vegetables and serve with rock sea salt, cornichons, and mustard.

# salade d'onglet

## INGREDIENTS

**12 ounces/340 g onglet steak,**
  cut into 1$^1/_2$-ounce/42-g pieces

### FOR THE MARINADE

**$^1/_2$ ounce/14 g fresh ginger,** grated
**2 garlic cloves,** finely chopped (if you
  use a garlic press, you shall surely
  burn in Hell)
**4 tbsp/56 ml soy sauce**

### FOR THE SAUCE

**salt and pepper**
**2 tbsp/28 g butter**
**$^1/_4$ cup/56 ml white wine**
**$^1/_4$ cup/56 ml dark chicken or veal stock**
  (an added spoon from your stash
  of demi-glace would be nice)
**2 tbsp/28 ml soy sauce**
**$^1/_8$ ounce/3 g fresh ginger,** grated
**1 garlic clove,** thinly sliced
**1 sprig of flat parsley,** chopped

### FOR THE SALAD

**4 ounces/112 g mesclun salad mix**
**1 shallot,** thinly sliced
**$^1/_4$ cup/56 ml red wine vinaigrette**
  (see page 256)

## EQUIPMENT

deep, nonreactive bowl
sauté pan
tongs
plate
wooden spoon
whisk
salad bowl
large serving platter

**SERVES 4**

**PREP**

Place the meat in the deep bowl. From the marinade recipe, add the $1/_2$ ounce/14 g ginger, the chopped garlic, and the soy sauce and mix well. Cover and refrigerate overnight. (If you don't have overnight to marinate the meat, 2 to 3 hours still makes it fairly tender and flavorful.)

**COOK THE MEAT AND MAKE THE SAUCE**

Remove the meat from the marinade and pat dry. Season lightly with salt and pepper. (Go easy on the salt, as the soy component will compensate.) Place the sauté pan over high heat and add 1 tablespoon/14 g of the butter. When the butter has foamed and subsided, add the meat, working in batches, if necessary, to avoid overcrowding the pan. Sear 3 minutes on each side, so that the meat is nicely browned. Using the tongs, set the meat aside on a plate.

Over high heat, stir in the wine, scraping the bottom, of course, with the wooden spoon. Cook until the pan is almost dry, then add the stock (and the demi-glace, if you have any) and the soy and reduce by half. Add the remaining $1/_8$ ounce/3 g ginger and the sliced garlic and cook for 30 seconds, then whisk in the remaining butter. Return the meat to the pan and cook for about a minute. Sprinkle with the chopped parsley and remove from the heat.

**SERVE**

Place the mesclun in the salad bowl and add the shallot. Season with salt and pepper and add the vinaigrette. Toss well and arrange the salad in the center of the serving platter. Arrange the meat around the salad and drizzle with the sauce. Serve right away.

# onglet gascon

This recipe calls for bone marrow, one of God's great gifts to serious eaters. The easiest strategy here is to ask your butcher to put a nice fat leg bone of veal on a bandsaw and saw you off four 2- to 3-inch/5- to 8-cm pieces. When you get home, soak the bones in cold water for a while and then, using your thumb, push the marrow through and out the other side of the bone. Hold in ice water until ready to use.

## INGREDIENTS

**4 6-ounce/168-g** *onglet* **steaks**
   (hanger steaks)
**salt and pepper**
**1 tbsp/14 ml oil**
**2 tbsp/28 g butter**
**marrow from 4 beef bones**
**2 ounces/56 ml white wine**
**$^1/_2$ cup/110 ml strong, dark veal stock**
   (nice to have a little demi-glace here, too)
**2 tbsp/28 g Dijon mustard**
**coarse sea salt**
**2 sprigs of flat parsley,** chopped

## EQUIPMENT

heavy-bottomed sauté pan
tongs
small roasting pan
plate
wooden spoon
whisk
serving platter

**SERVES 4**

### COOK THE STEAK AND THE MARROW

Preheat the oven to 375°F/190°C. Season the steaks with salt and pepper. Put the oil in the sauté pan and heat over high heat. When hot, add 1 tablespoon/14 g of the butter. When it has foamed and subsided, add the steaks, working in batches, as you don't want to overcrowd (and hence cool down) the pan. Using the tongs, turn the steaks, cooking about 2 minutes on each side. Put the pan aside without washing it.

Transfer the steaks to the small roasting pan and add the bone marrow. Place in the oven and cook for 5 minutes (maybe 8 for medium rare). Remove the meat from the pan, but leave in the marrow for seven additional minutes, until it's cooked through—meaning *no* pink, white, or red color remains. Place the steaks on the plate to rest.

### THE SAUCE

Return the sauté pan to the heat and stir in the wine with the wooden spoon. You know this by now, right? Or did you just jump to this recipe?

Okay. Fine. Make sure to scrape up the nice brown stuff with the spoon as you deglaze with the wine. Reduce the wine by half, stir in your stock (and now's the time to sneak in a little of our demi-glace stash). Reduce by half. Got any juices leaking out of your resting meat? I'll bet you do. Put that in the sauce, too. Whisk in the remaining butter (that's called *monter au beurre* if you wanted to know) and remove from heat. Off the heat, whisk in the mustard and adjust the seasoning.

## SERVE

Arrange the meat on the platter with the marrow around it. Spoon the mustard sauce over the steaks. Sprinkle the sea salt over the marrow. Sprinkle parsley over everything.

### SOME NOTES ON *ONGLET*

I can't say enough nice things about this wonderful cut of meat. And you shouldn't confine yourself to these recipes. Use it for steak frites, for the next time you fire up the backyard grill, for any occasion where you would otherwise be using sirloin or rib eye or filet. If you're planning on grilling outside, though, you might want to request the following of your butcher to allow for quicker grilling. "I want two hanger steaks" (this will get you four portions). "Please cut out the center seam" (the thin, white, tough tissue that runs right up the middle of every hanger steak). "Then, butterfly each half for me. Give each butterflied half a whack with the meat mallet. Not too much. Just to even the thickness. I don't want it too thin. I'm grilling." There will be some scraggly, dangly bits on the narrower end of each steak. You can trim those off and use for the *onglet* salad recipe on page 123.

If you really want to put on the beret and do it like they do it in wine country, see if you can score some old grapevines (next wine tour in the Napa Valley or the Hamptons, right?). Dry them out and use them to build a fire in your hibachi or outdoor grill. You can throw some on top of the charcoal if need be. When you've got enough heat, just toss some *onglets* on the grill, and cook as any other steak. At nearly the last minute, sprinkle some freshly chopped shallot over the meat and serve while still sizzling hot. To be eaten accompanied by vast amounts of red Bordeaux.

# faux-filet au beurre rouge

## INGREDIENTS

1/2 cup/110 ml red wine
1 shallot, finely chopped
8 ounces/225 g butter, softened
1 sprig of flat parsley, finely chopped
salt and pepper
4 8-ounce/225-g New York strip
   steaks (trimmed sirloin steaks)
1 tsp/5 ml oil

## EQUIPMENT

small pot
mixing bowl
food processor
rubber spatula
plastic wrap
brush
outdoor grill or grill pan

**SERVES 4**

**MAKE THE RED-WINE BUTTER**

In the small pot, combine the wine and shallot and bring to a boil over high heat. Cook until the wine has almost completely evaporated, taking care not to let the shallots burn. Transfer the mixture to the mixing bowl and let cool. In the food processor, add the softened butter, the shallot-wine mixture, the parsley, and salt and pepper to taste. Mix well.

Scrape the butter out of the food processor with the rubber spatula and place in the center of a large piece of plastic wrap. Gently form it into a 1-inch-diameter log, shaping and squeezing and rolling it like you would roll a joint—or a nori roll. Don't worry; you can't mess it up. It's like Play-Doh; you can always go back and do it again. When you've got it right, twist the ends of the plastic tightly and refrigerate in the rolled plastic until the butter is firm enough to slice.

Red-wine butter can be used on just about any steak you grill. Keeping a few logs of the stuff in the freezer is a good idea, as you never know when your deadbeat friends are going to drop by demanding meat.

**COOK AND SERVE THE STEAKS**

Take the steaks out of the refrigerator 10 minutes before cooking. Season the steaks with salt and pepper. Lightly brush them with the oil. Grill them, or cook them in the grill pan, to desired doneness. Put a slice of the red-wine butter on each steak just before serving.

# steak
# au poivre

You pick it, friend—whatever cut you want to use. Most restaurants opt for sirloin (at Les Halles we use the relatively obscure *pavé*), but because of the flavorful sauce it's perfectly appropriate to use filet mignon for this one. Filet, while tender as all get-out, lacks somewhat in the flavor arena. A healthy wallop of crunchy black peppercorns more than compensates.

## INGREDIENTS
4 8-ounce/225-g steaks
2 ounces/56 ml olive oil
2 ounces/56 g freshly cracked
   **peppercorns** (meaning crushed
   but not ground to powder!)
4 ounces/112 g butter
1 ounce/28 ml good Cognac
4 ounces/110 ml strong, dark veal stock
   (right now, you *really* could use a tiny bit
   of that demi-glace I told you to keep in
   your freezer)
salt and pepper

## EQUIPMENT
heavy skillet
tongs
wooden spoon
serving platter

**SERVES 4**

### COOK THE STEAKS
Preheat the oven to 425°F/220°C. Moisten the meat *very slightly* with oil, then dredge each of the steaks in the crushed peppercorns to thoroughly coat. Don't be shy with the pepper. Heat the remaining oil in the skillet over high heat. Once the oil is hot, add 2 ounces/56 g of the butter. Place the steaks in the pan and brown on all sides, about 5 minutes per side. Transfer the pan to the oven and cook to desired doneness, about 5 to 7 minutes for rare, 10 minutes for medium rare, and so on. Remove

the pan from the oven and remove the steaks from the pan to rest. Have I told you yet to *always* rest your meat after cooking? I've told you now.

## THE SAUCE

Return the skillet to the stovetop and *carefully* stir in the Cognac. As much fun as it is to create a column of flame as you add flammable material to an incredibly hot pan, it's not really desirable or necessary—especially in a home kitchen. Unless you're a pyromaniac, I recommend carefully adding the Cognac to the still-hot pan *off* the flame, stirring and scraping with the wooden spoon to get every scrap, every peppercorn, every rumor of flavor clinging to the bottom of the pan. *Now* place the pan on the flame again and cook it down a bit, by about half. Stir in the veal stock (and demi-glace) and reduce over medium heat until thick enough to coat the back of the spoon. Whisk in the remaining butter and season with salt and pepper. Serve immediately with French fries or sautéed potatoes.

## VARIATION

Incredible as it seems, this dish used to be a tableside standard at many restaurants, meaning waiters would prepare the dish in the dining room over Sterno, usually with great panache—and to inadvertent comic effect. My friend Jack used to order it just so everybody else in the dining room would go home smelling like his dinner. Often, waiters would sneak in a touch of heavy cream, ensuring a richer, easier, faster thickening of the sauce. As well, they'd sometimes offer the variation of a steak Diane, which was essentially the same dish but with a spoon of Dijon mustard and a touch of cream whisked into the final sauce.

## NOTE ON SEARING

With any recipe that calls for searing meat and then using the pan to make a sauce, be careful to avoid blackening the pan; your sauce will taste burnt. Adjust the heat to, say, medium high, so it will still sear the meat but not scorch the pan juices. But stoves and pans vary, so pay attention.

# steak tartare

Les Halles, the restaurant, was pretty much *created* to serve this dish. The key to a successful steak tartare is *fresh* beef, *freshly* hand-chopped at the very last minute and mixed tableside. A home meat grinder with a fairly wide mesh blade is nice to have, but you can and should use a very sharp knife and simply chop and chop and chop until fine. The texture will be superior. And *do not DARE* use a food processor on this dish—you'll utterly destroy it.

## INGREDIENTS

2 **egg yolks**

2 **tbsp/28 g Dijon mustard**

4 **anchovy fillets,** finely chopped

2 **tsp/10 g ketchup** (yes, ketchup—hard to believe, but true)

1 **tsp/5 g Worcestershire sauce**

**Tabasco sauce**

**freshly ground black pepper**

$^1/_4$ **cup/56 ml salad (i.e., corn or soy) oil**

1 **ounce/28 ml Cognac**

1 **small onion,** freshly and finely chopped

2 **ounces/56 g capers,** rinsed

2 **ounces/56 g cornichons,** finely chopped

4 **sprigs of flat parsley,** finely chopped

$1^1/_4$ **lb/560 g fresh sirloin,** finely chopped

## EQUIPMENT

large stainless-steel bowl

whisk

sharp knife or meat grinder

6 chilled dinner plates

3-inch/8-cm ring mold or a spatula

**SERVES 6**

### PREP

Place the egg yolks in the large stainless-steel bowl and add the mustard and anchovies. Mix well, then add the ketchup, Worcestershire sauce, Tabasco, and pepper and mix well again. Slowly whisk in the oil, then add the Cognac and mix again. Fold in the onion, capers, cornichons, and parsley.

### FINISH

Add the chopped meat to the bowl and mix well using a spoon or your hands (in clean rubber gloves, right? Yeah...right). Divide the meat evenly among the six *chilled* dinner plates and, using the ring mold or the spatula, form it into disks on the plates. Serve *immediately* with French fries and toasted bread points.

# côte de boeuf

Pound for pound, this is probably the best cut of beef on the animal—and one of the most expensive. For your serious meat-eating guests this is the way to go. When you approach the tableside with two of these intimidating monsters, and then carve them up in front of your guests, they will tremble with shock and awe, basking in your magnificence and casual impertinence. I suggest serving this dish with French fries and a staggeringly expensive bottle of Burgundy in cheap glasses. Just to show them who's their daddy.

INGREDIENTS
2 34-ounce/950-g rib steaks,
   bone still in
salt and freshly ground black
   pepper to taste
1 tsp/5 ml olive oil
1 recipe béarnaise sauce (see page 252)

EQUIPMENT
outdoor grill or grill pan
brush
tongs
roasting pan
cutting board
very sharp, bad-ass-looking knife
serving platter
novelty apron or vintage
   Ted Nugent T-shirt
ramekin (for béarnaise sauce)

**SERVES 6 TO 8**

**PREP**

This is a big, fat piece of meat. It's been in the refrigerator a long time and is hence chilled to the bone. Particularly if you plan on cooking this rare or medium rare (and you'd better be), you want to get that chill out. So, fuck the Health Department. Pull those big, beautiful beasts out of the fridge a good half hour before cooking time and let them come up to room temperature. It makes a real difference.

**COOK**

Preheat the grill or grill pan to high heat. Preheat the oven to 400°F/200°C. This cut is just too damn fat to cook all the way on the grill. Sear it on the grill or in the grill pan, turn it 180 degrees on each side to get that cool checkerboard pattern we all like, and continue grilling on both sides until you have a nice brown crust. Now toss those bad boys into the roasting pan and finish them in the oven. Should be about 8 to 10 minutes for medium rare.

When the steaks are cooked to desired doneness, allow them to rest for a good 10 minutes. This dish doesn't have to be served sizzling hot—in fact it shouldn't be. It's much more important that all those lovely juices distribute internally. Do not poke. Do not slice. Do not molest until rested. Now transfer to the cutting board, approach the table, and, wielding your razor-sharp slicing knife with terrifying aplomb, slice and serve in great bleeding, fat-rippled hunks. Serve accompanied by béarnaise sauce.

# filet of beef, sauce porto with roasted shallots

## INGREDIENTS
12 peeled whole shallots *plus*
  1 peeled, thinly sliced shallot
5 tbsp/70 g butter
4 8-ounce/225-g beef filets
salt and pepper
1 tbsp/14 ml oil
1 tsp/5 g flour
3 ounces/75 ml port
1 cup/225 ml strong dark veal stock
  (again, a tiny spoon of demi-glace
  would really boost this sauce)

## EQUIPMENT
small ovenproof sauté pan
foil
large sauté pan
tongs
roasting pan (large enough
  to hold 4 steaks)
wooden spoon
fine strainer
small saucepan
whisk
serving platter

**SERVES 4**

### PREP
Preheat the oven to 325°F/170°C. Place the peeled whole shallots in the small ovenproof sauté pan, throw in 2 tablespoons/28 g of the butter, cover with foil, and put in the oven. Cook low and slow, gently turning the shallots every once in a while, until they are brown and soft and slightly limp, but still recognizable and intact—about 45 minutes to an hour. Remove and keep warm.

### COOK
Jack the oven up to 375°F/190°C. Season the meat with salt and pepper. Heat the oil in the large sauté pan over high heat. Add 1 tablespoon/14 g of the butter, let it foam, and allow it to subside. Sear the meat on all

sides, using the tongs to turn the filets. Make sure the sides are seared, too. Transfer the meat to the roasting pan and place in the oven. Roast for about 7 minutes for rare, 10 minutes for medium rare.

Discard the fat from the large sauté pan and add 1 tablespoon/14 g of the butter. Heat over medium flame and, when hot, add the sliced shallot. Cook for 4 minutes, sprinkle in the flour, and cook for 2 minutes. Stir in the port and deglaze, scraping with the wooden spoon. Reduce the wine by half, then add the stock (and your demi-glace, I hope), bring to a boil, and reduce by half again, until the sauce coats the back of the spoon. Adjust the seasoning and strain through the fine strainer into the small saucepan. Bring the sauce back to a boil, remove from the heat, and whisk in the remaining tablespoon of butter.

### SERVE
Remove the filets from the oven, rest them a few moments, and arrange on the platter. Artfully nestle 3 of the cooked whole shallots next to each filet and spoon over the sauce. Good with mashed potatoes.

### ABOUT STEAK FRITES
Steak frites is, of course, simply grilled steak with French fries. But, please, don't confine yourself to sirloin. In my opinion, a true steak frites should be a slightly chewier, more flavorful experience. So by all means, experiment: Try *rumsteck,* which is a fairly thin, very lightly pounded slice off the top round (what we use at the restaurant); or *bavette,* which is flank steak; or *onglet;* or even *paleron* ("chicken steak"), if of prime quality, sliced and pounded.

Not surprisingly, when making steak frites, you'd better make a truly awesome French fry. In the "Potatoes" chapter, I'll explain how to do just that.

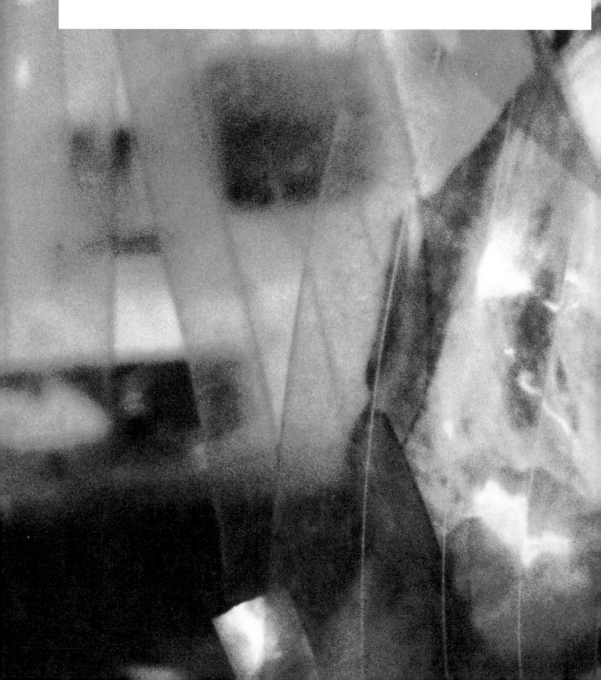

# veal & lamb

# VEAL

**Veal is prized largely for its tender, subtle-tasting cutlets, or scaloppines, its rib chops, its loin, and for the paillards off its legs. But veal is so much more.**

The shank, braised—as for osso buco—is a wonderment. Its cheeks and shoulders are fabulous for stewing or for blanquette. Its tongue, thymus glands, kidneys, tripe, brains, and liver are incomparable and irreplaceable. Compare a sautéed slab of beef liver with a calf's and you'll see immediately what I mean. Even a few lengths of veal leg bone, roasted plain, can be a magnificent meal. Dig out all that tasty, buttery cooked marrow, smear it on a piece of toasted baguette, and sprinkle with a little sea salt, and you have one of life's great treats. Almost nothing the human animal can cook or create beats that for pure pleasure. The bones are the foundation of so many classic stocks and sauces. The humble, ugly-looking feet impart magical flavor and natural gelatin to stocks, stews, and tripe preparations. The face—yes, the face—rolled, tied, and slowly simmered in court bouillon, can be a gourmet delight all too unfamiliar to most. And the beautiful white veal fat found around the kidneys, when rendered and used for frying, will make the best, most luxurious French fries you've ever imagined.

It's not nice what they do to calves to make that pale, tender, and attractive meat we so love. But if *I* tasted that good after being locked up and immobilized in a dark shed, I wouldn't blame anyone for trying.

# blanquette
# de veau

There are certain rules in the world of cooking. One of them is that color contrast is a good thing. A plate with too much white, for instance, cries out for some garnish, some color, something, *anything,* to distract the eye from all that monochrome. But not this dish. This dish is the exception to the rule. For a chef, it can be maddening to make it for the first time, as the natural impulse, the sum total of all one's training, says "Put some carrot in there—a little chopped parsley, for God's sake!" Resist the urge. It's supposed to be white. *All* white. Keep it that way. It makes something of a statement.

## INGREDIENTS

1 pint/560 g pearl onions

6 tbsp/84 g butter

1 pint/560 g small white
  button mushrooms

3 lb/1.35 kg veal neck or shoulder,
  cut into 2-inch/5-cm squares

1 bouquet garni (see Glossary)

1 large onion, cut in half and studded
  with 4 cloves

1 carrot, cut in half

1 celery rib

4 tbsp/56 g flour

$^{1}/_{2}$ cup/225 ml heavy cream

salt and white pepper

1 egg yolk

juice of $^{1}/_{2}$ lemon

## EQUIPMENT

2 small pots

large pot

strainer

medium pot

whisk

small bowl

measuring cup

**SERVES 6**

If you have a pristine, clear veal stock handy, you can replace half the water with it for better flavor.

### PREP

Peel the pearl onions, place in a small pot, and cover with cold water. Add 1 tablespoon/14 g of the butter and bring the water to a boil over high heat. Let it boil until the water evaporates (do not allow the onions to take on any color), then remove from the heat and set aside.

In the second small pot, repeat the procedure with the mushrooms, cooking them in water and 1 tablespoon/14 g of the butter just until they are tender. Set aside.

### COOK THE VEAL

Place the veal in the large pot. Cover with water and add the bouquet garni, onion, carrot, and celery. Bring the mixture to a boil, then reduce to a simmer. Let cook over low heat for 2 hours, periodically

skimming away and discarding meat scum, until the veal is fork-tender (meaning it can be easily cut with the side of a fork). Do not undercook. Do not overcook to mush! Strain the meat and set it aside. Strain the broth and keep it hot over heat. Discard the bouquet garni and the vegetables.

### THE SAUCE

*What you are doing, by the way—in case you didn't know—is making a roux.*

In the medium pot, melt the remaining 4 tablespoons/56 g of butter over medium heat, and once it has foamed and subsided, whisk in the flour, making sure it is completely incorporated. Cook over medium-low heat, stirring frequently. Do *not* color the flour. Gradually add 1 cup/450 ml of the hot broth, whisking constantly to incorporate smoothly. Add the remaining broth and bring to a boil, cooking and stirring until the mixture begins to thicken. Add the veal, pearl onions, mushrooms, and cream. Stir. Bring to a boil, reduce to a simmer, and heat for 5 to 8 minutes. Season with salt and white pepper.

### FINISH

Just before serving, place the egg yolk in the small bowl and add about a $^{1}/_{4}$ cup/112 ml of the hot sauce from the stew. Whisk well and add this mixture to the pot. Stir. Do *not* allow the sauce to come to a boil! Add the lemon juice, season again as needed, and serve with absolutely *white* rice.

# braised
# veal shank

## INGREDIENTS
$^1/_2$ calf's foot
salt and pepper
1 whole veal shank, on the bone
2 tbsp/28 ml olive oil
1 tbsp/14 g butter
2 medium onions, thinly sliced
1 carrot, cut into 1/2-inch/1-cm cubes
1 tbsp/14 g tomato paste
1 tbsp/14 g flour
1 cup/225 ml *plus* 2 tbsp/28 ml white wine
zest of 1 lemon
1 bouquet garni (see Glossary)
4 garlic cloves
1 tbsp/14 ml balsamic vinegar
2 sprigs of flat parsley, chopped

## EQUIPMENT
2 large pots
tongs
wooden spoon
strainer
small saucepan
small roasting pan

**SERVES 4**

### PREP
Place the calf's foot in a large pot, add 1 tablespoon/14 g of salt, and cover with water. Bring to a boil, then reduce to medium heat and cook for 1 hour, adding more water if necessary to keep the foot submerged. Remove the foot from the water with the tongs and set aside to cool.

## COOK THE SHANK

Preheat the oven to 325°F/170°C. Season the veal shank with salt and pepper. In the second large pot, heat the oil, then the butter, and when the butter stops foaming, add the shank and brown it on all sides, about 2 minutes per side. Using the tongs, remove the shank from the pot and set aside.

Add the onions and carrot to the pot and cook over high heat, stirring occasionally, until golden brown, about 5 minutes. Stir in the tomato paste and cook for 1 minute. Stir in the flour and cook for 2 minutes more. Whisk 1 cup/225 ml of the wine into the pot, scraping with the wooden spoon to get up the brown stuff. Put the foot and the shank in the pot, along with the lemon zest, bouquet garni, garlic, and 2 cups/450 ml of water. Bring the mixture to a boil and cover. Put the pot in the oven and cook for 2 hours and 30 minutes.

Later, using the tongs, remove the shank and the foot from the pot and set aside. Increase the oven temperature to 400°F/200°C (you'll need it later). Strain the hot cooking liquid into the small saucepan.

## THE SAUCE

Remove the bones from the calf's foot and discard. Cut the gelatinous portion of the foot into small pieces and add to the cooking liquid. Bring the liquid to a boil, reduce to a simmer, and cook for 15 minutes. Stir in the vinegar and parsley and adjust the seasoning with salt and pepper.

## FINISH

Place the cooked shank in the small roasting pan, cover with the remaining 2 tablespoons/28 ml of wine, and place in the oven for 15 minutes. Remove the meat from the bone and arrange on a serving platter. Serve with the sauce alongside.

# veal tenderloin with wild mushrooms

## INGREDIENTS

1 2-pound/900-g veal tenderloin
salt and freshly ground black pepper
1 tbsp/14 ml olive oil
3 tbsp/42 g butter
4 ounces/112 g fresh wild mushrooms
(porcini or morels preferred, but
cremini or shiitake if you must)
1 shallot, thinly sliced
4 ounces/110 ml Madeira
1 garlic clove, thinly sliced
4 ounces/110 ml dark chicken or veal stock
(and feel free to boost with demi-glace)
2 ounces/56 ml heavy cream
1 tbsp/14 ml sherry vinegar
1 sprig of flat parsley, finely chopped

## EQUIPMENT

large, ovenproof sauté pan
small sauté pan
wooden spoon
whisk
serrated knife, for slicing
serving platter

**COOK THE VEAL**

Preheat the oven to 350°F/180°C. Season the tenderloin with salt and pepper. Place a large, ovenproof sauté pan over high heat and add the oil. Drop in 1 tablespoon/14 g of the butter. Let it foam and subside. Place the tenderloin in the pan and sear on all sides until golden brown. Transfer the pan to the oven and cook for about 25 minutes, until the inside is nice and pink (*not* that you should be looking inside!).

In the small sauté pan, heat 1 tablespoon/14 g of the butter over medium-high heat. Once it has bubbled and come down again, add the mushrooms and cook over medium heat until they are golden brown. Then, add the shallot and continue to cook for another minute. Stir in 2 ounces/56 ml of the Madeira, scraping the bottom of the pan with the wooden spoon. Add the sliced garlic and continue to cook until the wine is reduced by half. Set aside.

**THE SAUCE**

Once the veal is cooked, remove from the oven and set aside. Return the pan to the stovetop over medium heat and stir in the remaining 2 ounces/56 ml of Madeira. As with the mushrooms, scrape up all the good stuff with the wooden spoon. Add the cooked mushroom mixture and the stock and bring to a boil. Let the liquid reduce by half, then add the cream. Continue to cook until the sauce is thick enough to coat the back of a spoon. Whisk in the remaining tablespoon/14 g of butter and drizzle in the sherry vinegar. Adjust seasoning with salt and pepper.

**SERVE**

Cut the veal into $1/4$-inch-/1-cm-thick slices with the serrated knife and arrange them on the serving platter. Pour the sauce over and garnish with the chopped parsley. Serve.

# veau viennoise

This recipe calls for scaloppine, which leaves your butcher with some latitude. Thin, boneless, fatless cuts of the leg, pounded flat with a meat mallet, are usually what you'll get (and that's fine). If you are independently wealthy and want the good stuff, demand that your scaloppine come entirely off the loin of veal. And if you're looking to have the very best—and are in a do-it-yourself mood—simply ask for four fat rib chops of veal. Back at the ranch, take two large pieces of plastic wrap, sandwich your chops, one at a time, between them, and with a meat mallet pound the living hell out of them until they flatten evenly and expand into massive cutlets with bone attached. In all your hammering, be careful not to tear the meat. You're flattening and tenderizing—*not* murdering the thing. This is not exactly French style, it's more of an Italian thing. But they know a thing or two down there. Even the French recognized that Catherine de Medici was no fool.

## INGREDIENTS

1 **hard-boiled egg**
4 **anchovy fillets** (make
  them *good* anchovies, please;
  white ones are nice.)
2 **tbsp/28 g capers,** rinsed and drained
1 **lemon,** peel and pith removed, flesh
  cut into $1/4$-inch/6-mm rounds
2 **eggs,** lightly beaten
2 **tbsp/28 ml water**
$1/4$ **cup/56 g flour**
**salt and pepper**
1 **cup/225 g fresh bread crumbs** (see NOTE)
4 **veal scaloppine,** about 6 ounces/168 g
  each (unless you went for the rib chops,
  in which case they'll be a bit larger)
1 **cup/225 ml peanut oil**
2 **tbsp/28 g chopped flat parsley**
2 **tbsp/28 g chopped onion**

## EQUIPMENT

knife
3 shallow bowls
whisk
plates
large, high-sided sauté pan (a bloody big
  one if you're using pounded chops)
slotted spatula
tongs (if using chops)
paper towels
serving platter

**SERVES 4**

## PREP

Separate the hard-boiled egg white from the hard-boiled egg yolk and chop both components separately. Roll each anchovy fillet around 1 caper, and reserve the remaining capers. Set these garnishes and the lemon slices aside for later.

Place the beaten eggs in a shallow bowl and whisk in the water. Place the flour in the second bowl and season it with salt and pepper. Place the bread crumbs in the third bowl and season them as well. Don't go nuts with the salt. It adds up. Dredge each piece of veal in the flour, then dip it in the eggs, then in the bread crumbs, taking care to shake off the excess coating at each step. When all the meat is thoroughly coated with bread crumbs, arrange it carefully—not stacked, but side by side—on plates, cover with plastic, and refrigerate for 2 hours. (If you're pressed for time, you can skip the refrigeration period.)

## COOK

Working in batches, heat the oil in the large, high-sided sauté pan until it's about 350°F/180°C—meaning hot, but *not* smoking! Remove the veal from the fridge and, one or two at a time, cook for 2 minutes on each side, or until the breading is a deep golden brown. Remove with a slotted spatula or tongs, carefully, and let rest on a plate lined with paper towels.

## SERVE

If you like a little more lubrication with your breaded, fried veal, a touch of *beurre blanc* (page 258) can help.

Arrange the scaloppine on the serving platter and top each piece with a few slices of lemon. Place one rolled anchovy atop each scaloppine and serve the parsley, onion, hard-boiled eggs, and remaining capers in small ramekins or in tiny, artful heaps alongside.

NOTE: Do I have to *tell* you to make *fresh* bread crumbs? How hard is that? You have a food processor, right? Then what's your problem? You want a lot of dried oregano and MSG and stable-dust in your nice veal, then be my guest—buy that prepared crap. Frankly, I don't think there's any excuse. If you insist on buying prepared bread crumbs, then you probably also own a salad shooter. I feel bad for you—and your victims/guests.

# roasted veal short ribs

## INGREDIENTS

4 veal short ribs, about 4 lb/1.8 kg total
$^1/_4$ **cup/56 ml extra-virgin olive oil**
**salt and pepper**
**1 cup/225 ml white wine**
$^1/_4$ **cup/56 ml sherry vinegar**
$^1/_2$ **bouillon cube or, much better,**
   **a spoon of demi-glace**
**1 large onion,** thinly sliced
**4 garlic cloves,** slightly crushed
**1 bouquet garni** (see Glossary)
**1 sprig of flat parsley,** chopped

## EQUIPMENT

small saucepan
whisk
roasting pan
bulb baster or brush
tongs
serving platter

**SERVES 4**

### PREP

Coat each rib with olive oil and season with salt and pepper. In the small saucepan, bring the wine and vinegar to a boil and whisk in the bouillon cube (or the demi-glace). Remove from the heat and set aside.

### COOK

Arrange the onion on the bottom of the roasting pan and pour in the wine-vinegar mixture. Add the garlic and the bouquet garni. Place the ribs in the pan, skin side up. Place the pan in a cold oven and crank the heat to 325°F/170°C. Let cook, undisturbed, for 1 hour.

After 1 hour, baste or brush the ribs with the pan juices and turn them with the tongs, every 15 minutes, for another hour, basting each time. Increase the heat to 400°F/200°C and cook for an additional 30 minutes, until the ribs are a lovely, dark brown. Remove from the oven and arrange on the platter. Spoon the pan sauce and onion over the ribs, garnish with the parsley, and serve.

# tournedos de veau au poivre rose

Pink peppercorns were one of the great missteps of the late 1970s. Every knucklehead (like me, sadly) who'd even read about nouvelle cuisine was busy chucking the damn things on everything. For a while, it seemed, you couldn't get a steak au poivre in New York without the menu reading "Steak with 3 peppercorns…" Many food crimes later, it's worth reevaluating the cute, pink little berries (they aren't even really a pepper), and after sifting through the wreckage, I've found *one* dish that actually benefits from their addition.

## INGREDIENTS

**8 small veal tournedos,**
about 3 ounces/75 g each, pounded
to 1$^1$/$_2$-inch/4-cm thickness
**1 tbsp/14 g cracked pink
peppercorns *plus* 1 tbsp/14 g
whole pink peppercorns**
**salt to taste**
**2 tbsp/28 ml olive oil**
**2 tbsp/28 g butter**
**1 shallot,** thinly sliced
**3 ounces/75 ml white wine**
**1 cup/225 ml chicken stock or broth**
**4 ounces/110 ml heavy cream**

## EQUIPMENT

heavy-bottomed sauté pan
tongs
plate
wooden spoon
strainer
small saucepan
serving platter
whisk

## COOK THE MEAT

Season the veal with the cracked peppercorns and salt. In the heavy-bottomed sauté pan, heat the oil, then the butter over high heat. Once the butter's ready, lower the heat to medium high and add the veal. Working in batches, cook each tournedos for 5 minutes on each side. Color you're looking for? You got it. Golden brown. Remove the veal to the plate and keep warm while you make the sauce.

## THE SAUCE

Discard the excess fat in the pan. (I'll bet you can practically see this dish coming at this point, right?) Add the shallot and, when brown, stir in 2 ounces/56 ml of the wine. Now *scrape*! Pick up your wooden spoon and scrape, you magnificent bastard! Reduce the wine over high heat to a glaze consistency, then stir in the stock or broth and reduce again, by half. Strain the mixture into the small saucepan.

When the sauce is in the saucepan, simmer over medium heat, add the cream, and reduce until the mixture coats the back of the spoon. Has your veal leaked any juice onto its plate? Good. Put that in the sauce. Arrange the veal on the platter (after a quick shot of heat in the oven if necessary). Add the remaining whole peppercorns to the sauce and whisk in the remaining butter. Spoon or pour it over the veal and serve immediately.

# tendron de veau lemon confit

The *tendron* is a special cut of veal from the breast. A good butcher can easily separate the short ribs from the meat (the *tendron*)—most of the time, the veal breast gets thrown out or ground up, so he should be happy to make some money off a cut that is ordinarily unpopular and unprofitable.

## INGREDIENTS

3$^1/_2$ lb/1.675 kg veal *tendron*, cut into 1$^1/_2$-inch/4-cm cubes

salt and pepper

2 tbsp/28 ml olive oil

1 tbsp/14 g butter

1 medium onion, finely chopped

2 small carrots, finely chopped

8 ounces/225 g canned whole Italian plum tomatoes, drained

1 tbsp/14 g flour

$^1/_2$ cup/110 ml white wine

2 cups/450 ml chicken stock or broth

4 garlic cloves, crushed

1 bouquet garni (see Glossary)

$^1/_2$ preserved lemon (see page 264), rinsed

4 sprigs of flat parsley, finely chopped

## EQUIPMENT

Dutch oven

tongs

wooden spoon

large pasta bowl

**SERVES 6**

### PREP

Season the veal with salt and pepper. In the Dutch oven, heat the oil over high heat, and when it is almost smoking, add the butter. When the butter is sizzling, add the veal cubes, in batches, browning on all sides. Once the veal is browned, remove it from the pan with the tongs and set aside.

### COOK

Add the chopped onions and carrots to the still-hot Dutch oven and cook over medium heat until browned. Add the tomatoes and cook for about 2 minutes, then stir in the flour and cook another 2 minutes. Add the wine and scrape with the wooden spoon. Let the wine reduce by half, add the chicken stock, and bring to a boil. Add the veal, garlic, and bouquet garni and reduce to a simmer. Let the mixture simmer for 2 hours, until the veal is fork-tender. Discard the bouquet garni and bring the mixture again to a boil. Add the preserved lemon and cook for 1 minute. Garnish with the chopped parsley and serve in the pasta bowl.

# tournedos d'agneau with fig confit

Ordinarily, the "tournedos" of lamb is a special cut available, as far as I know, at few places other than from our skilled in-house butcher at Les Halles. It's a piece that marks the end of the lamb's saddle (the loin) and the beginning of the gigot (the leg). It's tender, tasty, and boneless. I'd suggest that if you can't make a special trip to New York, asking your butcher to completely bone out a saddle of lamb, cutting the completely trimmed meat into $1^1/_2$-inch-/4-cm-thick medallions, would do the trick. Alternatively, he could completely "seam" and bone out a leg of lamb—separating out the muscles—which would leave you some very nice pieces of skinless, boneless, fatless lamb that you could then cut into similarly sized portions. It's worth trying.

## INGREDIENTS
**4 dried figs**
**1 cup/225 ml Banyuls wine**
**4 lamb "tournedos" or 4 8-oz/225-g portions of boneless lamb** (of same general size and shape)
**salt and pepper**
**1 tbsp/14 ml oil**
**2 tbsp/28 g butter**
**1 small onion,** finely chopped
**1 tsp/5 g flour**
**1 cup/225 ml dark chicken, veal, or lamb stock** (a spoon of demi-glace might help boost the sauce)
**2 sprigs of mint, leaves only,** finely chopped
**splash of sherry vinegar**

## EQUIPMENT
small pot with cover
heavy-bottomed sauté pan
roasting pan
wooden spoon
whisk
serving platter

**SERVES 4**

### PREP THE FIGS
Combine the figs and the wine in the small pot and let sit for 2 hours. After 2 hours, bring the mixture to a boil over high heat. Once the mixture boils, remove from the heat, cover, and set aside.

## COOK THE LAMB

Preheat the oven to 375°F/190°C. Season the lamb with salt and pepper. Heat the oil in the heavy-bottomed sauté pan over high heat. Once the oil is hot, add 1 tablespoon/14 g of the butter, and allow to foam and subside. Add the lamb and sear for 3 minutes per side. Transfer the lamb to the roasting pan and place in the oven for about 15 to 20 minutes (depending very much on the size of the cut). Press the meat with a fingertip to judge doneness. The more resistance, the more cooked. Remove from the oven and let rest for 10 minutes.

## THE SAUCE

Add the chopped onion to the hot sauté pan and cook over medium heat until soft and caramelized. Stir in the flour and cook for 2 minutes. Remove the figs from the wine and, using the wooden spoon, stir the wine into the pan, scraping up any good brown stuff from the bottom. When the wine has reduced by half, add the stock (and a teaspoon of demi-glace, if you have it) and the figs. Bring the mixture to a boil and reduce until it coats the back of the spoon. Add any juices accumulated from the cooked lamb. Season with salt and pepper and whisk in the remaining tablespoon/14 g of butter, the chopped mint, and the vinegar.

## SERVICE

Arrange the meat on the serving platter and spoon over the sauce, making sure there's a fig perched atop each piece.

# carré d'agneau au moutarde

Yee-hah! Rack of lamb! Just like they make it on ocean liners, in hotels, at fancy rug joints, in revolving restaurants…and at Les Halles. Some classics, I guess, you just don't mess with. "French cut" means the excess fat has been trimmed and the bones have been scraped down to expose the ribs. Your butcher will take care of this.

INGREDIENTS
2 racks of lamb, French cut
salt and pepper
2 tbsp/28 ml olive oil
2 tbsp/28 g butter
1 cup/225 ml red wine
2 cups/450 ml strong, dark lamb stock
1 garlic clove, slightly crushed
1 bouquet garni (see Glossary)
1 pinch of fresh thyme leaves
1 pinch of fresh rosemary leaves
2 tbsp/28 g Dijon mustard
2 tbsp/28 g fresh bread crumbs

EQUIPMENT
large, heavy-bottomed sauté pan
tongs
wooden spoon
fine strainer
small pot
roasting pan
serving platter
whisk

**SERVES 4**

For full "Dining Room of the *Titanic*" effect, I suggest serving this on a large platter with a dazzling medley of sautéed vegetables of contrasting colors. And for potatoes? The recipe for *gratin dauphinois* (page 240) was made for this dish. Or else some cute, football-shaped *rissolé* potatoes.

### PREP

Season the racks with salt and pepper. Heat the olive oil in the sauté pan and, when the oil is hot, add 1 tablespoon/14 g of the butter. Once the butter has foamed and subsided, put the racks in, fat side down, and sear, turning with the tongs, until brown on all sides, about 5 minutes total. Remove from the pan and set aside.

Discard the fat from the sauté pan and, over high heat, stir in the wine, scraping the bottom with the wooden spoon. Reduce by half, then add the lamb stock, garlic, and bouquet garni. Bring to a boil, reduce to a simmer, and cook down until thick enough to coat the spoon. Strain into the small pot and set aside.

### FINISH

Preheat the oven to 375°F/190°C. Sprinkle half the thyme and rosemary leaves over the lamb. Then spoon the mustard over the fat side of the lamb rack and cover the area with bread crumbs. Press the bread crumbs into the mustard with your hands, so that they adhere to the mustard, forming a thick layer over the outside. Place the lamb in the roasting pan and cook in the oven for 17 minutes (for medium rare). Remove from the oven and let rest 10 minutes before slicing into double chops and arranging on the serving platter. Bring the sauce to a boil and add the remaining thyme and rosemary. Whisk in the remaining 1 tablespoon/14 g of butter and serve alongside the lamb.

# gigot de sept heures

That's right: seven-hour leg of lamb. That leaves you plenty of time for prepping additional courses, a long nap, and catching up on the taped episodes of *The Simpsons* you've been meaning to watch.

## INGREDIENTS
1 leg of lamb, about 6 lb/2.7 kg
4 garlic cloves, thinly sliced,
  *plus* 20 whole garlic cloves
$1/_4$ cup/56 ml olive oil
salt and pepper
2 small onions, thinly sliced
4 carrots, peeled
1 bouquet garni (see Glossary)
1 cup/225 ml dry white wine
1 cup/225 g flour
1 cup/225 ml water

## EQUIPMENT
paring knife
Dutch oven with lid
medium mixing bowl
wooden spoon

SERVES 8

### PREP THE LAMB
Preheat the oven to 300°F/150°C. Using the paring knife, make many small incisions around the leg. Place a sliver of garlic into each of the incisions. Rub the lamb well with olive oil and season it all over with salt and pepper. Place it in the Dutch oven and add the onions, carrots, bouquet garni, and wine. Put the lid on the Dutch oven.

### SEAL THE PAN AND COOK THE LAMB
In the medium bowl, combine the flour and water to form a rough "bread dough," mixing it well with the wooden spoon. (Don't worry, you don't have to eat it.) Use the dough like grout or caulking material to create a seal that connects the lid to the Dutch oven. Place the Dutch oven in the oven and cook for 7 hours.

Remove the Dutch oven from the oven and break the seal. Ideally, that leg of lamb will be so damn tender that you'll be able to eat it with a spoon.

# grilled lamb steaks

## INGREDIENTS

**4 8-ounce/225-g lamb steaks,**
  from the leg
**6 garlic cloves,** sliced thin
**2 sprigs of rosemary**
**4 sprigs of thyme**
**6 tbsp/84 ml olive oil**
**1 small onion,** finely chopped
**4 sprigs of flat parsley,** finely chopped
**salt and pepper**

## EQUIPMENT

nonreactive casserole dish
  (such as glass or crockery)
small bowl
outdoor grill or grill pan
tongs

**SERVES 4**

### MARINATE THE LAMB

Place the meat in the nonreactive casserole dish and add the garlic, rosemary, thyme, and 4 tablespoons/56 ml of the olive oil. Cover and refrigerate overnight.

### MAKE THE PERSILLADE

In the small bowl, combine the onion, parsley, salt, pepper, and the remaining 2 tablespoons/28 ml of olive oil. Mix well and set aside.

### COOK THE LAMB

Remove the steaks from the refrigerator about 20 minutes before cooking. Preheat the outdoor grill to high, or place a grill pan on the stove and crank the heat. Remove the steaks from the marinade and brush off excess oil, garlic, and herbs. Season each steak on both sides with salt and pepper and place on the grill or grill pan. Cook for 2 minutes, then use the tongs to turn each steak 180 degrees to create that crisscross pattern on the underside that cookbook photographers love so well. After 2 minutes, flip the steak and repeat the process. Just before removing the steaks from the heat, top each steak with some of the persillade mixture, then serve immediately.

# daube provençale

The best cut of meat for this dish is the neck, bone still in. But if you can't, for some reason, find neck, or prefer boneless meat (you poor deluded bastard), then use shoulder.

## INGREDIENTS

2 tbsp/28 ml olive oil
2 tbsp/28 g butter
3 lb/1.35 kg lamb neck and shoulder, with bones **or 2 lb/900 g boneless lamb shoulder,** cut into 2-inch/5-cm pieces
salt and pepper
1/2 lb/225 g slab bacon, cut into lardons (see Glossary)
1 small onion, finely chopped
1 celery rib, finely chopped
2 garlic cloves, crushed
1 tbsp/14 g tomato paste
1 tbsp/14 g flour
1 cup/225 ml white wine
1 cup/225 ml strong, dark veal, chicken, or lamb stock (got some demi-glace? sneak in a spoonful)

1 small carrot, coarsely chopped
1 bouquet garni (see Glossary)
zest of 1 orange
2 potatoes, peeled and "turned," meaning cut into small football shapes, *or* just cube the damn things into large dice
4 sprigs of flat parsley, chopped

## EQUIPMENT

Dutch oven with cover
tongs
wooden spoon
serving bowl

**SERVES 4**

### PREP THE LAMB

Heat the olive oil in the Dutch oven on high heat. Add the butter. Foam it. Let it subside. Season the meat with salt and pepper. Sear it on all sides in the hot pan, in batches if need be, until all of it is deep, dark brown. When browned, remove from the pan with the tongs and set aside.

## COOK THE STEW

Add the bacon to the still-hot pan and cook until it's crispy and has rendered out its fat. Remove the bacon from the pan and set aside. Discard most of the fat and then add the onion, celery, and garlic to the pan. Cook over medium-high heat until the vegetables have caramelized (browned), about 5 minutes. Using the wooden spoon, stir in the tomato paste and cook it for about 1 minute. Stir in the flour and cook for an additional minute. Stir in the wine and scrape up all that brown stuff. Bring the wine to a boil, reduce by half, then add the stock (and a teaspoon of demi-glace if you have any). Bring back to a boil and reduce immediately to a simmer. Add the lamb, carrot, bouquet garni, orange zest, and bacon. Season with salt and pepper, cover the pot, and simmer over low heat for about 90 minutes, occasionally skimming the fat from the surface of the stew.

After 90 minutes, add the potatoes to the stew and cook until they are tender, about 12 to 15 minutes. Skim the stew a final time, making sure there's no film of fat floating on the surface, then serve in a big old bowl, garnished with the chopped parsley.

This same recipe, omitting the bacon and the potatoes, is really nice with the addition of a little extra orange zest, some chopped fresh rosemary and thyme, and, at the last minute, some diced tomato, pitted niçoise and green olives, and fava beans.

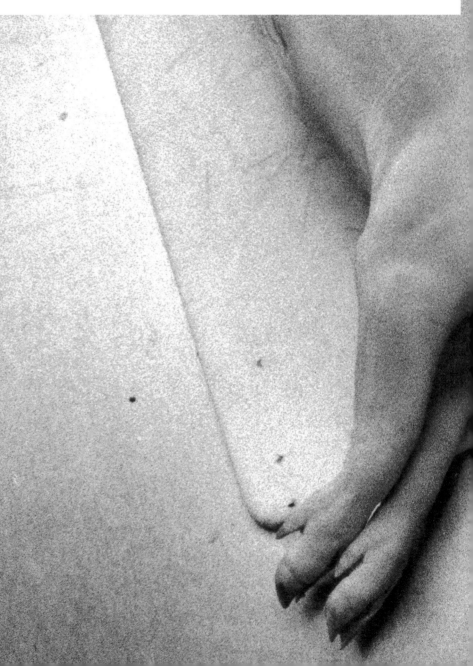

pig

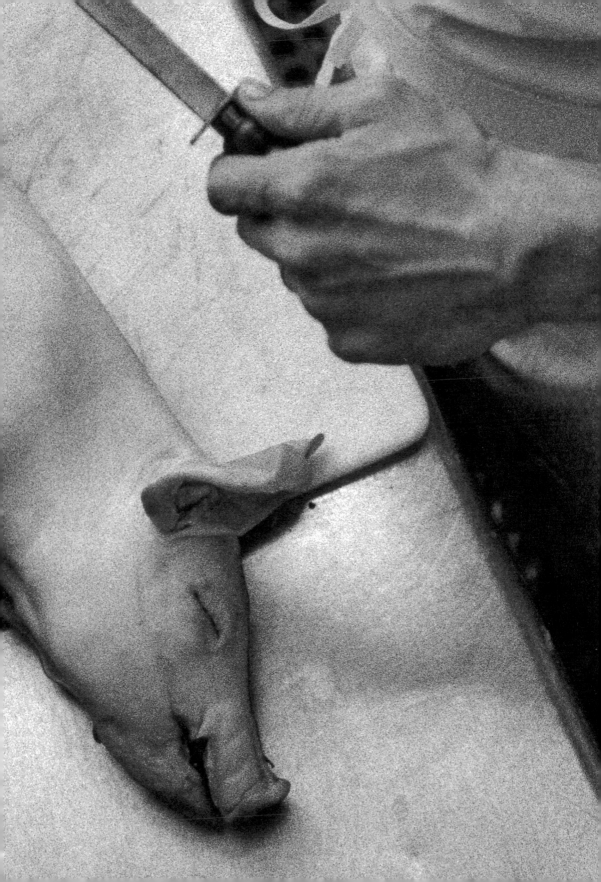

# PIG

**Is there any better, more noble, more magical animal than the pig? Not from a cook's perspective there isn't. Virtually every single part of a pig can be made into something delicious. Pork makes just about everything taste better, and no beast offers more variety, more possibilities, more traditional, time-tested recipes per ounce than the humble piggy.**

Here, more than anywhere else, it is necessary to jettison *right now* any squeamishness or preconceptions about what you can and cannot eat. Unless you are an observant Jew, Muslim, or Hindu, there is no reason at all not to throw yourself with abandon into the veritable magical mystery tour that is pork. From nose to tail, from beard to butt, it's all good, all useful, a walking, snorting, squealing specialty store of valuable and versatile ingredients. Turn whatever ideas you might have about "the other white meat" right on their head, because the lean, white, relatively fat-free chops and roasts the pork industry would like you to think are the best parts are in fact the most limiting and uninteresting. It is a severe Food Crime when the major pork producers breed pigs for leanness, as all chefs know that the fattier stuff is by far the best and most useful.

The pig's tail, slow roasted, then breaded and fried; or used in soup; or salted, cured, and stewed, is good good *good*. Its legs and shoulders become gorgeously cured hams of countless cultures: Parma (prosciutto), Smithfield, Bayonne, *jambon blanc,* the incredible and life-changing Spanish *patas negras*...Salt pork, fatback, smoked hock, and *poitrine* (belly), whether fresh, semi-cured, or cured (as with bacon), were essential ingredients in many ancient cultures, and in many ways, the history of interplay between salt and pork is the history of the world. Few things are not made better with the addition of a fat, smoky lardon of bacon.

Every strip of gut makes any number of wonderful sausages, both fresh and cured. The blood can be used for soup, for little blood

cakes, for the straight-from-heaven *boudin noir,* or as a thickening and flavoring agent for sauces and stews. Nearly every other culture in the world gets this, has gotten it for centuries. Only we lag behind.

Ears, when confited, are crunchy delicious; the jowls, when roasted, are the best a roast can be; and the bones make a hearty soup base. The skin is good for cracklin's, or for lining a cassoulet pot. The fat—whether from hams, sausages, bacon, or fresh pork—is a potential secret ingredient. The cheeks are great, and the trotters, or feet, though labor intensive, are one of the great workingman's classics of everyday French cuisine. That they sell well at Les Halles is a principal joy.

Love pork in all its many-faceted glory. Respect it. Do not waste it. Use it carefully and well. Cook with it, at all times, as if you were dirt poor; it is imperative that you not waste a scrap. A highly intelligent animal died so you could have bacon. So don't overcook it.

A good starting point, a simple, real-world introduction to just how good pork really is, is the recipe for rillettes on page 086. Here's an ancient preparation involving little more than fresh pork, its fat, and a little water. Prepared with love and attention, it will reward you with joy and enlightenment. You will understand. And you will be better for it.

# mignons de porc à l'ail

**This is one of the most popular dishes at Les Halles. Yet another dish that would really benefit from a stash of good demi-glace.**

## INGREDIENTS

**4 heads of garlic confit** (see page 262)
**4 pork tenderloins,**
  about 10 ounces/280 g each
**2 slices of bacon**
**1 tbsp/14 ml olive oil**
**3 tbsp/42 g butter**
**salt and pepper**
**2 shallots,** thinly sliced
**$^1/_4$ cup/56 ml white wine**
**$^1/_2$ cup/110 ml strong,**
  **dark chicken or veal stock**
**1 sprig of flat parsley,** finely chopped

## EQUIPMENT

fork
small bowl
cutting board
plastic wrap
kitchen string
sauté pan
small roasting pan
wooden spoon
large plate
whisk
serving platter

**SERVES 4-6**

### PREP

Use the fork to mash half of the garlic cloves. Reserve the remaining cloves separately in the small bowl. Lay two of the tenderloins down across the cutting board. Lay some plastic wrap across them and give them a light pounding with the heel of your hand. You're looking to flatten the tenderloins ever so slightly on the fatter end. Remove and discard the plastic wrap.

Top the tenderloins with the mashed garlic, spreading the pastelike substance evenly along the length of the tenderloins. Lay the bacon slices across the garlic the long way. Now lay the other two tenderloins on top of the first two, the fatter ends pointing in the opposite direction from the ones on the bottom, so that they nestle together in a yin-yang sort of a way, creating a fairly even-shaped tube. Using kitchen string, tie each double tenderloin together tightly and evenly at several points along the tube (that way it can be sliced into medallions without cutting the string). Refrigerate overnight.

## COOK

Preheat the oven to 350°F/180°C. Remove the tenderloins from the refrigerator. In the sauté pan, heat the olive oil over high heat. Add 1 tablespoon/14 g of the butter. When the butter stops foaming, season the pork, then add it to the pan, working in batches so as not to overcrowd the pan. Cook the pork over high heat for about 6 to 8 minutes per side, after which the meat should be nicely browned. Place the meat in the roasting pan and finish cooking in the oven for about 20 minutes. When cooked through, but still moist in the center, remove from the oven and allow to rest on the plate.

Discard the fat from the sauté pan and add 1 tablespoon/14 g of the butter. Heat over medium-high heat, then add the shallots. Cook for 2 minutes, or until the shallots are soft. Stir in the wine with the wooden spoon, scraping the bottom to dislodge the good stuff. Cook over high heat until the wine is reduced to a glaze consistency, then stir in the stock. Cook over high heat until it's reduced by half. (At this point you should, if you can, whisk in a spoon of that good demi-glace from your stash.) Add any drippings from the plate that's holding your cooked pork. Whisk the remaining tablespoon/14 g of butter into the sauce, as well as the remaining cloves of garlic confit and the parsley. A little splash of raw wine at this point is nice, too.

## SERVE

Slice the pork into 1$^{1}/_{2}$-inch/4-cm medallions, arrange them around the platter, and spoon over the sauce. This dish is very good with mashed potatoes, in which case, you might want to arrange the medallions on and around the potatoes, with the garlic confit–studded sauce also poured over and around. Delicious.

**If you're in a hurry, you can slice the pork into medallions when raw, then individually sear each medallion. That way you won't need to use the oven.**

# côte de porc à la charcutière

**INGREDIENTS**

**1 tbsp/14 ml oil**
**1 tbsp/14 g butter**
**4 rib chops of pork,**
   about 10 ounces/280 g each
**salt and pepper**
**1 small onion,** finely chopped
**1 teaspoon Wondra flour** (see Suppliers),
   *or* **all-purpose flour**
**$^1/_2$ cup/110 ml white wine**
**1 cup/225 ml dark, strong chicken**
   **or veal stock**
**2 tbsp/28 g Dijon mustard**
**10 cornichons,** thinly sliced
**1 sprig of flat parsley,** chopped

**EQUIPMENT**

oven-safe sauté pan
tongs
platter
aluminum foil
wooden spoon
whisk
serving platter

**SERVES 4**

Let's assume you don't *have* any "good strong stock" and are unlikely to make some. Here's another reason to load up your freezer once or twice a year with demi-glace, portioned in small amounts. To make up for a ball-less stock, all you have to do is spoon in a little of that beautiful demi-glace. It'll change everything for you.

Preheat the oven to 375°F/190°C. In the oven-safe sauté pan, heat the oil, then the butter. Season the chops with salt and pepper, then sear in the hot pan for about 4 minutes per side, or until golden brown. Transfer the pan to the oven and cook for another 8 minutes. Remove the pan from the oven and remove the chops. Set them aside on the platter, loosely covered with foil, while you make the sauce.

Return the sauté pan to the heat, and add the onion. Cook until golden brown. Add the flour and cook, stirring, for 1 minute. Stir in the wine and reduce by half, scraping, scraping, of course. Add the stock (and you really *do* need a good, dark, strong stock for this). Reduce the liquid by half. Remove the pan from the heat and whisk in the mustard. Add the cornichons, the parsley, and any nice juice that has run off the cooked pork chops. Adjust the seasoning. Arrange the chops on the platter and pour over the sauce. Eat.

# rôti de porc au lait

## INGREDIENTS
3 lb/1.35 kg boneless pork loin roast
salt and pepper
2 tbsp/28 ml olive oil
1 tbsp/14 g butter
1 **medium onion,** chopped
1 **carrot,** finely chopped
1 **leek, white part only,** finely chopped
1 **garlic clove,** finely chopped
1 tablespoon flour
2 cups/450 ml whole milk
1 **bouquet garni** (see Glossary)

## EQUIPMENT
Dutch oven
large plate
wooden spoon
strainer
small pot
hand blender
carving knife or other
   very sharp knife
serving platter

**SERVES 6**

### COOK THE PORK
Season the pork with salt and pepper. Heat the oil in the Dutch oven. When the oil is hot, add the butter. Brown the roast on all sides, 6 to 7 minutes total. Remove the roast from the pan and set aside on the large plate. Add the onion, carrot, leek, and garlic and stir over high heat until soft and caramelized, about 10 minutes. Stirring constantly, add the flour and cook for 2 minutes, then add the milk and the bouquet garni. Bring to a boil and cook over high heat for 5 minutes. Add the pork and any juices that have collected on the plate. Reduce the heat to a simmer. Cover and cook over low heat for 1 hour, making sure to periodically rotate the pork (the sugars in the milk can cause sticking and scorching). Remove the pork and allow to rest for 15 minutes.

### FINISH THE SAUCE AND SERVE
Remove and discard the bouquet garni. Strain the cooking liquid into a small pot and bring to a boil. Using a hand blender, purée the sauce until foamy. Adjust the seasoning as needed. Carve the pork and arrange on a serving platter. Spoon the sauce over and around and serve immediately.

# palette de porc à la bière

## INGREDIENTS

**4 to 6 lb/1.8 to 2.7 kg pork shoulder**
(the palette), bone in
**salt and pepper**
**4 tbsp/56 ml olive oil**
**2 tbsp/28 g butter**
**2 small onions,** thinly sliced
**2 carrots,** chopped
**4 garlic cloves**
**2 tbsp/28 g flour**
**$1/4$ cup/56 ml cider vinegar**
**12 ounces/340 ml beer**
**1 cup/225 ml chicken stock or broth**
**4 tbsp/56 ml Dijon mustard**
**2 tbsp/28 g bread crumbs**
(unseasoned, not toasted)

## EQUIPMENT

large pot
tongs
plate
wooden spoon
baking sheet
small brush
cutting board
strainer
small saucepan
whisk

**SERVES 4**

### COOK THE PORK

Season the pork all over with salt and pepper. Heat 2 tablespoons/28 ml of the oil in the large pot over high heat. Then add the butter. Let it foam, right? Like always. Is it hot? Okay. Lay the pork in the pot and cook over high heat for 5 minutes. Then roll the beast over using your tongs and cook for another 5 minutes on the other side. Nice brown color on both sides? Remove the pork from the pan and set aside on the plate.

Take the pot off the heat, discard the blackened butter, and add 2 tablespoons/28 ml of fresh oil. Now add the onions, carrots, and garlic to the pot. Cook over medium heat until soft and brown. Add the flour and stir well so it coats the vegetables, then cook for 2 minutes, stirring occasionally.

Stir in the vinegar and beer, scraping up all the good stuff with the wooden spoon. Bring to a boil and cook until the liquid is reduced by half. Stir in the chicken stock or broth. Bring to a boil. Reduce to a simmer and return the pork to the pot, being sure to incorporate any juices from the meat. Reduce to a very low simmer, cover the pot, and let cook for about 2 hours, stirring occasionally.

### MAKE THE CRUST
Preheat the oven to 450°F/230°C. Remove the pork from the pot and place on the baking sheet. Brush the meat evenly with 2 tablespoons/28 ml of the mustard, then press bread crumbs into the mustard-covered surface of the meat. Place in the oven for 15 minutes, or until the crumbs form a firm, browned crust. Remove from the oven, and allow to rest on the cutting board for 5 minutes while you finish the sauce.

### FINISH THE SAUCE
Strain the cooking liquid into the small saucepan. Bring to a boil, then reduce to a simmer. Simmer for about 15 minutes, then season with salt and pepper. Remove from the heat and whisk in the remaining 2 tablespoons/28 ml of mustard. Slice the meat and serve with sauce either on the side or poured around the slices.

# poultry & game

# poule au pot

## INGREDIENTS

1 cup/225 g stale bread,
cut into cubes
1 cup/225 ml heavy cream
$^1/_2$ lb/225 g chicken livers, chopped
1 shallot, finely chopped
$^1/_2$ bunch of flat parsley
(about $1^1/_2$ ounces/32 g)
1 egg yolk
1 lb/450 g pork sausage,
squeezed from casing and crumbled
salt and pepper
1 6-lb/2.7-kg chicken or capon
(basically a big, tough old bird)
6 whole cloves
2 medium onions, peeled and
cut in half
6 leeks, white part only, thoroughly
washed and rinsed
4 carrots, cut into 3-inch/8-cm sticks
(big, chunky, Flintstones-like batons
are fine)
2 celery ribs, cut into 3-inch/8-cm sticks

2 small turnips, peeled and cut into
4 pieces each
1 bouquet garni (see Glossary)
1 tbsp/14 g whole black peppercorns
1 head of cabbage, cut into 8 pieces
6 small potatoes
$^1/_2$ lb/225 g cornichons
$^1/_2$ cup/112 g sea salt
$^1/_2$ cup/112 g Dijon mustard

## EQUIPMENT

mixing bowl
kitchen string
trussing needle
*huge* pot
3 small ramekins
serving platter
soup terrine
ladle
6 large soup bowls

**SERVES 6**

## PREP

In the mixing bowl, combine the bread and the heavy cream. Allow the bread to absorb the liquid. Add the chicken livers, shallot, parsley, egg yolk, sausage, and salt and pepper and mix well, taking care to not crush the ingredients. Wash the interior of the chicken, stuff it with the mixture, and then sew the cavity closed with the string and trussing needle. It's easy. Even I can do it. Press 3 cloves into each onion, as if you were sticking tacks into a bulletin board. Tie the leeks into 2 bundles of 3 each.

## COOK

In the huge pot, combine the chicken, onions, leeks, carrots, celery, turnips, and bouquet garni. Add the peppercorns and salt to taste, and fill the pot with water. Bring to a simmer and let cook over low heat for about 2 hours. After 2 hours, add the cabbage and potatoes and cook for an additional 30 minutes.

Discard the bouquet garni and the onions. Place the cornichons, sea salt, and mustard in separate ramekins or crocks and situate on your table. Carefully transfer the chicken to the serving platter and use a sharp knife to cut and remove the string. Arrange the cooked vegetables around the chicken and place the broth in a soup terrine.

## SERVE

Each guest should get a piece of white meat, a piece of dark meat, some vegetables, and a spoonful of stuffing. Ladle broth over each portion and serve with the condiments.

# poulet roti

**That's *roast chicken,* numbnuts! And if you can't properly roast a damn chicken then you are one helpless, hopeless, sorry-ass bivalve in an apron. Take that apron off, wrap it around your neck, and hang yourself. You do not deserve to wear the proud garment of generations of hardworking, dedicated cooks. Turn in those clogs, too.**

Perhaps I'm being a little unfair. Perhaps I'm being unreasonable. Given that ninety-five percent of the chickens roasted in this country are clearly the result of insensitive and murderous overcooking by food-hating orangutans, why should I expect *you* to know how to roast a damn bird? Most people seem to think that if you just scatter some salt and pepper and, God forbid, *paprika* on a chicken, then throw him, legs askew, into an oven and cook every bit of blood and moisture out of him—that *that's* roasting a chicken. Hell, most people figure that if the crispy skin tastes good, and there's no yucky blood or pink stuff near the bone, that's a fine roast chicken. It is not. This is the kind of thinking that makes fried batter a favorite menu item in this country. This is the kind of dangerously low expectation that explains the Chicken McNugget. A good-quality chicken, of noble birth and upbringing, respectfully prepared by someone who loves and understands it, is a beautiful thing. Many chefs claim to be able to tell everything about a prospective cook by how he or she roasts a chicken—and I can well believe it.

There are many ways to roast a chicken. Put twelve chefs in a room, with the mission of defining once and for all how best to roast a chicken, and you will never get agreement. Only spirited discussion, some heavy drinking, and maybe fisticuffs. But this recipe works

for us at Les Halles. It's simple, it's good, it requires minimal technique—and the possibilities of failure are few. Yes, you *can* sear the skin of the chicken in a pan *before* roasting. Yes, you *can* sear the skin, then vacuum-seal the bird, then roast it slowly. Yes, you *can*—and should (if you know how)—truss a bird up like Betty Page. But this bird will do. It'll do fine.

Before we begin we should talk about the chicken. Perhaps you think that a drugged-up supermarket bird that's spent its whole life jammed into a cramped pen with a bunch of similarly unhealthy specimens, eating its neighbor's droppings (really!), is adequate for your kitchen. It is decidedly *not.* Fortunately for you, free-range chickens are becoming more widely available every day (see Suppliers). If not, there are kosher chickens to be had. You want them. Chicken is *not* a medium for sauce. Chicken should taste like chicken. Understand also that legs and breasts cook at slightly different rates. In your zeal to make sure that there is no pink (eek!) or red (oooohh!) anywhere in the legs, you are often criminally overcooking your breasts. Find a happy medium. A little pink color by the thigh bone does *not* necessarily mean you are eating rare poultry.

Okay. Let's go…

## INGREDIENTS
**1 whole chicken, about 4 lbs/1.8 kg,**
  giblets reserved
**salt (preferably sea salt) and**
  **freshly crushed black pepper**
**1/2 lemon**
**1 onion,** peeled and cut in half
**1 sprig of fresh rosemary**
  (do not get that dried trash
  anywhere near my bird!)
**1 sprig of fresh thyme**
  (what did I just say?)
**2 tbsp/28 g herb butter** (see page 259)
**3 tbsp/42 g butter,** softened
**1 1/2 cups/340 ml white wine**
**a little chopped flat parsley**

## EQUIPMENT
flameproof *roasting pan*
basting brush
wooden spoon
serving platter
whisk
sauceboat or gooseneck

**SERVES 2**

**Do *not* remove the
"pope's nose" (the ass).
That's flavor.**

### PREP THE CHICKEN
Preheat the oven to 375°F/190°C. Cut off the wing tips, leaving the last joint only. With fingers, remove excess fat from the chicken's inside cavity. Trim off excess skin at the neck (and at the head, if you've bought a head-on bird in Chinatown; good for you, by the way, if you did). You removed the giblets packet, right? You'd better have, 'cause you're gonna need them. Wash the inside of the chicken thoroughly with cold running water. Allow to dry. Season the inside cavity with salt and pepper.

Okay…now, I'm not going to try and explain how to truss a chicken with twine—as much fun as that is. Here's a shortcut instead. First: Lie on your back on the floor, put your knees together, and draw them both up to your chest with your arms. Press them against your chest. You should look pretty funny down there—but that's exactly the position I want you to put your chicken in. Knees up, ass out.

Undignified, but effective. Now, take a paring knife and just below the end of the chicken's legs (approximately below where your heels would be), poke a small hole on each side, and tuck the leg carefully inside, pinioning the legs in a position approximating what you just did on the floor. Try not to tear the skin, okay? Now gently give the outside of your bird a good rubdown with salt and pepper. All over. Don't miss any spots. Put the lemon half, half of the onion, the rosemary, and the thyme inside the chicken cavity.

Carefully taking hold of the edge of the skin on each side of the chicken, lift the skin and gently push a tablespoon of herb butter underneath, prodding it along so that one lump of herb butter sits on each side of the bird's breastbone. Rub the outside of the chicken with about half of the plain (softened) butter. Gently! *Don't rip the freaking skin!*

**COOK THE CHICKEN**
Remove the giblets from the bag and place them and the remaining half of the onion in the center of the roasting pan. Place the chicken on top of same. Pour $^1/_2$ cup/110 ml of white wine into the pan and roast for 30 minutes, basting occasionally with the fat and butter that collects. When you baste, it's a very good idea to move the roasting pan around in the oven a little, even rotating it, as many ovens have "hot spots" that might color or cook your bird unevenly.

After 30 minutes, crank the oven temperature up to 450°F/230°C and cook for another 25 minutes. Remove the chicken from the oven and allow to rest for 15 minutes before carving. If you're worried about undercooking, with the point of a *small* knife or with a skewer or cake tester, you can poke the fat part of the thigh. If the liquid that runs out is clear—not pink or red—your bird is cooked.

**FINISH**

If you are unhappy or insecure about your sauce, yank a cube of frozen *dark* chicken stock out of the freezer and chuck that in with the wine. Using commercial broth or base, in this instance, would destroy all your good work to this point—a crime against food, God, and man.

Place the roasting pan on the stovetop over high heat. Stir in the remaining wine and scrape the bottom of the pan with the wooden spoon to dislodge the *fond* (the brown bits). Bring the wine to a boil and cook until it is reduced by half. Discard the giblets and onion and whisk in the remaining softened butter. Stir in the parsley, season with salt and pepper, and serve alongside the chicken in a boat or gooseneck.

# poulet basquaise

## INGREDIENTS

1 whole chicken, about 4 lb/1.6 kg,
 cut into 8 pieces
salt and black pepper
pinch of cayenne pepper or
 piment d'esplète (see Suppliers)
2 tbsp/28 ml olive oil
1 tbsp/14 g butter
2 red bell peppers,
 cut into fine julienne
2 green bell peppers,
 cut into fine julienne
1 onion, thinly sliced
16 ounces/450 g canned Italian
 plum tomatoes

$^1/_2$ cup/110 ml white wine
$^1/_2$ cup/110 ml water
$^1/_2$ cube chicken bouillon or $^1/_2$ cup/110
 ml light chicken stock or broth (this is
 one dish that can handle a bouillon cube)
3 sprigs of flat parsley, finely chopped

## EQUIPMENT

large pot with cover
tongs
plate
wooden spoon
serving platter

**SERVES 4**

Season the chicken all over with salt, black pepper, and cayenne. Heat
the large pot over medium-high heat and add the oil. When the oil is
hot, add the butter. When the butter has foamed and subsided, add the
chicken, skin side down, and brown on that side *only*. Remove the
chicken with the tongs and set aside on the plate. Add the peppers and
the onion to the pot and reduce the heat to medium low. Cook for
about 10 minutes, then add the tomatoes and cook until the liquid is
reduced by half. Stir in the wine, scraping, scraping—as always—to
get the good stuff up. Cook until the wine is reduced by half, then add
the water and the bouillon (or the $^1/_2$ cup/110 ml of chicken stock).
Return the chicken to the pot, making sure to add all the juice that's
accumulated on the plate while it rested. Cover the pot and allow to
cook on low heat for about 25 minutes, then remove the chicken to the
serving platter.

Crank up the heat to high and reduce the sauce for 5 minutes. Season
with salt and pepper and add the parsley. Pour the sauce over the
chicken and serve immediately, with rice pilaf.

# chartreuse
# of quail

This dish is basically a combination of three main ingredients—quail, foie gras, and cabbage—that are cooked separately, then assembled in ramekins and baked in the oven. It looks tough, but it's not. If you have your *mise en place* together and your prep done, the actual cooking and assembly are easy.

Keep the quail carcasses for making the sauce, and if you want to be arty-farty, reserve the drumsticks, too—for garnish.

## INGREDIENTS

8 quail, breasts boned out
  and separated (see Suppliers)
salt and freshly ground pepper
8 tbsp/112 g whole butter, *plus*
  2 tbsp/28 ml melted butter
4 large cabbage leaves, *plus*
  1 cup/225 g shredded cabbage
1 ounce/28 g slab bacon,
  very finely diced
1 carrot, finely chopped, *plus*
  1 carrot, coarsely chopped
1 onion, finely chopped, *plus*
  1 onion, coarsely chopped
$^1/_4$ cup/56 ml *plus* $^1/_2$ cup/
  110 ml Madeira
3 sprigs of flat parsley
1 sprig of fresh thyme
1 bay leaf
1 tsp/5 g whole black peppercorns

2 cups/450 ml dark chicken stock
8 ounces/225 g foie gras, cut into 4
  even slices, *plus* 1 ounce/28 g foie gras
  (see Suppliers)
4 $^1/_2$-inch/1-cm slices white bread,
  crusts removed

## EQUIPMENT

small sauté pan
2 medium pots
roasting pan
2 medium saucepans
fine strainer
whisk
4 8-ounce/225-ml ovenproof ramekins
pastry brush
roasting pan
4 warmed dinner plates

SERVES 4

## PREP THE MAIN INGREDIENTS

*The quail.* Preheat the oven to 375°F/190°C. Season the breasts with salt and pepper. Heat 1 tablespoon/14 g of the butter in the sauté pan until it foams and subsides, then add the breasts, skin side down. Let cook undisturbed over medium heat for 5 minutes.

Remove them from the pan and set both breasts and pan aside. If you want to use the quail legs for garnish, cut off the drumsticks, sauté them in the same pan until brown, and also set aside.

*The cabbage leaves.* Bring a medium pot of water to a boil, add 2 tablespoons/28 g of salt, then add the cabbage leaves. Cook for 5 minutes, remove from the water, and set aside.

*The stuffing.* Brown the bacon in the other medium pot over high heat for about 3 minutes, then add the finely chopped portions of the onion and the carrot. (No! *Not* the *coarsely* chopped stuff, numbnutticus!) Cook for 5 minutes, or until the vegetables are browned, then add the *shredded* cabbage and cook over low heat for about 30 minutes. Season with salt and pepper and set aside.

### MAKE THE SAUCE

Heat the pan you sautéed the quail in and, when hot, deglaze with $^1/_4$ cup/56 ml of the Madeira—meaning, add the booze to the pan and scrape up all that good stuff. Put it aside. Place the bird carcasses and thighs in the roasting pan and add the *coarsely* chopped onion and carrot and 1 tablespoon/14 g of the whole butter. Roast, uncovered, in the oven for about 25 minutes, or until both bones and vegetables are browned. Remove the pan from the oven. Deglaze with $^1/_2$ cup/110 ml of the Madeira, scraping the bottom to get every brown bit. Transfer the bones, vegetables, and pan juices to a medium saucepan and add the parsley, thyme, bay leaf, and peppercorns. Add the liquid from the pan you cooked the quail in and the chicken stock. Bring the mixture to a boil, then reduce to a simmer and let it cook until the liquid is reduced by half. Pour through a fine strainer into a clean saucepan. Bring to a boil and cook for 15 minutes. Turn down the heat to low and whisk in 2 tablespoons/28 g of the whole butter and the 1 ounce/28 g of foie gras. Season with salt and pepper.

### ASSEMBLE

Butter each of the 4 ramekins with 1 tablespoon/14 g of the whole butter. Line each ramekin with 1 precooked cabbage leaf. Hopefully, the cabbage will extend, like an overlarge piecrust, beyond the ramekin, leaving extra to wrap with later. Start to fill each ramekin with a few tablespoons of the bacon-cabbage mixture, then add 1 slice of foie gras. Top that with 2 quail breasts, followed by more bacon-cabbage mix. Fold each cabbage leaf around the ingredients to seal it from the top. Brush each of the slices of bread with the melted butter and place on top of each ramekin, butter side down, trimming to fit.

Take a break and picture this: You have layers of cabbage and bacon and quail and foie gras, wrapped up inside a cabbage leaf inside the mold of each ramekin, plugged nicely at the top with the bread. When you finally unmold, the bread will form a nice base at the bottom. Can you see it? If you're uncomfortable with the ramekin for some reason, you can do the same damn thing with a heavy soup cup. Got it? *Capisce?*

### BAKE

Decrease the oven temperature to 325°F/170°C. Carefully place the ramekins in a roasting pan and cook for about 25 minutes, until the juices start to bubble around the edges. If you want to garnish your chartreuse with the quail drumsticks, simply pop them in the oven for a few minutes until cooked through, then keep warm.

### SERVE

Place 1 ramekin, upside down, in the middle of each of the 4 warmed dinner plates. Carefully slip the ramekins off. (You *did* remember to butter the ramekins like I said, right?) Spoon sauce around each portion and, if you wish, garnish with the quail drumsticks, 2 to a portion.

Congratulations. You have completed one fancy-ass dish.

# roulade of wild pheasant

Okay, this is a little more luxurious than standard bistro fare—and more complicated. But you can do it. Just make sure you're organized, and that you've got everything you need on hand before you begin. Do things in stages. And stay relaxed. If it doesn't come out perfect the first time, you'll get it right the next. Have fun. Look at it like building a model airplane. Be fussy, precise, and attentive to details.

You will definitely want to get your trusted butcher to bone out your pheasant. Keep the bones! You'll need them.

## INGREDIENTS

1 **wild pheasant,** completely boned out, with skin intact, in one piece, bones reserved (see Suppliers)
4 **leeks,** thinly sliced
1 **cup/225 ml** *plus* **¹/₂ tbsp/7 ml** *plus* **¹/₄ cup/56 ml port**
4 **ounces/112 g lean veal**
**¹/₄ cup/56 ml heavy cream**
**salt and pepper**
6 **ounces/168 g foie gras,** cut into equal finger or log shapes (see Suppliers)
1 **tbsp/14 ml olive oil**
3 **tbsp/42 g butter**
2 **shallots,** thinly sliced
1 **tbsp/14 g flour**
1 **cup/225 ml dark chicken stock**
1 **bouquet garni** (see Glossary)
**¹/₂ cup/110 ml truffle juice** (see Suppliers)
2 **tbsp/28 g chopped truffles**

## EQUIPMENT

nonreactive bowl or casserole
food processor
kitchen string
cheesecloth (coffee filters work in a pinch)
plastic wrap
medium saucepan
wooden spoon
strainer
small saucepan
large pot (sizable enough to hold pheasant without folding it)
large sauté pan
carving knife
serving platter
whisk

**SERVES 4**

**PREP THE BIRD**

In the nonreactive bowl or casserole, combine the pheasant, 2 of the sliced leeks, and 1 cup/225 ml of the port. Marinate for 24 hours, covered, in the refrigerator.

Place the veal in the food processor and purée the living hell out of it, while slowly adding the cream, $1/2$ tablespoon/7 ml of the port, and salt and pepper. Eventually, you want to attain a mousse-like consistency, meaning smooth, baby, smooth. Now, remove the pheasant from the marinade, pat it dry with paper toweling, and lay it out, skin side down, on a clean, dry work surface. Season the flesh with salt and pepper. Now spread the veal mixture in an even layer on the inside of the pheasant, as if you were slathering peanut butter on a piece of white bread, only a little thicker. Lay the logs of foie gras end to end right down the middle—the long way—on top of the veal mix. You see what's happening here? We're making a nori roll. You're going to want the foie gras to be a center garnish, surrounded by a layer of veal mixture, itself surrounded, or wrapped, by the pheasant meat and skin. Can you picture it? Good. 'Cause now it's time to do it. Here's how:

*Roll* the pheasant carefully around the foie gras the long way, *not* squeezing too hard. The skin and meat should overlap slightly when rolled. If you can roll a decent joint, this part should be way easy. And just like with a joint, you don't want it fat in the middle and skinny on the ends. You want a nice even shape. Be gentle.

Secure the "joint" with kitchen string, at three or four points, not tying it too tightly. You're looking at this point to shape it and hold it together. Season the pheasant with salt and pepper and wrap it tightly in a layer of cheesecloth. Then wrap the whole thing again in plastic wrap, very tightly. If you've done it right to this point, you can be a little rougher, as everything has been secured with string and cheesecloth. Make

Now have a cocktail.
You deserve it. The hard
part is over.

sure the ends are twisted and secured by either knotting the plastic
or securing with more string.

### MAKE THE SAUCE

In the medium saucepan, heat the oil over medium-high heat. Add
1 tablespoon/14 g butter and let foam and subside. Add the pheasant
bones and brown them well. Add the shallots and the remaining 2 leeks
and cook over medium-high heat until they are caramelized and
brown. You may need to add more butter if the veggies stick or look
like they're thinking about scorching. Stir in the flour and cook for 2
minutes, then stir in $1/4$ cup/56 ml of the port and the reserved marinade.
Reduce by half over high heat. Then add the chicken stock and the
bouquet garni. Bring to a boil, reduce to a simmer, and cook for 1 hour.
(If you have some of that good demi-glace in your freezer, feel free to
sneak in a teaspoon.) Remove from the heat and strain into the small
saucepan. Stir in the truffle juice and the truffles and cook for 2
minutes. Hold in a warm place.

### COOK THE BIRD

Bring water to a boil in the large pot. Add the wrapped pheasant
(still in the plastic wrap), cover the pot, and shut off the heat. Let the
pheasant sit undisturbed in the water with the lid on the pot for 2
hours. Remove the pheasant from the water and let it rest for an hour.
Unwrap it from the plastic and the cheesecloth but keep the string on.

Now heat 1 tablespoon/14 g of the butter in the large sauté pan over
medium-high heat. Brown the roulade of pheasant for about 4 minutes
on all sides, until golden brown. Remove the string and slice the roulade
into $1/2$-inch/1-cm slices. Arrange the slices artfully on the serving
platter, crank up the heat on the sauce, and whisk in the remaining
1 tablespoon/14 g of butter to finish. Drizzle the sauce *around* the slices of
roulade and serve.

# canard sauvage

## INGREDIENTS
1 tbsp/14 ml olive oil
2 **wild ducks,** 2$^1/_2$ **lb/1.1 kg each,**
   breasts removed (with skin intact),
   legs with thighs removed, bones
   hacked into 4 or 5 pieces, all
   innards reserved (see Suppliers)
2 **small leeks,** finely chopped
3 **shallots,** finely chopped
3 to 4 tbsp/42 to 56 g **butter**
$^1/_2$ **cup/110 ml** *plus* **2 tbsp/28 ml**
   **Calvados**
2 cups/450 ml **dark chicken stock**
1 **bouquet garni** (see Glossary)
**salt and pepper**
1 tbsp/14 g **flour**

2 tbsp/28 ml **cider vinegar**
1 **duck liver,** liquefied in blender

## EQUIPMENT
2 medium pots
wooden spoon
strainer
medium bowl
tongs
plate
small sauté pan
serving platter
slicing knife
gooseneck

**SERVES 4**

### PREP THE DUCK STOCK

In a medium pot, heat 1 tablespoon/14 ml olive oil over high heat. Add the duck bones and brown them well, then add the leeks and 2 of the shallots. Cook over medium-high heat, stirring occasionally, until the vegetables are caramelized. You might need to drop in a little butter if the vegetables begin sticking to the pan or look like they're going to scorch. Don't let that happen. Stir in $^1/_2$ cup/110 ml of the Calvados, scraping the bottom of the pan with the wooden spoon, of course. Reduce the liquid until it's almost gone, then stir in the dark chicken stock and add the bouquet garni. Bring to a boil, reduce to a simmer, and let cook over low heat for 1 hour. Strain the stock into the medium bowl and throw out all the solids.

## BRAISE THE DUCK LEGS

Season the duck legs with salt and pepper. In the other medium pot, heat 1 tablespoon/14 g of the butter until it foams and subsides. Brown the duck legs in the butter, turning with the tongs to evenly cook all sides. Remove the legs to the plate and set aside. Now add the remaining shallot to the pot, as well as the duck gizzards and hearts. Cook over medium heat until well caramelized, stirring frequently. Stir in the flour and cook for 2 minutes, then stir in the cider vinegar. Reduce over high heat until the vinegar nearly evaporates, then return the legs to the pot. Add the reserved duck stock, bring to a boil, then reduce to a simmer. Let simmer for 1 hour, or until the legs are very tender.

## COOK THE BREASTS

Season the breasts with salt and pepper. Heat 1 tablespoon/14 g of the butter in the small sauté pan until it foams and subsides. Add the breasts *skin side down* and cook for 3 minutes, then turn them over and cook for 2 minutes on the flesh side. Remove the breasts from the pan and set aside. Stir the remaining 2 tablespoons/28 ml of Calvados into the pan, reduce by half, then strain this in with the duck-braising liquid.

## FINISH THE DISH

Remove the legs, gizzards, and hearts from the braising liquid and arrange on the serving platter. Slice the breasts as thin as possible and arrange the slices, shingled and slightly overlapping, alongside the legs. Bring the braising liquid to a boil, check the seasoning, and whisk in 1 tablespoon/14 g of the butter. Remove from the heat and whisk in the liquefied liver. Pour some of the sauce over the duck—careful not to cover the beautiful red and pink slices completely—and serve the rest in a gooseneck.

NOTE: You should really never cook duck breasts more than medium rare. Beyond that, they get tough as hell, and nowhere near as pretty. If you must overcook your duck, simply toss in the oven for a few more minutes after searing in the pan. And may God forgive you. For a little height and color—and because it tastes good—you might consider serving this with sautéed Swiss chard or spinach, and parsnip purée (page 265).

# duck à l'orange

**When you prepare the duck, trim the floppy excess skin and fat where the head used to be, and the soft stuff just inside the butt end of the body cavity. Make sure to *save* this. It's very useful for making confit, sautéing potatoes, etc.**

## INGREDIENTS
**1 fresh duck,** trimmed of excess fat
**salt and pepper**
**$^1/_2$ orange,** cut into 4 pieces
**1 lemon,** cut into 6 pieces
**$^1/_2$ cup/100 ml red wine vinegar**
**2 ounces/56 g sugar**
**2 cups/450 ml dark duck stock or
  chicken stock**
**3 ounces/75 ml Grand Marnier**
**2 tbsp/28 g butter**
**zest of 2 oranges,** confited
  (see citrus zest confit, page 263)
**juice of $^1/_2$ orange**
**juice of $^1/_2$ lemon**
**2 oranges,** peeled and segmented

## EQUIPMENT
kitchen string
roasting pan or baking sheet
wire rack (optional)
tongs
medium saucepan
pastry brush
fine strainer
small saucepan
whisk
serving platter

**SERVES 2**

### COOK THE DUCK
Preheat the oven to 250°F/130°C. After thoroughly washing the insides (and removing the giblets), season the cavity and outside of the duck with salt and pepper. Place the 4 orange pieces and the 6 lemon pieces inside the cavity. With the kitchen string, truss the duck, just like I told you to truss a chicken (see page 182). Legs up tight against the body. And get rid of the wing tips; they scorch.

Place the duck in the roasting pan or on a baking sheet and cook for 25 minutes at the relatively low temperature of 250°F/130°C. Then remove from the oven and cool to room temperature.

Crank up the oven heat to 350°F/180°C. Place the duck back in the roasting pan or on the baking sheet, but this time, elevate it from the bottom with a wire rack. If you don't have a wire rack, use duck bones, or carrots and onions, or English muffins to keep the bird from sticking to the bottom, and to allow for the copious amounts of drainage that'll be going on as all that lovely fat oozes out of your bird. Cook in the oven for about 1 hour and 15 minutes, until the skin is crispy and deep, golden brown. It's a good idea to spin the pan around to avoid uneven cooking.

## THE SAUCE

Meanwhile, in the medium saucepan, combine the vinegar and sugar and bring to a boil. Using a wet pastry brush to keep the sugar from hardening on the sides of the pan, continue to cook until the sugar has completely dissolved and the liquid has the consistency of a light caramel. Do I need to remind you that this stuff is godawful hot? That it will stick to you like napalm if you touch it? Good. Remove from the heat and stir in your stock. Do this *very* gradually and carefully. Even if your stock is boiling, it is in no way anywhere *near* as hot as that sugar-vinegar mix. The stock could come up in a boiling foam and scald the living hell out of you if you're not careful.

Got through that without third-degree burns? Outstanding. Now simmer the sauce for 45 minutes on low heat. When the duck is cooked, remove it from the oven and allow it to rest. Discard the excess fat from the roasting pan (though using it to roast or sauté potatoes is a superb idea). Place the now greaseless pan over high heat and add the Grand Marnier. Watch out, as it might well flame up and set your hair and eyelashes alight. When you've scraped up all that duck goodness, pour it all into the simmering sauce. Simmer until the sauce is reduced by half, then strain through the fine strainer into the small saucepan. Add the juices dribbling out of your resting duck if you like. Season the sauce with salt and pepper to taste and bring to a boil. Whisk in the butter and add the confited orange zest, orange juice, and lemon juice. Check the seasoning again.

## SERVE

On the serving platter, arrange the orange segments around the duck, and pour the sauce over and around it. The rest of the sauce can go in a sauceboat or gooseneck if you like. Carve the duck like a chicken, but expect less meat. It's not a typo; one duck will feed two reasonably hungry adults.

**If you were smart enough and cool enough to use your duck fat to roast some potatoes, you will be eating very, very well.**

# lapin aux olives

## INGREDIENTS
4 rabbit legs
1 small onion, coarsely chopped
1 small carrot, coarsely chopped
1 celery rib, coarsely chopped
4 garlic cloves, crushed
2 bay leaves
2 sprigs of thyme, *plus* 1 sprig
  of thyme, leaves only, finely chopped
1 sprig of rosemary, *plus* 1 sprig of
  rosemary, leaves only, finely chopped
1 sprig of flat parsley, *plus* 1 sprig of
  flat parsley, leaves only, finely chopped
1 tbsp/14 g whole black peppercorns
$1^1/_2$ cups/340 ml white wine
salt and pepper

$^1/_4$ cup/56 g flour (for dredging), *plus*
  1 tbsp/14 g flour (for sauce)
2 tbsp/28 ml olive oil
1 tbsp/14 g butter
1 tbsp/14 g tomato paste
$^1/_4$ cup/56 ml red wine vinegar
2 cups/450 ml chicken stock
$^1/_4$ lb/112 g picholine olives, pitted

## EQUIPMENT
large mixing bowl
Dutch oven or other heavy, large pot
wooden spoon
strainer
serving platter

SERVES 4

### PREP THE BUNNY
In the large mixing bowl, combine the rabbit legs, onion, carrot, celery, garlic, bay leaves, whole sprigs of thyme, rosemary, and parsley, the peppercorns, and the wine. Let marinate for 2 hours.

### COOK THE BUNNY
Drain the marinade and reserve the liquid and the vegetables separately. Pat the legs dry and season with salt and pepper. Dredge the legs in $^1/_4$ cup/56 g of the flour. Heat the olive oil over high heat in the Dutch oven and, once the oil is hot, add the butter. Brown the legs on both sides until they are dark golden brown, about 3 to 4 minutes per side. Remove the legs from the pot and set aside.

Add the vegetables from the marinade to the pot and cook over high heat until they are browned and caramelized. Stir in the tomato paste and the remaining tablespoon/14 g of flour and mix well with the wooden spoon. Cook for 1 minute, then stir in the vinegar and the reserved marinade liquid. Cook over high heat until the liquid is thick enough to coat the back of the spoon. Stir in the chicken stock and bring to a boil. Add the rabbit legs and reduce to a simmer. Cook over low heat for 1 hour, or until the meat is very tender. Remove the legs and set aside.

**FINISH AND SERVE**
Strain the cooking liquid and return it to the pot. Return the legs to the pot and bring the liquid to a boil. Stir in the olives and the chopped herbs, season with salt and pepper, and serve on the platter.

# civet of wild boar

## INGREDIENTS

**2 lb/900 g wild boar shoulder,** cut
   into 2-inch/5-cm cubes (see Suppliers)
**1 small onion,** thinly sliced
**1 small carrot,** cut into
   2-inch/5-cm pieces
**1 leek,** finely chopped
**4 garlic cloves,** crushed
**1 cup/225 ml** *plus*
   **$^{1}/_{2}$ cup/110 ml red wine**
**salt and pepper**
**1 tbsp/14 ml olive oil**
**4 tbsp/56 g butter**
**1 tbsp/14 g flour**
**1 cup/225 ml veal stock**
**1 bouquet garni** (see Glossary)
**2 tbsp/28 ml red wine vinegar**
**1 tbsp/14 g shaved bitter chocolate**
**$^{1}/_{4}$ cup/56 g chopped flat parsley**

## EQUIPMENT

2 large mixing bowls
plastic wrap
colander
Dutch oven
tongs
wooden spoon
strainer
medium bowl
slotted spoon
serving bowl
whisk

**SERVES 4**

**PREP**

Place the boar cubes in a large mixing bowl and add the onion, carrot, leek, and garlic. Cover with 1 cup/110 ml of the wine, then cover the bowl with plastic wrap and let the meat marinate for 24 hours in the refrigerator.

**COOK**

Place the colander inside the other large mixing bowl. Pour the meat, vegetables, and marinade into the colander, then remove the liquid and set aside. Reserve the vegetables separately. Pat the meat dry and season with salt and pepper. Heat the oil in the Dutch oven and, once it is hot, add the butter. When the butter has foamed and subsided, add the meat, working in batches, turning with the tongs to brown on all sides. As the meat is browned, remove it from the pan and set aside. Add the reserved vegetables and cook them over medium heat until they are brown and caramelized. Stir in the flour and cook for 2 minutes. Stir in the remaining red wine and reduce it by half, then add the veal stock, the reserved marinade, the bouquet garni, and the meat. Bring to a boil, reduce to a simmer, and season with salt and pepper.

Simmer over low heat for about $1^1/_2$ hours, or until the meat is *very* tender. Remove the meat and carrots from the cooking liquid and set aside. Strain the liquid into the medium bowl, then discard any solids remaining in the strainer and skim any foam or fat or schmutz from the liquid. Return the liquid to the pot and add the meat and carrots. Bring the mix to a boil, immediately reduce to a simmer, and cook until the meat is hot. With the slotted spoon, transfer the meat and carrots to the serving bowl. Remove the sauce from the heat, add the vinegar, and whisk in the bitter chocolate. Bring the sauce to a boil for a few seconds, then pour over the meat. Garnish with the chopped parsley and serve.

# the big classics

# boeuf bourguignon

Traditionally, this dish is cooked entirely with red wine. And that's fine, just fine. But if you listened to me earlier, and keep a stash of good, strong demi-glace kicking around in your freezer, a couple of spoonfuls give the sauce a nice flavor boost. This is one of the easiest dishes in this book, and also one of the best.

## INGREDIENTS

2 lb/900 g *paleron* of beef, or
   "chicken steak" (see Glossary), *or*
   same amount of shoulder or neck,
   cut into 1$^1$/$_2$-inch/4-cm pieces
salt and pepper
$^1$/$_4$ cup/56 ml olive oil
4 onions, thinly sliced
2 tbsp/28 g all-purpose flour
1 cup/225 ml red Burgundy
6 carrots, cut into 1-inch/2.5-cm pieces

1 garlic clove
1 bouquet garni (see Glossary)
a little chopped flat parsley

## EQUIPMENT

Dutch oven, or large,
   heavy-bottomed pot
wooden spoon
large spoon or ladle

**SERVES 6**

### STAGE ONE

Season the meat with salt and pepper. In the Dutch oven, heat the oil over high heat until it is almost smoking. Add the meat, in batches—NOT ALL AT ONCE!—and sear on all sides until it is well browned (*not gray*). You dump too much meat in the pot at the same time and you'll overcrowd it; cool the thing down and you won't get good color. Sear the meat a little at a time, removing it and setting it aside as it finishes. When all the meat is a nice, dark brown color and has been set aside, add the onions to the pot. Lower the heat to medium high until the onions are soft and golden brown (about 10 minutes). Sprinkle the flour over them. Continue to cook for about 4 to 5 minutes, stirring occasionally, then add the red wine. Naturally, you want to scrape up all that really good *fond* from the bottom of the pot with your wooden spoon. Bring the wine to a boil.

## STAGE TWO

Return the meat to the pot and add the carrots, garlic, and bouquet garni. Add just enough water (and two big spoons of demi-glace, if you have it) so that the liquid covers the meat by one third—meaning you want a ratio of 3 parts liquid to 2 parts meat. This is a stew, so you want plenty of liquid, even *after* it cooks down and reduces. Bring to a boil, reduce to a gentle simmer, and let cook for about 2 hours, or until the meat is tender (break-apart-with-a-fork tender).

You should pay attention to the dish, meaning check it every 15 to 20 minutes, stirring and scraping the bottom of the pot to make sure the meat is not sticking or, God forbid, scorching. You should also skim off any foam or scum or oil collecting on the surface, using a large spoon or ladle. When done, remove and discard the bouquet garni, add the chopped parsley to the pot, and serve.

This dish is much better the second day. Just cool the stew down in an ice bath, or on your countertop (the Health Department is unlikely to raid your kitchen). Refrigerate overnight. When time, heat and serve. Goes well with a few boiled potatoes. But goes *really* well with a bottle of Côte de Nuit Villages Pommard.

# pot-au-feu

You want to make a Frenchman cry? Make him a nice bowl of pot-au-feu. This is soul food for socialists. There are no tricky parts to the recipe. The colors are gorgeous, and it's a great main course for a casual dinner party. Who would have thought that a big pile of boiled meat and vegetables could be so good?

## INGREDIENTS

1 lb/450 g *paleron* of beef, or
  "chicken steak" (see Glossary),
  *or* brisket
6 pieces of oxtail,
  cut $1^1/_2$ inches/4 cm thick
6 beef short ribs
1 veal shank, on the bone
8 whole cloves
2 onions, cut in half
6 leeks, white part only
2 small celery roots (celeriac),
  cut into quarters
4 carrots, cut into 4-inch/10-cm lengths
1 bouquet garni (see Glossary)
salt and pepper
4 medium potatoes,
  peeled and cut in half
1 head of cabbage, cored and
  cut into 6 to 8 wedges
$1/_2$ lb/225 g cornichons
1 cup/225 g large-grained
  sea salt (gros sel)
1 cup/225 g hot prepared mustard

## EQUIPMENT

a really big pot
tongs
ladle
3 medium ramekins
marrow spoon (you can use the
  back end of an iced-tea spoon)
serving platter (a bloody big one)
soup terrine

**SERVES 6**

## COOK

In the huge pot, combine the steak, oxtail, short ribs, and veal shank and cover with cold water. Bring to a boil over high heat and as soon as the water comes to a boil, remove from the heat. Set the meats aside and throw out the water. *Clean the pot*. Seriously, do it. *Then* put the meat right back inside. Push 2 cloves into each onion half and add the onions to the pot, along with the leeks, celery roots, carrots, and bouquet garni. Season with salt and pepper and cover with cold water.

Bring the pot to a slow simmer, gradually, and let cook over medium-low heat for around $2^{1}/_{2}$ hours, or until the meat is tender. Skim the cooking liquid with a ladle periodically to remove scum and foam. Add the potatoes and cabbage and cook for an additional 30 minutes, until soft. You want to maintain the structural integrity of the meat and vegetables. Adjust the seasoning as needed.

## SERVE

Put the cornichons, sea salt, and mustard in the ramekins and set on the table. Remove the chicken steak (or brisket) from the pot and cut into 6 pieces. Remove the veal shank from the pot and cut the meat off the bone, again into 6 to 8 pieces. Using the marrow spoon, dig out all that lovely marrow from the inside of the veal bone. Arrange the oxtails, the meats, the marrow, and the vegetables in an attractively disheveled fashion on the serving platter and spoon some of the cooking liquid over and around it. Serve the rest of the liquid in a soup terrine.

Alternatively, you can arrange the meats uncarved, with the vegetables around them, swimming in broth in a big, beautiful pile in a deep serving platter, and let your friends just tear at it like the savage animals they are. (I'm getting hungry just writing this recipe.)

# coq au vin

Another easy dish that looks like it's hard. It's not. In fact, this is the kind of dish you might enjoy spending a leisurely afternoon with. There are plenty of opportunities for breaks. It's durable, delicious, and the perfect illustration of the principles of turning something big and tough and unlovely into something truly wonderful. I know it looks like a lot of ingredients, and that the recipe might be complicated. Just take your time. Knock out your prep one thing at a time, slowly building your *mise en place.* Listen to some music while you do it. There's an open bottle of wine left from the recipe, so have a glass now and again. Just clean up after yourself as you go, so your kitchen doesn't look like a disaster area when you start the actual cooking. You should, with any luck, reach a Zen-like state of pleasurable calm. And like the very best dishes, coq au vin is one of those that goes on the stove looking, smelling, and tasting pretty nasty, and yet later, through the mysterious, alchemical processes of time and heat, turns into something magical.

## INGREDIENTS

**1 bottle/1 liter** *plus* **1 cup/225 ml**
  **of red wine**
**1 onion,** cut into a 1-inch/2.5-cm dice
**1 carrot,** cut into $^1/_4$-inch/6-mm slices
**1 celery rib,** cut into $^1/_2$-inch/1-cm slices
**4 whole cloves**
**1 tbsp/14 g whole black peppercorns**
**1 bouquet garni** (see Glossary)
**1 whole chicken, about 3.5 lb/1.35 kg,**
  "trimmed"—meaning guts, wing tips, and
  neckbone removed
**salt and freshly ground pepper**
**2 tbsp/28 ml olive oil**
**6 tbsp/75 g butter,** softened
**1 tbsp/14 g flour**
**$^1/_4$ lb/112 g slab or country bacon,**
  cut into small oblongs (lardons) about
  $^1/_4$ by 1 inch/6 mm by 2.5 cm
**$^1/_2$ lb/225 g small, white button
  mushrooms,** stems removed

**12 pearl onions,** peeled
**pinch of sugar**

## EQUIPMENT

3 large, deep bowls
plastic wrap
fine strainer
large Dutch oven or heavy-bottomed pot
tongs
wooden spoon
small sauté pan
small saucepan
1 sheet of parchment paper (you can
  always beg a sheet off your local
  bakery—they've got lots)
whisk
deep serving platter

**SERVES 4**

**DAY ONE**

The day before you even begin to cook, combine the bottle of red wine, the diced onion (that's the *big* onion, *not* the pearl onions), sliced carrot, celery, cloves, peppercorns, and bouquet garni in a large, deep bowl. Add the chicken and submerge it in the liquid so that all of it is covered. Cover the bowl with plastic wrap and refrigerate overnight.

**DAY TWO**

Remove the chicken from the marinade and pat it dry. Put it aside. Strain the marinade through the fine strainer, reserving the liquids and solids separately. Season the chicken with salt and pepper inside and out. In the large Dutch oven, heat the oil and 2 tablespoons/28 g of the butter until almost smoking, and then sear the chicken, turning with the tongs to evenly brown the skin. Once browned, remove it from the pot and set it aside again. Add the reserved onions, celery, and carrot to the pot and cook over medium-high heat, stirring occasionally, until they are soft and golden brown. That should take you about 10 minutes.

Sprinkle the flour over the vegetables and mix well with the wooden spoon so that the vegetables are coated. Now stir in the reserved strained marinade. Put the chicken back in the pot, along with the bouquet garni. Cook this for about 1 hour and 15 minutes over low heat.

Have a drink. You're almost there…

While your chicken stews slowly in the pot, cook the bacon lardons in the small sauté pan over medium heat until golden brown. Remove the bacon from the pan and drain it on paper towels, *making sure* to keep about 1 tablespoon/14 g of fat in the pan. Sauté the mushroom tops in the bacon fat until golden brown. Set them aside.

Now, in the small saucepan, combine the pearl onions, the pinch of sugar, a pinch of salt, and 2 tablespoons/28 g of the butter. Add just enough water to just cover the onions, then cover the pan with the parchment paper trimmed to the same size as your pan. (I suppose you can use foil if you must.) Bring to a boil, reduce to a simmer, and cook until the water has evaporated. Keep a close eye on it. Remove the paper cover and continue to cook until the onions are golden brown. Set the onions aside and add the remaining cup/225 ml of red wine to the hot pan, scraping up all the *fond* on the bottom of the pot. Season with salt and pepper and reduce over medium-high heat until thick enough to coat the back of the spoon.

Your work is pretty much done here. One more thing and then it's wine and kudos...

When the chicken is cooked through—meaning tender, the juice from the thigh running clear when pricked—carefully remove from the liquid, cut into quarters, and arrange on the deep serving platter. Strain the cooking liquid (again) into the reduced red wine. Now just add the bacon, mushrooms, and pearl onions, adjust the seasoning with salt and pepper, and swirl in the remaining 2 tablespoons/28 g of butter. Now pour that sauce over the chicken and dazzle your friends with your brilliance. Serve with buttered noodles and a Bourgogne Rouge.

### IMPROVISATION
If you are a bold adventurer, and live near a live-poultry market or friendly pork butcher, you might want to play around a bit after doing this recipe a few times. By cutting back on the flour and thickening with fresh pig or chicken blood, you will add a whole new dimension to the dish. Be warned, though: add the blood slowly. It doesn't take much to make the sauce sit up like a rock. (Blood freezes nicely, by the way, so you might consider keeping a stash in small, individual packets. You never know when you'll need it.)

# bouillabaisse

What is an "authentic" bouillabaisse? That's an invitation to a fistfight if there ever was one. Frenchmen living in Marseille can't agree, so there'll be no consensus here, I assure you. Above and beyond the "lobster, *oui*?" or "lobster, *non*" question—and the various interpretive issues, which we could spend the rest of our natural lives discussing—there's the issue of fish. You're simply not going to be finding any congre, loup de mer, rascasse, or rouget near you. This, my boss José assures me, is as close to the real deal (whatever that might be) as you're likely to get. It's pretty damn tasty.

## INGREDIENTS

2 ounces/56 ml olive oil
2 **leeks,** white part only, washed
   and thinly sliced
2 **small onions,** thinly sliced
1 **fennel bulb,** thinly sliced
4 **garlic cloves**
3 **fresh plum tomatoes,** seeded
   and chopped (or 18 ounces/500 g
   canned Italian plum tomatoes)
2 **lb/900 g tiny little fish, like porgies
   or whiting,** guts out but heads on
1¹/₂ **lb/675 g whole red snapper,
   dourade, or striped bass,** head
   removed and set aside (you'll need it),
   scaled and gutted but skin still on, cut
   right across the spine into 4 steaks
1 **bouquet garni** (see Glossary)
**peel of** ¹/₂ **orange**
3 **pistils (strands) of saffron**
1 **healthy shot/28 ml of Pernod**
8 **small red bliss potatoes**
1 **lb/450 g monkfish tail,** skinned,
   on the bone, cut into 4 pieces
1 **lb/450 g skate wing,** skinned,
   on the bone, cut into 4 pieces
**salt and pepper**
**extra-virgin olive oil**

12 **fresh shrimp,** heads on and
   unpeeled (I guess you *could* live
   without the heads. Philistine!)

FOR THE AÏOLI GARNISH:
8 **garlic cloves**
**small pinch of sea salt**
5 **strands of saffron**
1 **egg yolk**
2 **ounces/56 ml extra-virgin olive oil**
**juice of 1 lemon**
16 **croutons of sliced, toasted baguette**

## EQUIPMENT

large, wide, heavy-bottomed pot
mallet or heavy object
fine strainer
food processor or mortar and pestle
large ramekin
plastic wrap
small pot
large, shallow casserole dish
ladle
serving platter
tureen

**SERVES 4 VERY
HUNGRY PEOPLE**

**STAGE ONE**

In the large, wide, heavy-bottomed pot, heat the oil. Add the leeks, onions, fennel, and garlic and let them sweat over medium heat for about 4 minutes. Add the tomatoes and cook for another 4 to 5 minutes. Add the small fish (porgies or whiting) and the fish head. Cook for about 15 minutes, rolling the ingredients all around in the pan. Add water to cover, the bouquet garni, and the orange peel. Add the 3 strands of saffron. Add half/14 ml of the Pernod now. Lower the heat and let simmer for about an hour. Remove from the heat. (Smells good, huh?)

With the mallet or heavy object, crush the hell out of everything in the pot. Don't be delicate about it—but don't splash boiling liquid all over yourself, either. Crush it all up and then run all the contents of the pot through the fine strainer. Be sure to squeeze out every damn drop. Hold the liquid on the side.

### STAGE TWO: THE GARNISH

First purée the garlic and salt together. Then add the saffron and egg yolk. Mix well until smooth. Now, while the machine is running, slowly, *slowly* drizzle in the extra-virgin olive oil until you get a mayonnaise consistency. Add the lemon juice at the very end. Adjust thickness with a little additional olive oil if needed, as the lemon juice will thin the mix. Remove from the machine and put in the large ramekin. Cover with plastic and reserve for later.

**You *can* make aïoli the old-school way by using a mortar and pestle and a lot of patience, like my Tante Jeanne. *She* didn't have a Cuisinart...but then she didn't have an indoor toilet, either. I suggest you use your food processor.**

### STAGE THREE: COOK THE FISH AND FINISH THE DISH

In the small pot, boil the potatoes until *nearly* cooked all the way. You're going to finish cooking them with the fish, so only cook them until they are around three-fourths done. Hold them in cold water.

In the large, shallow casserole dish, arrange the remaining fish (*except* the shrimp), being careful not to stack them on top of one another; season them with salt and pepper as you put them in. Remove the potatoes from the water, cut them in half, and arrange them among the pieces of fish. Sprinkle a little extra-virgin olive oil over the fish like you see Mario do on TV all the time. Ladle about half the liquid you made earlier and the remaining Pernod over the fish and potatoes, or just barely to cover. Bring to a simmer and cook for about 15 minutes.

Two minutes before the fish is done, add the shrimp and the remaining liquid. Simmer the whole glorious mess until everything is cooked through. Carefully transfer the solid ingredients to an attractive serving platter, arranging it all in artful style. Ladle some hot liquid over the fish, and serve the rest in the tureen.

The aïoli and croutons should be served on the side. Invite your guests to slather the garlicky, saffrony mayonnaise onto the croutons and dip as they eat.

# cassoulet

This is a great, not very difficult dish to make, and it doesn't take much time—*if* you spread the work over three days: a few easy, fairly uninvolved small tasks per day. You will also need to know how to make duck confit, a skill that will serve you well should you ever want to serve it as an appetizer or use the meat as ravioli filling (very tasty). Let's begin with the confit and move on from there. As it will survive happily in your refrigerator for weeks, you can make it way in advance.

INGREDIENTS FOR THE DUCK CONFIT
4 duck legs
sea salt
2 cups/450 g duck fat (see Suppliers)
black pepper
4 sprigs of fresh thyme
1 sprig of fresh rosemary
1 garlic clove

EQUIPMENT
shallow dish
plastic wrap
saucepan
ovenproof casserole
foil

**SERVES 4**

### DAY ONE

Rub the duck legs fairly generously with sea salt, place in the shallow dish, cover with plastic, and refrigerate overnight. At all times, keep your work area clean and your ingredients free of contamination— meaning don't allow any other foodstuffs like bread crumbs or scraps to get into your duck or duck fat or confit, as they will make an otherwise nearly nonperishable preparation suddenly perishable.

### DAY TWO

Preheat the oven to 375°F/190°C. Render (melt) the duck fat in the saucepan until clear. After seasoning with the black pepper (not too much), place the duck legs in the *clean*, ovenproof casserole, nestle the thyme, rosemary, and garlic in with it, and pour the duck fat over the legs to just cover. Cover the dish with foil and put in the oven. Cook for about an hour, or until the skin at the "ankle" of each leg pulls away from the "knuckle." The meat should be tender.

Allow to cool and then store *as is* in the refrigerator, sealed under the fat. When you need the confit, you can either warm the whole dish, in which case removing the legs will be easy, or dig them out of the cold fat and scrape off the excess. I highly recommend the former. A nice touch at this point is to twist out the thighbone from the cold confit. Just place one hand on the drumstick, pinioning the leg to the table, and with the other hand, twist out the thighbone, plucking it from the flesh without mangling the thigh meat. Think of someone you hate when you do it.

## INGREDIENTS FOR THE CASSOULET

5 cups/1100 g Tarbais beans
  (see Suppliers) **or white beans**
2 lb/900 g fresh pork belly
1 **onion,** cut into 4 pieces
1 lb/450 g pork rind
1 **bouquet garni** (see Glossary)
**salt and pepper**
$^1/_4$ **cup/56 g duck fat**
6 pork sausages
3 **onions,** thinly sliced
1 **garlic clove,** thinly sliced
4 **confit duck legs** (which you
  already have, *non?*)

## EQUIPMENT

large bowl
large pot
strainer or colander
sauté pan
paper towels
blender
large, ovenproof
  earthenware dish
measuring cup
kitchen spoon

## DAY ONE

Place the beans in the large bowl and cover with cold water so that there are at least two or three inches of water above the top of the beans. Soak overnight. That was hard, right?

## DAY TWO

Drain and rinse the beans and place in the large pot. Add the pork belly, the quartered onion, $^1/_4$ lb/112 g of the pork rind, and the bouquet garni. Cover with water, add salt and pepper to taste, and bring to a boil. Reduce to a simmer and cook until the beans are tender, about an hour. Let cool for 20 minutes, then discard the onion and the bouquet garni. Remove the pork belly, cut it into 2-inch/5-cm squares, and set aside. (If you plan to wait another day before finishing the dish, wait to cut the pork belly until then.) Strain the beans and the rind and set aside, reserving the cooking liquid separately.

In the sauté pan, heat all but 1 tablespoon/14 g of the duck fat over medium-high heat until it shimmers and becomes transparent. Carefully add the sausages and brown on all sides. Remove and set aside, draining on paper towels. In the same pan, over medium-high heat, brown the sliced onions, the garlic, and the reserved squares of pork rind from the beans (*not* the unused pork rind; you'll need that later). Once browned, remove from the heat and transfer to the blender. Add 1 tablespoon/ 14 g of the remaining duck fat and purée until smooth. Set aside.

Preheat the oven to 350°F/180°C. Place the uncooked pork rind in the bottom of a deep ovenproof earthenware dish. You're looking to line the inside, almost like a piecrust. Arrange all your ingredients in alternating layers, beginning with a layer of beans, then sausages, then

**Don't get fancy. Just pile, dab, stack, and pile. It doesn't have to be pretty.**

more beans, then pork belly, beans, duck confit, and finally more beans, adding a dab of the onion and pork rind puree between each layer. Add enough of the bean cooking liquid to just cover the beans, reserving 1 cup/225 ml in the refrigerator for later use. Cook the cassoulet in the oven for 1 hour, then reduce the heat to 250°F/130°C and cook for another hour. Remove from the oven and allow to cool. Refrigerate overnight.

## DAY THREE

Preheat the oven to 350°F/180°C again. Cook the cassoulet for an hour. Break the crust on the top with the spoon and add $^1/_4$ cup/56 ml of the reserved cooking liquid. Reduce the heat to 250°F/130°C and continue cooking another 15 minutes, or until screamingly hot through and through. Then serve.

# choucroute garnie

Oh, steaming heap of pork! Thy glistening hues of white and gray and pink! The aromatic waft of sauerkraut, redolent of Germans pouring across the border (yet again) into France with their bacon and their sausages! This is not a dish. This is a party! Just promise me: *no* oompah music! This is one dish, by the way, for which readers from the Midwest and Pennsylvania might actually have an advantage over their brethren on the coasts, suppliers of German specialty items being, one would hope, closer at hand. You ain't likely to get smoked pork loin from anybody *but* a German. And if you can buy *fresh* pork belly, cover it with a mound of sea salt and let it sit in the refrigerator for two nights. Then simply rinse or wipe it clean and use.

## INGREDIENTS

2 lb/900 g *high-quality* sauerkraut
   (find a German specialty store if
   you can, or see Suppliers)
4 peeled, boiled new potatoes
2 tbsp/28 g rendered duck fat
   (or pork fat, if you must)
1 onion, finely chopped
10 juniper berries
1 small garlic clove, crushed
3 cups/675 ml dry white wine
   (Riesling, naturally)
1 bay leaf
1 tsp/5 g coriander seed
salt and pepper
4 slices of salted pork belly

4 slices of smoked pork loin
4 frankfurters (good-quality, from a
   German pork butcher if possible)
4 *boudins blancs* or German white
   veal sausage (as above)
grainy mustard, for garnish

## EQUIPMENT

colander
2 large pots, one with lid
wooden spoon
tongs
large serving platter
ramekin for mustard

## PREP

Rinse the sauerkraut in cold water and let it drain in the colander. Peel and boil your potatoes, if you haven't yet.

## COOK

Heat the duck (or pork) fat in a large pot over medium heat. Once it's hot, add the onion and cook until translucent, about 5 minutes. Add the sauerkraut, juniper berries, garlic, white wine, bay leaf, coriander seed, salt, and pepper. Cover and bring to a simmer. Add the pork belly and the smoked pork loin. Cover the pot and simmer for $1^1/_2$ hours. In a separate pot, bring $^1/_2$ gallon of water to a simmer and add the frankfurters, *boudins blancs,* and potatoes. Simmer until hot.

## SERVE

Place the sauerkraut in the center of the large serving platter. Arrange all the meats and boiled potatoes around it. Serve with the grainy mustard.

## VARIATIONS

You can, and *should,* improvise on this recipe. We do at the restaurant. Just handle the sauerkraut (including the pork belly) the same way. Then add, for instance:

### FOR DUCK CHOUCROUTE
**4 confit duck legs** (heat that in the kraut)
**4 duck foie gras sausages** (see Suppliers)
**4 duck sausages** (see Suppliers)
**4 confit duck gizzards** (see Suppliers)

### FOR CHOUCROUTE LES HALLES
**4 smoked ham hocks** (which have been simmered, separately, until very tender)
**4 *boudins noirs* or blood sausages** (see Suppliers)
**4 smoked garlic sausages**
**4 slices of smoked pork loin**

The hardest part of this dish is the shopping. Once you have your ingredients, you can almost *not* screw this dish up. As long as you get your sauerkraut right, you can even go caveman style and just dump all your remaining ingredients right into the cabbage and heat it all up together. Then, just pick it all out, pretty it up, and arrange nicely.

# tournedos rossini

Sometimes, too much of a good thing is just enough. Case in point, this over-the-top classic from ocean liners and hotels past. This is not bistro food, though we do run it at Les Halles now and again. It always quickly sells out. But then, any dish with the words *tournedos, foie gras,* and *truffles* in it usually does.

## INGREDIENTS

4 tournedos of beef
   (about 7 ounces/196 g each)
**salt and pepper**
**1 tbsp/14 ml oil**
**3 tbsp/42 g butter,** softened
**8 ounces/225 g fresh foie gras,**
   sliced into 4 equal portions,
   *plus* 1 tbsp/14 g foie gras scraps
$^1/_4$ **cup/56 ml** *plus* **2 tbsp/28 ml Madeira**
**2 shallots,** sliced thin
**1 cup/225 ml veal demi-glace**
**1 tbsp/14 g chopped truffles**

## EQUIPMENT

2 heavy-bottomed sauté pans
tongs
small roasting pan
plate
wooden spoon
fine strainer
small saucepan
serving platter
whisk

**SERVES 4**

### COOK THE MEAT

Preheat the oven to 375°F/190°C. Season the beef with salt and pepper. Heat the oil in a heavy-bottomed sauté pan over medium-high heat. When the oil is hot, add 1 tablespoon/14 g of the butter and, once it foams and subsides, add the meat and sear on both sides, about 3 minutes per side. Hold the meat with the tongs against the surface of the pan on all sides so that it is completely browned all over. I *highly* recommend you do this one or two tournedos at a time, as you probably do not have anything like the gas pressure or heat we have in the restaurant. Too much meat in the pan at one time and you'll cool it down and get a lousy sear.

If you think you want it medium well or well, you don't deserve to eat this dish. See you at Sizzler.

When the meat is seared, transfer to the roasting pan and put in the oven. Cook the meat about 7 minutes for rare, 10 minutes for medium rare. Anything beyond that will ruin this dish. Medium? Okay... maybe, 15 minutes.

### COOK THE FOIE GRAS

Season the slices of foie gras with salt and pepper. Heat another heavy-bottomed sauté pan (a separate pan—this is essential) over high heat. When the pan is very hot, quickly sear the foie gras for about 45 seconds a side. Remove the foie gras and set aside on the plate. Reduce the heat to medium high and stir in the 2 tablespoons of Madeira with the wooden spoon, scraping up any good stuff left in the pan. Set aside.

### MAKE THE SAUCE AND SERVE

Discard the fat from the first sauté pan and add 1 tablespoon/14 g of the butter. Cook over medium-high heat until it foams and subsides, then add the shallots. Cook for about 4 minutes, then stir in the remaining $^1/_4$ cup/56 ml of Madeira and the demi-glace and reduce by half, or until it coats the back of the spoon. Adjust the seasoning and strain the sauce through a fine strainer into the small saucepan, and return to a very low heat.

When the meat is done, remove from the oven and let rest for 5 minutes without poking, cutting, or in any way molesting it. Don't even talk loudly to it. When it is rested and ready, put it on the serving platter, perhaps atop a nice cloud of mashed potatoes, and quickly finish the sauce by bringing it back to a boil, whisking in the foie gras scraps, the truffles, and the remaining tablespoon/14 g of butter. Pour it over and around the meat and serve.

# blood & guts

# BLOOD & GUTS

**This is the good stuff, the dishes chefs get all misty-eyed about when they talk about food. The "nasty bits" have always been the principal challenge of great cooks throughout history, and when we look back on "what went wrong" with American cuisine, in the era following the Second World War, it began when stuff like this started disappearing off menus.**

If you look at turn-of-the-century American menus you'll find that we *used* to eat like champions. Kidneys, brains, tongues, hearts, feet, and jowls were all over the place. But, with postwar prosperity, the eating of liver was transformed from a pleasure to an occasional odious chore, reinforced by generations of well-intentioned mothers who urged their kids to eat liver with the blood-chilling admonition, "It's *good* for you!" Well,

let's pretend it's *not* good for you. Pretend it's illegal. Hell, if the PETA folks and the Health Taliban have their way, it soon may well be. So, for now, take a chance, take a trip down memory lane—only this time, do it right. A perfunctory, overfried piece of calf's liver can indeed be the worst thing in the world. But as I hope you will discover, a lovingly prepared one can be sublime.

# tripes
# 'les halles"

C'mon, bold adventurer! Depending on who you hang with, this dish will either make or lose you a lot of friends. One thing's for sure: They'll never forget you. Even at Les Halles, we seldom get away with serving this dish. But once a year, we invite our fellow brasserie, bistro, and French-restaurant workers, some regular customers, hard-core Francophiles, and lonely French expats to a midnight party where we ply them with cheap Beaujolais and serve them from a big old pot of tripe. Almost everybody seems to love it. Even me (and I generally think tripe smells like wet sheepdog). As this recipe serves twelve, I suggest throwing a big, rowdy party, getting your guests all liquored up, and, when they finally start complaining, "Where's the guacamole and the remaki?" hauling out a big, beautiful tub of steaming hot guts. Those who don't run screaming from the room—or frantically calling out to Domino's—might well have a revelatory experience.

This is a three-day dish, to be prepared at a relaxed pace.

## INGREDIENTS

2 lb/900 g honeycomb tripe
  (see NOTE)
2 lb/900 g feathered tripe
1 calf's foot, cut into 4 pieces (have
  your butcher cut it; he has a band saw)
salt and pepper
2 onions, skin on, cut in half,
  *plus* 1 onion, peeled and thinly sliced
1 lb/450 g pork belly
4 pig's ears
2 lb/900 g great northern beans
1/2 lb/225 g Serrano ham scraps
  (an end piece would be good; try
  your local overpriced gourmet deli)
1 bouquet garni (see Glossary)
4 tbsp/56 g pork fat

4 garlic cloves, crushed
1 tbsp/14 g ground cumin
2 carrots, cut into 1/4-inch/6-mm slices
1 tbsp/14 g tomato paste
10 ounces/280 g Spanish chorizo
3 *boudins noirs* or blood sausages
  (see Suppliers)

## EQUIPMENT

2 very large pots, 1 with lid
colander
large bowl
2 large pots
4-quart/3.6-liter storage container
large earthenware casserole
  or baking dish

**SERVES 12**

**DAY ONE**

To prep the meat…place both types of tripe and the calf's foot in a very large pot and cover with water. Add 2 tablespoons/28 g salt and one of the halved onions. Bring to a boil, reduce to a simmer, and cook for about 2 hours, until the tripe is tender. *I know, I know,* it doesn't smell too good yet…Patience. Patience. It gets better.

Drain the tripe, allow it to cool, then cut it into 2-inch/5-cm squares. Remove the meat and gelatinous material from the calf's foot, and cut into 1-inch/2.5-cm pieces. (This stuff is *gold,* baby—natural gelatin like you wouldn't believe!) Discard the bones. Refrigerate the tripe and the foot meat.

In a separate very large pot, combine the pork belly and the pig's ears and cover with cold water. Bring to a boil, reduce to a simmer, and cook for about $1^1/_2$ hours, or until the meat is tender. Drain the meats, reserving a gallon of the cooking liquid, and allow to cool. Cut the pork belly into $1^1/_2$-inch/3-cm squares and the pig's ears into 1-inch/2.5-cm pieces. Refrigerate. Soak the beans in cold water overnight.

**DAY TWO**

Drain and rinse the beans and place in a large pot. Cover with cold water and add the Serrano ham scraps, the bouquet garni, and the remaining halved onion. Bring to a boil, reduce heat to a simmer, and cook for about 45 minutes, or until the beans are tender. Strain the beans and set aside. Chuck out the bouquet garni.

In the other large pot, heat 2 tbsp/28 g pork fat until melted and sizzling. Add the sliced onion, garlic, and cumin and cook until soft and translucent, stirring occasionally. Add the carrots and cook for a minute, then stir in the tomato paste. Cook for 2 minutes, then add all of the cooked meats and 1 cup of the reserved cooking liquid. Bring the mixture to a simmer and season with salt and pepper. Cover and let simmer for 15 minutes. Now, add the beans and the remaining cooking liquid. Bring to a boil, reduce to a low simmer, cover, and cook for 2 hours. Let cool and *refrigerate overnight*. (It'll be *so* much better tomorrow.)

### DAY THREE

Preheat the oven to 325°F/170°C. Transfer the mixture to a large earthenware casserole or baking dish. Add the chorizo and the *boudins noirs*. Top the mixture with the remaining pork fat (2 tbsp/28 g) and put in the oven. Cook for $1^1/_2$ hours. Remove from the oven and let rest 15 minutes before serving.

Now bask in the moral certainty that you are the baddest-ass king hell, fearless fucking gourmet in your area! In fact, send me a photo (c/o the publisher) of yourself, holding up this completed recipe, with some friends in the background (and I want to see *ears* in there!) and I'll send you a personal letter of commendation and devotion.

**NOTE: The recipe calls for both frisée (feathered) and honeycomb tripe. When you're talking good tripe (not to mention pig's ears!), unless you have a really good butcher who'll order it for you fresh, you're talking about a trip to Chinatown. They've got it good. Calf's foot should be a little easier but should also be ordered in advance. Hell, half the fun of this dish is getting the ingredients. (There should be some surprised looks.)**

# rognons de veau à la moutarde

I was recently in Paris, walking down a narrow street in Saint-Germain-des-Prés with a friend, and as we passed an intersection, she stopped and pointed out a shabby-looking bistro halfway down the block. "That place there," she said, beginning to breathe heavily, "they have *the best rognons* in Paris. Soo divine!" She stood there wistfully, as if remembering a former lover, before moving on. I recall thinking, "This is someone who must really love kidneys—to have apparently searched Paris until finding the 'best' at this forlorn little dive." But then kidneys do inspire that kind of devotion among the cognoscenti. Judge for yourself.

## INGREDIENTS
**2 whole veal kidneys,** trimmed (have your butcher clean them up for you)
**salt and pepper**
**1 tbsp/14 ml vegetable oil**
**2 tbsp/28 g butter**
**2 shallots,** thinly sliced
**$1/_4$ cup/56 ml white wine**
**$1/_2$ cup/110 ml chicken stock** (dark would be nice, but you can use broth)
**2 tbsp/28 g Dijon mustard**

## EQUIPMENT
heavy-bottomed sauté pan
tongs
wooden spoon
whisk
slicing knife
serving platter

**SERVES 4**

Season the kidneys with salt and pepper. Place the oil in the heavy-bottomed sauté pan and heat over high heat. When the oil is hot, add 1 tablespoon/14 g of the butter. Once it begins to foam, add the kidneys, cooking them for 2 minutes on each side. Reduce the heat to medium and cook for 2 minutes more per side, then remove and set aside in a warm place (such as a very low oven).

The snowy white fat that surrounds the veal kidneys, when rendered, is absolutely the best frying medium you could use for the perfect French fry. Consider that when buying your kidneys.

Discard the fat from the pan and add the remaining tablespoon/14 g of butter. Cook the shallots in the butter until soft, about 3 minutes, then stir in the wine and reduce by half over high heat. Add the chicken stock or broth, bring to a boil, and cook for 5 minutes. Turn off the heat and whisk in the mustard. Slice the kidneys and arrange them on the serving platter, then spoon the sauce over them and serve.

# cœur de porc
# à l'armagnac

## INGREDIENTS

**1 tbsp/14 g pork fat**
**1 medium onion,**
  cut into 1-inch/2.5-cm cubes
**1 sprig of thyme,** chopped
**1 sprig of flat parsley,** chopped
**1 pig's heart,** trimmed of excess sinew
**salt and pepper**
**2 tbsp/28 ml Armagnac**
**$^1/_2$ cup/110 ml chicken stock or broth**
**8 cloves of garlic confit** (see page 262)
**2 tbsp/28 g butter**

## EQUIPMENT

small pot
ovenproof sauté pan
ovenproof casserole dish
whisk
slicing knife
serving platter

SERVES 2

### PREP

In the small pot, heat the pork fat over medium-high heat and add the onion. Sweat for about 5 minutes, then add the chopped herbs and remove from the heat. Season the heart with salt and pepper and stuff the arteries with the onion-herb mixture.

### COOK

Preheat the oven to 375°F/190°C. Place the heart in the sauté pan and cook for about 12 minutes (for medium rare). Remove the heart from the pan and set aside in a warm place. Set the pan aside. Place the casserole on the stovetop on high heat. Carefully add the Armagnac, which should flame up—so watch out. Reduce to nearly dry, then stir in the chicken stock and bring to a boil. Reduce by half, add the pan drippings from the sauté pan the heart was cooked in. Add the garlic confit and whisk in the butter. Season with salt and pepper.

### SERVE

Slice the heart into very thin slices and arrange on the serving platter. Spoon over the sauce and serve right away.

# boudin noir aux pommes

Good *boudin noir* is some of the best eating on earth. But you're not making *boudin noir*. I'm not making *boudin noir*. Unless you live on a farm, slaughter your own pigs, and know how to make sausages, you'll likely have to buy it. So check out the Suppliers section for a source. The stuff does freeze well, so buy a bunch and keep it around.

## INGREDIENTS
2 tbsp/28 g sugar
2 tbsp/28 g butter
1 **apple,** peeled and cored and
   cut into 8 wedges
1 **pinch of cumin seed** (optional)
4 **blood sausages**
1 tbsp/14 ml oil
**salt and pepper**

## EQUIPMENT
2 sauté pans, one of them ovenproof
wooden spoon
serving platter

**SERVES 4**

In a sauté pan, combine the sugar and butter and cook over medium heat until the mixture is bubbling and caramel colored. Do I have to tell you that if you get any of this on your hands or elsewhere, it will burn (and likely scar) the living hell out of you? Good. Now be careful. Carefully add the apple wedges and even more carefully toss them over medium heat for about 3 minutes. Don't worry, the sugar—which probably firmed up on you for a few moments there, when you put in the cold apple—will melt again. Gather up the caramel mixture with the wooden spoon so that it coats the wedges. If you care to sprinkle a little cumin seed in with the apple, do it now. Remove from the heat while the wedges are still slightly firm.

Preheat the oven to 375°F/190°C. Gently prick the skin of the sausages with a fork—not too much—and sprinkle with salt and pepper. What

you're trying to do is prevent the heating, expanding contents of the sausages from rupturing the skins. (If that happens, don't worry; it'll look ugly but still taste delicious.) In the clean, ovenproof sauté pan, heat the oil over high heat, then add the sausages. Cook for 2 minutes per side, being always gentle, then transfer the pan to the oven and cook for an additional 10 minutes.

Arrange the cooked apple wedges on the platter, add the sausages, and serve. Nice with mashed potatoes, too.

# veal tongue with madeira

## INGREDIENTS
1 veal tongue
2 tbsp/28 ml olive oil
1 small onion, thinly sliced
1 leek, white part only, thinly sliced
1 small carrot, thinly sliced
1 tbsp/14 g flour
1 cup/225 ml *plus* 1 tbsp/14 ml
   Madeira
2 tbsp/28 ml sherry vinegar
1 cup/225 ml strong, dark chicken
   or veal stock
1 bouquet garni (see Glossary)

salt and pepper
2 sprigs of flat parsley, leaves only, chopped
1 to 2 tbsp/14 to 28 g butter,
   softened (optional)

## EQUIPMENT
large pot
medium pot
wooden spoon
serving platter
fine strainer

**SERVES 4**

Place the tongue in the large pot and cover with water so that the water comes at least 3 inches/8 cm above the tongue. Bring to a simmer and cook for 1 hour and 15 minutes. Remove from. Cool it down enough to handle, then peel off the outer skin and set aside.

In the medium pot, heat the oil over medium heat and, when it's hot, add the onion and the leek. Cook, stirring occasionally, until they're golden brown, then add the carrot and cook for another 2 minutes. Stir in the flour, cook for 2 more minutes, then stir in 1 cup/225 ml of the Madeira and 1 tablespoon/14 ml of the sherry vinegar. Add the stock, the bouquet garni, and the tongue to the pot. Bring to a boil, reduce to a simmer, and season with salt and pepper. Cover and allow to simmer over low heat for $1^1/_2$ hours, or until the tongue is tender.

Remove the tongue to a cutting board, cut it into thin slices, and arrange it on the serving platter. Bring the sauce to a boil and add the remaining Madeira and vinegar. Discard the bouquet garni, strain the sauce through a fine strainer, return to the heat, and adjust the seasoning. Add the chopped parsley and swirl in a small knob of softened butter if you like. Pour over the tongue slices and serve.

# foie de veau lyonnaise

Here's a perfect example of a dish that doesn't *need* but would very much *benefit* from a single spoon of decent demi-glace. Have some in the freezer? Slip it in at the appropriate moment. If you don't have any? Not to worry. It's still really good.

Cleaning and peeling liver is a tricky business. I could explain it all day long; it's still going to take trial and error and a score of ruined livers to get it right. You are probably better off having your butcher do it. Just make sure he knows you want it peeled and cleaned and sliced into two 7-ounce slices.

## INGREDIENTS

2 tbsp/28 ml olive oil
2 tbsp/28 g butter (*plus* 1 tsp/5 g softened
   butter if you use demi-glace)
2 medium onions, thinly sliced
1/2 cup/110 ml *plus*
   2 tbsp/28 ml sherry vinegar
2 liver steaks, about 7 ounces/200 g each
salt and freshly cracked peppercorns
1/4 cup/56 g flour
2 heaping tbsp/28 g demi-glace (optional)
chopped flat parsley, for garnish

## EQUIPMENT

2 sauté pans
wooden spoon
plate
spatula
serving platter

SERVES 2

### COOK THE ONIONS

In a sauté pan, heat 1 tablespoon/14 ml of the oil over high heat. When the oil is hot, add 1 tablespoon/14 g of the butter. Allow the butter to foam and subside, then add the onions and cook over medium heat, stirring frequently with the wooden spoon, until they are soft and golden brown, about 10 minutes. Stir in 1/2 cup/110 ml of the sherry vinegar and scrape up the good stuff, incorporating it into the onion mix. Remove from the heat and set aside.

## THE LIVER

Season the liver with salt and freshly cracked pepper. Place the flour
on the plate and dredge each slice of liver in the flour. Shake off any
excess. Heat the remaining tablespoon/14 ml of oil in a clean sauté pan
over high heat, then add the second tablespoon/14 g of butter; wait a
few seconds and then add the liver to the pan. Cook for about
2 minutes per side, turning carefully with the spatula; this should get
you medium rare. Remove the liver to the serving platter and stir in the
remaining 2 tablespoons/28 ml of vinegar, scraping, scraping…(At this
point, if you have demi-glace, stir that in too.) Reduce over high heat
for 1 minute, then add the cooked onions. (If you added demi-glace,
swirl in a small knob of softened butter if you like.) Stir in the chopped
parsley and spoon the onions and sauce over the liver. Goes well with
mashed or Lyonnaise potatoes.

## TWEAKS AND IMPROVS

It shouldn't take a genius to figure out that one could add some nicely
cooked lardons of country bacon to the onions. Or that if you use the
same recipe—only substituting Calvados for the sherry vinegar, and
sautéed apple slices (along with demi-glace) for half the onions—you
might get something really nice. Sautéed liver, the pan deglazed with
raspberry vinegar, then boosted with demi-glace, is surprisingly,
disturbingly good as well. Ditto red wine vinegar. Just sauté the liver,
remove from the pan, add some chopped shallots, sauté, deglaze with a
bit of red wine vinegar, add demi-glace, reduce. Swirl in a knob of butter
and some chopped parsley at the end. Pour over your liver and eat.

**potatoes**

IDAHO® POTATOES
GPOD OF IDAHO : SHELLEY, IDAHO 83274
GPOD
IDAHO® POTATOES
GPOD OF IDAHO : SHELLEY, IDAHO 83274
GPOD
IDAHO® POTATOES
GPOD
IDAHO® POTATOES
GPOD
POTATOES
GPOD
IDAHO® POTATOES
GPOD OF IDAHO
50
GPOD
GPOD
POTATOES

# les halles fries

**There were surely few lowlier, more stupid moments in American history than when a few boobish media whores started talking about changing the name of French fries to "Freedom Fries." First of all, the French call them *frites*—and could hardly care less what we call them. (I'm sure that, if anything, they were amused at the mini-controversy, as it seemed to confirm their worst assumptions about the savage and "uncultured" Americans.)**

Second of all, frites are very likely a Belgian invention. Third, if you really want to hurt the French, just keep opening McDonald's franchises and Euro Disneys. And, of course, continue making better movies and popular music than they do. They really hate that. Which is to say it's never a good idea to mix politics and food. I'm no fan of Donald Rumsfeld, for instance; but if he makes a good sandwich, I'll certainly eat it.

We're famous for our fries at Les Halles. Many have said that we make the best fries in New York. Naturally I agree. Your fries, on the other hand, very likely suck. Most people don't bother to make fries at home. There's the oil disposal problem for one. After cooking one batch of fries for dinner, you're stuck with a few quarts of heavy, messy, used oil that you can't dump down the drain, can't pour in the garbage, and can't throw over the fence into Flanders's yard. Unlike a restaurant, which can and will reuse the oil until it's dead (and get money for selling the used oil to renderers), it's not likely you'll be regularly frying spuds at your place. As well, restaurants have large, professional deep fryers that are drained at the end of the night by a dishwasher or porter.

There's plenty of room to cook lots of fries in those things—and you don't even have to clean up afterward. Chances are, the first time you made fries, you put too many potatoes in the oil at one time, and they became greasy, limp, and inadequately caramelized. Maybe you didn't even bother to blanch them. In the end, no matter how hard you tried to suspend disbelief, you knew your fries just didn't make it.

Reasonably cheap deep fryers are available for home use. They cost around fifty dollars and are probably your best option for trying the following at home. You can regulate the temperature. Most make it easier to dispose of the oil. There's plenty of room. And there's all sorts of other fun you can have: making chips, spring rolls, croquettes, frizzled garnishes, batter-fried fish, and so on. Alternatively, you *can* fill a heavy-bottomed pot with a load of oil, crank up the flame, and use a thermometer to tell you when it's at the right temperature. Later, presumably when it's cool, you can pour the oil back in the containers it came in and dispose of it.

There are a few very important factors in the making of a really good French fry:

**THE OIL.** You need lots of it. You can't make a decent fry in a skillet with a pathetic inch of oil in it. The fries won't cook evenly. Peanut oil is what we use at Les Halles. And peanut oil is what you should use. In a perfect world, we'd *love* to render down some beef fat, or the kidney fat from veal, and fry in that. But these fats break down quickly and would be prohibitively expensive and difficult to work with in a busy restaurant situation. You're chucking out your oil after one use anyway, though, right? So you might, after mastering the peanut oil version, try that out yourself. It makes a real difference.

**THE POTATO.** An Idaho potato, roughly peeled, is what we use. Specifically, we use what's called a GPOD 70 potato—meaning it's an Idaho potato of a certain size conducive to perfect fry-dom. It comes 70 to a case.

**BLANCHING.** If you don't blanch your fries first, you'll get a scandalously bad result. Blanching is a *must*.

**FRYING.** To the right doneness. Not too many at a time. The fries should float free in the hot oil, not be lumped together so they stick.

**DRAINING AND SEASONING.** So, let's make fries. But do it right. There's no half-ass way to make a French fry. Respect and observe the tenets of fry-dom and you'll be well on your way.

**PREP**

**BLANCH**

**FRY**

**SERVE**

**INGREDIENTS**
4 **Idaho potatoes,** big, long ones
2 **quarts/2.25 liters or more**
   **peanut oil to fill fryer (or pot)**
**table salt**

**EQUIPMENT**
2 large bowls
deep fryer or heavy-bottomed pot
skimmer or wire basket (if using a pot)
baking sheet
towel

**SERVES 4**

**STEP ONE: PREP**
Fill a large bowl with ice water. Peel the potatoes and cut them into
$1/_2$-inch/1-cm-thick sticks. Put them immediately into the bowl
of ice water to keep them from oxidizing. Leave them in the water
anywhere from 30 minutes to overnight, then rinse well in cold water
to take out much of the starch.

**STEP TWO: BLANCH**
In a deep fryer or heavy-bottomed pot, heat the oil to 280°F/140°C.
Cook the potatoes in batches, about 6 to 8 minutes for each batch,
until they are soft and their color has paled from opaque white to a
semitranslucent white. Do *not* get impatient and yank them out early.
Remove them from the oil with the skimmer or wire basket and
spread evenly on the baking sheet. Let them rest at least 15 minutes.

**STEP THREE: FRY**
Bring the oil up to 375°F/190°C. No hotter, no cooler. Fry the blanched
potatoes in batches for 2 to 3 minutes each, or until they are crispy and
golden brown. Remove from the oil with the skimmer or wire basket,
shake off the excess oil, and…

**STEP FOUR: SERVE**
…immediately drop the fries into the other large bowl, which has been
lined with a clean, dry towel. Add salt to taste and whip out the towel.
Toss the fries around in the bowl and serve while still hot.

# gratin dauphinois

**INGREDIENTS**

**8 Yukon Gold potatoes,** peeled
    and cut into $1/4$-inch/6-mm slices
**2 cups/450 ml heavy cream**
**5 garlic cloves,** slightly crushed
**1 sprig of thyme**
**1 sprig of rosemary**
**1 sprig of flat parsley**
**salt and white pepper**
**freshly ground nutmeg** (go *easy*)
**1 tbsp/14 g butter**
**4 ounces/112 g grated Gruyère cheese**

**EQUIPMENT**
large pot
large ovenproof gratin dish

**SERVES 4**

**PREP**

Preheat the oven to 350°F/180°C. Place the potatoes in the large pot and add the cream, 4 of the garlic cloves, and the herbs. Season with salt, white pepper, and nutmeg. Bring to a boil, then reduce to a simmer. After 10 minutes of simmering, remove from the heat and discard the garlic and herbs.

**COOK**

Use the remaining garlic clove to rub around the inside of the gratin dish. Butter the inside of the gratin dish as well so that it is evenly coated. Transfer the potatoes and cream to the gratin dish and sprinkle the top with the Gruyère cheese. Cook in the oven for 40 minutes, or until the mixture is brown and bubbling. Remove from the oven and allow to rest for 10 to 15 minutes before serving.

# pommes fondants

## INGREDIENTS
4 large Idaho potatoes, scrubbed
2 tbsp/28 g duck fat
$^1/_2$ cup/110 ml light chicken
  stock or broth
2 garlic cloves, thinly sliced
1 sprig of thyme, *plus* 1 generous
  pinch of thyme leaves
salt and pepper

## EQUIPMENT
paring knife
large bowl filled with cold water
paper towels
sauté pan

**SERVES 4**

Think tiny zeppelins.
(And don't be too hard
on yourself, odds are
they won't be perfect.)

### PREP
Cut each potato in half, across its equator, and cut each half into 3 equal-size pieces. Use the paring knife to "turn" (or whittle, if necessary) each piece into a football shape—hopefully with six sides. Place the pieces in the bowl of cold water to keep them from turning brown.

### COOK
Once all the potatoes have been shaped, remove them from the water and pat dry with paper towels. Place the sauté pan over high heat and add the duck fat. When the fat is hot, add the potatoes and cook for 4 to 5 minutes, tossing occasionally, until they are golden brown on all sides. Remove the pan from the heat and add the chicken stock, the garlic, and the sprig of thyme. Bring to a boil and cook for 2 minutes. Reduce to a simmer and cook for 12 minutes, or until the potatoes are very tender. Bring to a boil again and cook until the liquid has almost completely evaporated. At this point, the potatoes should be coated with pan sauce. Discard the thyme sprig; sprinkle the potatoes with the thyme leaves, salt, and pepper; and serve.

# pommes purée

**Everybody knows how to make mashed potatoes, right? But these are a little better...**

## INGREDIENTS
**6 Idaho potatoes,**
  cut in half lengthwise
**1 tbsp/14 g salt** (*plus* more to taste)
**2 cups/450 ml heavy cream**
**6 tbsp/75 g butter**
**freshly ground black pepper**

## EQUIPMENT
large pot
strainer
small pot
potato masher

**SERVES 6**

### COOK THE POTATOES
Place the potatoes in the large pot and add enough cold water to completely cover them. Add the 1 tablespoon/14 g of salt and bring to a boil. Let the potatoes cook in the boiling water for about 15 minutes, or until they are easily pierced with the tip of a paring knife.

Drain the potatoes, discarding the hot water, and when they are cool enough to handle—but still hot—slip them from their skins. This might take some effort, and unless you're a magician, there will probably remain a few tiny bits of skin. Not a big deal. Just discard the skins as best you can and move on.

**MAKE THE PURÉE**

In the small pot, combine the heavy cream and butter and bring the mixture to a boil. (It boils over quickly, so keep an eye on it.)

In the meantime, return the potatoes to the large pot and mash them with the potato masher. Once the cream mixture has come to a boil, pour it in increments into the potatoes and mix well. Add cream. Mash. Add cream. Mix. Do not overwork the potatoes. When the mixture is creamy and smooth, season with salt and pepper and serve.

**IMPROVISATION**

There are a lot of chefs in this country who are getting a lot of mileage from "Truffle Mashed Potatoes." Now, fresh truffles are very expensive, and I doubt you'll want to use them for something as simple as mashed potatoes. But don't worry. Most of these chefs aren't using fresh stuff either. Simply make the recipe above, drop a teaspoon of the relatively inexpensive canned "black truffle peelings" into the mix, then jack it with a few drops of white truffle oil.

Chive mashed potatoes? Sure! Simply drop a bunch of chives into boiling water for about 30 seconds. Immediately cool in ice water to retain the bright green color. Chop roughly, then purée in a blender with a little oil to moisten. Push through a fine strainer, then fold the result into your potatoes, along with some fresh chopped chives.

Roasted pepper mashed potatoes? Roast red peppers. Peel off skins. Remove seeds and stem. Purée. Mix with spuds.

# pommes sautées au lard

**INGREDIENTS**
**3 ounces/75 g slab bacon,**
  cut into $1/4$-inch/6-mm cubes
**2 Yukon Gold potatoes,** peeled,
  cut in half, then cut into
  $1/4$-inch-/6-mm-thick slices
**1 garlic clove,** thinly sliced
**2 sprigs of flat parsley,** finely chopped
**salt and pepper**

**EQUIPMENT**
sauté pan
wooden spoon

**SERVES 4**

Heat the sauté pan over medium heat and add the bacon. Cook until most of the fat is rendered and the meat is crispy, about 5 to 8 minutes. Remember to turn the bacon occasionally for even cooking. Add the potatoes and cook for 15 minutes, stirring and tossing frequently. Add the garlic and cook for 2 minutes, then season with parsley, salt, and pepper. Serve immediately.

# pommes en croûte de sel

**INGREDIENTS**
**2 egg whites**
**1 lb/450 g rock salt**
**4 Idaho potatoes**

**EQUIPMENT**
large mixing bowl
whisk
gratin dish

**SERVES 4**

Preheat the oven to 400°F/200°C. In the large bowl, whisk the egg whites to soft peaks. Add the salt and mix well. Place the potatoes in a gratin dish large enough to hold them in a tight configuration. Cover the potatoes with the egg and salt mixture and bake in the oven for 1 hour. Remove from the oven, break the crust, and serve the potatoes immediately.

# miscellaneous meez & other useful recipes

# basic pie dough

## INGREDIENTS
9 ounces/250 g pastry flour
pinch of salt
1$\frac{1}{2}$ tbsp/20 g sugar
$\frac{1}{2}$ cup/125 g butter,
   chilled and cut into small cubes
1 egg, beaten
1$\frac{1}{2}$ tbsp/20 ml water

## EQUIPMENT
sifter or sieve
clean wooden board or large bowl
pastry cutter or 2 butter knives
plastic wrap
rolling pin

MAKES ONE
10-INCH/
25.5-CM CRUST

### METHOD 1—BY HAND
First, make sure you are working in a cool room, on a cool surface. Sift the flour onto the clean wooden board or into the large bowl, and add the salt and sugar. Use your hand to form a well in the center of the mixture, about 3 inches/8 cm in diameter. Add the butter, egg, and water, and knead the mixture together, using the pastry cutter or two butter knives. The goal is to evenly distribute the butter throughout the matrix of flour without causing it to melt. Form the dough into a ball and do not worry if some chunks of butter remain. Wrap the dough in plastic wrap and refrigerate for at least 1 hour.

Once you are ready to use the dough, remove from the refrigerator, unwrap, and press the dough down with the heel of your hand to flatten. Use a floured rolling pin to roll the dough out, on a floured work surface, to the desired thickness.

**Does not require use of a pastry cutter or knives. Also, it's worth noting, *infinitely* easier.**

## METHOD 2—IN THE FOOD PROCESSOR

In the bowl of the food processor, combine the flour, salt, sugar, egg, and butter and turn the machine on, processing until the ingredients form a cohesive whole. Keeping the machine on, add the water all at once, watching carefully so that you can turn off the machine as soon as the dough binds and comes away from the sides of the bowl. Roll the dough into a ball, wrap with plastic wrap, and refrigerate for 1 hour.

Once you are ready to use the dough, remove from the refrigerator, unwrap, and press the dough down with the heel of your hand to flatten. Use a floured rolling pin to roll the dough out, on a floured work surface, to the desired thickness.

## ROLL OUT DOUGH AND LINE THE PAN

Working from the center of the dough, use short, quick strokes with a rolling pin to get your dough to the desired thickness (which is about $^1/_4$ inch/6 mm thick for most pies and tarts). Tears can be repaired by patting the dough back together with fingers, but take care to avoid too many patches, as this will interfere with the proper and even cooking of the dough. When you're ready to transfer the dough to the pan, gently fold the dough in half on itself (so that the circle becomes a half-moon), and gently lift and place it in the pan (which should not be very far away). Gently unfold the dough so that its shape roughly mirrors the shape of the pan. Use gentle pressure to pat the dough into the corners of the pan, and once you are satisfied that the dough is truly lining the pan, either fold over or cut away the excess.

# basic tart dough

**INGREDIENTS**
1 cup/250 g pastry flour
$^1/_2$ cup/125 g butter
1 egg
$^1/_2$ cup/125 g sugar
a few drops of vanilla extract

**EQUIPMENT**
sifter or sieve
large bowl
electric mixer
wooden spoon
pastry cutter or 2 butter knives
plastic wrap
rolling pin
wooden cutting board

**MAKES ONE 10-INCH/
25.5-CM CRUST**

Sift or sieve the flour into the large bowl. In the bowl of the electric mixer, cream the butter (whipping on medium speed to soften and lighten it). Turn the butter into the bowl with the flour and quickly mix the two ingredients, using the wooden spoon. Make a well in the center of the mixture and add the egg, sugar, and vanilla. Use the pastry cutter or two knives to combine the mixture into a dough. Roll it into a ball, wrap in the plastic wrap, and let sit in the refrigerator for 1 hour.

Once you are ready to use the dough, remove it from the refrigerator, unwrap, and press the dough down with the heel of your hand to flatten it. On a floured work surface, use a floured rolling pin to roll the dough out to the desired thickness.

**ROLL OUT THE DOUGH AND LINE THE PAN**
Working from the center of the dough, use short, quick strokes with the rolling pin to get your dough to the desired thickness—generally about $^1/_4$ inch/6 mm thick for most pies and tarts. Tears can be repaired by patting the dough back together with fingers, but take care to avoid too many patches, as this will interfere with the proper and even cooking of the dough. When you're ready to transfer the dough to the pan, gently fold the dough in half on itself (so that the circle becomes a half-moon), and gently lift and place it in the pan (which should not be very far away). Carefully unfold the dough so that its shape roughly mirrors the shape of the pan, and using delicate pressure, pat the dough into the corners of the pan. Once you are satisfied that the dough is truly lining the pan, either fold over or cut away the excess dough.

Tart dough is much more delicate than pie dough, so it is essential that your ingredients be cold, that the work surface and rolling pin be amply floured, and that you work with a quick and delicate hand.

# sauce gribiche

## INGREDIENTS

**1 hard-boiled egg,** yolk and white
separated and finely chopped
**4 cornichons,** finely chopped
**1 tbsp/14 g capers,** finely chopped
**1 sprig of flat parsley,** chopped
**2 ounces/56 ml peanut oil**
**1 ounce/28 ml red wine vinegar**
**salt and pepper**

## EQUIPMENT

mixing bowl

**YIELDS ³/₄ CUP/170 ML**   In the mixing bowl, combine the egg, cornichons, capers, and parsley and mix well. Fold in the oil and vinegar, mix well, and season with salt and pepper.

# béarnaise sauce

## INGREDIENTS
$^1/_2$ cup/110 ml sherry vinegar
  or red wine vinegar
2 shallots, finely chopped
1 tsp/5 g cracked black peppercorns
1 bunch of tarragon, leaves only,
  finely chopped, *plus* 1 sprig of
  tarragon, finely chopped
8 ounces/225 g butter
4 egg yolks
salt and pepper

## EQUIPMENT
2 small pots
warm metal mixing bowl
double boiler
whisk
tall narrow container (optional)
sharpening steel (optional)
thermos (optional)

**YIELDS 8 OUNCES/225 G**

### THE REDUCTION
In a small pot, combine the vinegar, shallots, cracked pepper, and tarragon leaves. Bring to a boil and reduce until nearly dry. Remove from the heat and set aside.

### CLARIFY THE BUTTER
Place the butter in the other small pot over low heat. As the butter melts, a foam will rise at the top. Skim it off and discard. Remove from the heat and set aside, undisturbed, so that the milk solids settle to the bottom.

### ANOTHER CLARIFYING STRATEGY
Melt down your butter until it foams and turns liquid. Pour into a tall, narrow container. Refrigerate overnight. The next day, scrape the solidified fat off the top, peeling it away carefully and discarding it. With a sharpening steel, punch a hole in the solidified butter, extending the hole all the way to the bottom of the container. Turn the

container upside down and the milk solids and water should pour right out. Now slowly heat the remaining product until it is liquid and clear. You're ready to go.

**MAKE THE SAUCE**
Place the egg yolks in the warm metal mixing bowl. Add the tarragon reduction (and, if you're feeling cowardly and unambitious, a few drops of water to give a little insurance against curdling). Bring a few cups of water to a boil in the bottom half of the double boiler and place the metal bowl with the eggs over the simmering water. Whisk the eggs *constantly,* pulling the bowl away from the heat if the eggs start to curdle or harden. You are *not* making scrambled eggs here, okay? So be careful.

Once the eggs have become very foamy and start to thicken, slowly begin to incorporate the clarified butter, whisking as you add it. (A "collar" made of a moistened kitchen towel can be helpful as a base for the bowl, to keep it in place while you whisk.) Keep whisking. You're making an emulsion here. Whisk until all the butter is incorporated. Season with salt and pepper and mix in the fresh chopped tarragon sprig. Serve immediately, or hold in a thermos (but not for longer than an hour).

NOTE: Know this. If you haven't made béarnaise from scratch before, you will surely fuck this sauce up. Don't worry. Just do it again. This and hollandaise, more than any other sauces, seem to *smell* fear and uncertainty. Once you've got it down, however, your self-confidence will become a vital ingredient. Most professionals don't even use the double boiler. They just whip the yolks over a low direct flame, dropping in the butter in seemingly careless amounts—and they get it right every time. How come? 'Cause they're confident. 'Cause they've done it before...many times. Because they can.

Béarnaise and hollandaise are recipes well worth practicing. The technique of gradual emulsification once learned will serve you well with all other emulsified sauces. And allow you the dubious privilege of being able to make real eggs Benedict. That prepared hollandaise mix you can buy at the supermarket? That's not food.

# sauce béchamel

**INGREDIENTS**
**1¹/₂ ounces/42 g butter**
**1¹/₂ ounces/42 g flour**
**2 cups/450 ml milk**
**salt and white pepper**
**pinch of nutmeg**

**EQUIPMENT**
2 heavy saucepans
wooden spoon
whisk

**YIELDS 2 CUPS/450 ML**

Melt the butter in a saucepan until it foams and subsides. Add the flour and stir with the wooden spoon to combine with the butter. Reduce the heat and cook for a few minutes, but don't allow the flour-butter mixture to take on any color. In the other saucepan, heat the milk to a simmer, then whisk that gradually into the pan with the flour-butter mixture (the roux). Continue to whisk until smooth. Season with salt and white pepper and add the nutmeg. As always, be very careful with the nutmeg. Do *not* add too much. Heat on low heat until the sauce is thick enough to coat the back of the spoon.

# chicken liver vinaigrette

## INGREDIENTS

**4 ounces/56 g chicken livers,**
"trimmed"—meaning remove the
tissue that connects liver sections
to each other, and any fat
(there shouldn't be much)
**salt and pepper**
**1 tbsp/14 g butter**
**2 ounces/56 ml red wine vinegar**
**2 ounces/56 ml olive oil**

## EQUIPMENT

sauté pan
blender
wooden spoon

**SERVES 4**

Season the livers with salt and pepper. Heat the butter in the sauté pan over medium heat until it foams and subsides. Add the livers to the pan and sear on both sides, about 3 minutes per side. Remove the livers and allow to cool for a few minutes.

Place the livers in the blender. Return the pan to the heat and stir in the vinegar, scraping all that goodness from the bottom of the pan with the wooden spoon. Remove the pan from the heat and add the vinegar to the blender with the livers. Add the olive oil and blend until smooth. Season with salt and pepper as needed.

# red-wine vinaigrette

## INGREDIENTS
<sup></sup>$^1/_2$ cup/110 ml red wine vinegar
1 garlic clove, crushed
salt and freshly ground black pepper
1 tsp/5 g Dijon mustard
1 cup/225 ml extra-virgin olive oil

## EQUIPMENT
medium mixing bowl
fork or whisk

**YIELDS**
$1^1/_2$ **CUPS/335 ML**

In the mixing bowl, combine the vinegar, garlic, and salt and pepper to taste. Let sit 30 minutes, then remove and discard the garlic. Add the mustard and slowly whisk in the oil, continuing to whisk until the mixture is emulsified.

# aïoli

## INGREDIENTS
**4 garlic cloves,** germ removed
(that's the tough little green bit in
the center of the clove)
**large-grain sea salt** (*gros sel*)
**1 cup/225 ml extra-virgin olive oil**
**1 egg yolk**

## EQUIPMENT
food processor

**YIELDS 1¹/₄ CUPS/28 G**     Place the garlic cloves in the food processor. Add the salt and half the olive oil. Process for a few seconds, then add the yolk and mix well. With the machine running, slowly drizzle in the rest of the olive oil and process until smooth. Keep refrigerated until needed (no more than 2 days).

# beurre blanc

## INGREDIENTS
**1 shallot,** thinly sliced
**2 tbsp/28 ml white wine**
**juice of 1 lemon**
**8 ounces/225 g butter,** cut into
   small cubes and softened slightly
**1 ounce/28 ml heavy cream**
   (optional cheat)
**salt and pepper**

## EQUIPMENT
small pot
whisk
strainer
wide-mouthed thermos
   (optional)

**YIELDS**
**1 1/2 CUPS/335 ML**

In the small pot, combine the shallot, wine, and lemon juice and bring to a boil. Continue to cook until the liquid has almost evaporated. Remove from the heat and slowly begin to incorporate the butter, a bit at a time, using the whisk. Once all the butter has been emulsified, season with salt and pepper and strain.

### A COUPLE OF THINGS YOU SHOULD KNOW

Beurre blanc is very unstable. Held too hot or too cold, it will break, so make it at the last minute and serve immediately, or hold it in a wide-mouthed thermos. It should be about blood warm, or a little warmer.

For a slightly more durable beurre blanc, do what most chefs do: cheat. Though cream is not part of the classic recipe, many of us sneak a little heavy cream into the pot after the lemon juice and wine have reduced. We reduce the cream down to a thick emulsion and then remove the pot from the heat and whisk in the butter. It makes a sauce that holds together better and longer. If you do decide to use this method, though, be sparing with the cream. This is a butter sauce, not a cream sauce.

# herb butter

**INGREDIENTS**
$^1/_2$ **cup/110 g butter,** softened
**1 tbsp/14 g fresh basil,**
  finely chopped
**1 tbsp/14 g fresh parsley,**
  finely chopped
$^1/_2$ **tbsp/7 g fresh thyme,**
  finely chopped
$^1/_2$ **tbsp/7 g fresh rosemary,**
  finely chopped
$^1/_2$ **tbsp/7 g honey**
**pinch of salt**
**pinch of finely ground white pepper**

**EQUIPMENT**
mixing bowl
wooden spoon
plastic wrap

**YIELDS
APPROXIMATELY
$^3/_4$ CUP/170 G**

Combine all the ingredients in the mixing bowl and mix well with the wooden spoon. Gently roll the mixture into a log about the same length and width as a stick of butter. Roll tightly in plastic wrap and refrigerate until use.

# rouille

**INGREDIENTS**
**3 garlic cloves,** crushed
**1 red bell pepper,**
  roasted, peeled, and seeded
**2 egg yolks**
**1 tsp/5 ml freshly squeezed lemon juice**
**pinch of saffron threads**
**$^1/_2$ cup/110 ml extra-virgin olive oil**
**salt and freshly ground black pepper**

**EQUIPMENT**
food processor

**YIELDS
APPROXIMATELY
$^3/_4$ CUP/170 G**

In the bowl of the food processor, combine the garlic, red pepper, egg yolks, lemon juice, and saffron. Pulse until smooth, then slowly drizzle in the oil and process continuously until the mixture thickens. Season with salt and pepper to taste, and use immediately.

# basil oil
# and parsley oil

**INGREDIENTS**
**20 leaves of basil (or a good
    handful of parsley leaves)**
**extra-virgin olive oil**
**salad oil** (optional)

**EQUIPMENT**
small pot
bowl of ice water
blender
*fine* strainer
small ladle or spoon
squeeze bottle

**YIELDS
APPROXIMATELY
$^3/_4$ CUP/170 G**

Take about 20 leaves of basil (or in the case of parsley oil, a good
handful of parsley leaves). Drop the leaves into boiling water for five
or six seconds and immediately remove them to the bowl of ice water
(this will get you a nice, bright, electric green color). When cool, squeeze
out *all* the moisture you can. Chop roughly and place in the blender.
For basil oil, add just enough olive oil to cover. For parsley oil, I suggest
a less strong-tasting salad oil. Blend the living hell out of everything.
Pour and scrape the purée into the strainer and push the green sludge
carefully with the small ladle or spoon, squeezing through every bit of
color, goodness, and flavor. Discard what remains in the strainer. Keep
the oil in a squeeze bottle and use where desired or needed.

# garlic confit

**This is good stuff. Sweeter and more full-bodied than raw garlic, it's a nice garnish or flavoring agent.**

**INGREDIENTS**
**2 heads of garlic,**
  broken into unpeeled cloves
**2 tbsp/28 ml olive oil**
**1 sprig of thyme**
**coarse sea salt**

**EQUIPMENT**
aluminum foil

**YIELDS 1 CUP/225 G GARLIC CLOVES**

Preheat the oven to 350°F/180°C. Leaving the skin intact on each clove, gather the cloves together into a bunch and wrap with foil, adding the oil, thyme, and salt before sealing the packet.

Cook in the oven for 30 minutes (you may want to agitate the bunch a few times during cooking to ward off uneven roasting, i.e., brown spots). Set aside and allow to cool before popping the garlic cloves from their skins.

# citrus zest confit

**INGREDIENTS**
1 grapefruit *or* 2 limes
   *or* 2 lemons *or* 2 oranges
1 cup/225 ml water
4 ounces/112 g sugar

**EQUIPMENT**
paring knife
small pot with lid
strainer
airtight container

**YIELDS APPROXIMATELY**
**1/2 CUP/110 G**

With the paring knife, remove the peel from the fruit. Cut away the white pith from the peel and cut the remaining zest into thin strips. (You can also use a *canneleur,* a tool that makes nice strips of zest.)

Combine the water and sugar in the small pot and bring to a boil. Add the strips of zest and reduce to a simmer. Loosely cover the pot and let the liquid cook until it is reduced by half. Remove from the heat and allow to cool completely. Strain the zest and store in the airtight container.

# preserved lemons

**INGREDIENTS**
6 lemons, *plus* juice of 3 lemons
3 cups/675 g kosher salt
1 bay leaf
pinch of black peppercorns
pinch of coriander seeds

**EQUIPMENT**
sharp knife
medium mixing bowl
sterile crock or Mason jar large
   enough to hold all ingredients

**MAKES 6
PRESERVED LEMONS**

Scrub each lemon under hot running water to remove wax and other impurities from the skin. Cut each lemon in half through its equator, then make two deep perpendicular cuts through each half, stopping short of cutting the pieces apart. The effect is that of creating deep canyons through the lemons' flesh.

In the mixing bowl, combine the lemon juice, salt, bay leaf, peppercorns, and coriander seeds. Place a 1-inch/2.5-cm layer of this mixture in the bottom of the crock or Mason jar, then add a layer of lemons. Repeat the process until you have added all of the salt mixture and all of the lemon halves. Pack everything tightly so that each lemon half is surrounded by curing mixture. Cover tightly and let cure for 30 days.

**Use the preserved
lemons in recipes or
sliced as a condiment,
taking care to rinse off
excess salt.**

The lemons will keep for 6 months at room temperature or 1 year in the refrigerator.

# parsnip purée

**INGREDIENTS**
**8 parsnips,** peeled and
   chopped into 2-inch/5-cm hunks
**salt**
**1 stick/112g of butter**
**white pepper**

**EQUIPMENT**
medium pot
strainer
food processor
rubber spatula

**SERVES 4**

In the medium pot, boil the parsnips in salted water until cooked through and soft, about 20 minutes. Strain, discarding the water. Put the still-hot parsnips in the food processor and pulse, adding butter a bit at a time until rich and smooth, but *not* soupy. Don't overprocess; you want the stuff to stand up a bit. Season with salt and white pepper. Delicious.

# desserts

# îles flotantes

## INGREDIENTS
8 egg whites
pinch of salt
10 ounces/280 g sugar
2 cups/450 ml milk
$^1/_2$ **vanilla bean,** cut in half lengthwise
4 egg yolks
1 ounce/28 g slivered almonds

## EQUIPMENT
electric mixer with whisk
  attachment (optional)
large, shallow pan
2 large soupspoons
plate lined with paper towels
strainer
small pot
medium mixing bowl
whisk
wooden spoon
large bowl, filled with ice and water
4 soup bowls, for serving

**SERVES 4**

**You can opt to just whisk by hand, but it's a lot more work.**

### PREP THE MERINGUE
Place the egg whites in the bowl of the mixer and add the salt. Using the whisk attachment, mix the whites slowly to break them up, then increase the speed and beat them until they hold soft peaks. Reduce the speed and slowly add 6 ounces/168 g of the sugar. Continue beating until the sugar is incorporated and the eggs once again hold soft peaks.

### COOK THE MERINGUE
Place the milk in the large, shallow pan and bring it to a boil. Reduce the heat to a simmer. Using the two large spoons, scoop 12 "quenelles"

from the egg whites and gently add them to the simmering milk to poach, 2 minutes per side. Carefully remove the quenelles, place them on the plate lined with paper towels, and set aside to drain and cool. Reserve the milk.

## MAKE THE SAUCE (CREME ANGLAISE)
Strain the milk into the small pot, adding more milk if necessary so that you have exactly 2 cups/450 ml. Add the vanilla bean and bring the milk back to a boil. Turn off the heat and let the vanilla infuse into the milk. Meanwhile, in the medium mixing bowl, whisk together the egg yolks and the remaining 4 ounces/112 g of sugar. Bring the milk back to a boil and, while whisking the yolk mixture, add to it half the boiling milk. Once this mixture is homogenous, add it back to the pot with the remaining milk, whisking constantly. Switch to a wooden spoon and stir the mixture constantly, using a figure-eight motion and making sure to reach all edges of the pot. Continue to stir over low heat until the mixture coats the back of the spoon. Remove the sauce from the heat, discard the vanilla pod, and carefully place the pot into the ice-water bath, making sure that the water does not leak into the custard.

## SERVE
Place 3 quenelles in the center of each of the four soup bowls. Ladle crème anglaise into each bowl. Garnish with slivered almonds and serve immediately.

# crème brûlée

**INGREDIENTS**
1 quart/900 ml heavy cream
1 vanilla bean
6 ounces/168 g granulated sugar
10 egg yolks
6 tbsp/84 g brown sugar

**EQUIPMENT**
large pot
paring knife
large mixing bowl
whisk
6 8-oz. ramekins
9 by 13-inch/22.5 cm by 32.5-cm
  baking pan
propane torch

**SERVES 6**

**PREP**

Put the heavy cream in the large pot. Split the vanilla bean lengthwise with the paring knife and scrape the insides into the cream. Put the empty pod in as well. Add half the granulated sugar to the cream, stir well, and bring the mixture to a boil.

Place the egg yolks in the large mixing bowl and whisk in the remaining granulated sugar, continuing to whisk until the mixture is pale yellow and slightly foamy. Remove the cream mixture from the heat and *slowly,* gradually whisk it into the yolk mixture. Make sure to whisk constantly to prevent the hot liquid from curdling the yolks. Remove the vanilla bean pod and discard.

**BAKE**

Preheat the oven to 300°F/150°C. Place the ramekins in the baking pan and fill the pan with water so that it comes halfway up the sides of the ramekins. Divide the custard evenly among the ramekins and cook them in the oven for about 45 minutes, or until the top is set but still jiggly. Remove the ramekins from the oven and let cool to room temperature. The custards can be held overnight, covered with plastic in the refrigerator.

**SERVE**

Sprinkle 1 tablespoon/14 g brown sugar over the top of each custard. Carefully run the propane torch's flame over each custard to caramelize the sugar. Wait a minute, then serve the custards with spoons.

# tarte alsacienne

## INGREDIENTS

3 tbsp/42 g butter

3 ounces/75 g sugar

4 **Golden Delicious apples,** peeled,
cored, and cut into $^1/_2$-inch/1-cm slices

4 **eggs**

$^1/_2$ **cup/110 ml milk**

$^1/_2$ **cup/110 ml heavy cream**

1 **tsp/5 g vanilla extract**

1 **10-inch/25.5-cm prebaked piecrust**
(see basic pie dough, page 248)

## EQUIPMENT

2 baking sheets

2 sheets of parchment paper

large mixing bowl

whisk

small saucepan

**SERVES 8**

### PREP THE APPLES

Preheat the oven to 300°F/150°C. Line a baking sheet with parchment paper and grease the paper with 1 tablespoon/14 g of the butter. Sprinkle the paper with 1 tablespoon/14 g of the sugar and arrange the apples on the paper so that they do not overlap. Cut the remaining 2 tablespoons/28 g of butter into very small pieces and dot the apples with the butter. Sprinkle another tablespoon/14 g of the sugar over the apples and bake in the oven for about 40 minutes, or until the apples are soft but still holding their shape. Remove from the oven and allow to cool.

### PREP THE CUSTARD

In the mixing bowl, combine the eggs and the remaining sugar and whisk. In the small saucepan, combine the milk, cream, and vanilla extract and bring it to a boil. Remove this mixture from the heat and slowly add it to the egg mixture, whisking constantly until it is all incorporated and the mixture is slightly thickened.

### ASSEMBLE

Increase the oven heat to 350°F/180°C. Line the other baking sheet with parchment paper and place the piecrust on it. Arrange the apple slices in a circular pattern in the crust. The apples should fill up the shell. Pull the oven rack out halfway and place the baking sheet and crust on the rack. Now, carefully pour the custard mixture into the piecrust, filling to the top but *not* over-filling it. Carefully push the rack back into the oven and bake until the custard is set, about 25 minutes. Allow to rest for 15 minutes before serving.

# chocolate mousse

It's all about the chocolate, isn't it? Use second-rate chocolate, get second-rate mousse. My pastry chef always insists—and I mean *insists*—on expensive Valrhona chocolate (see Suppliers). And as she knows a helluva lot more about pastry than I do, I figure I'd better agree.

## INGREDIENTS

6 ounces/168 g bittersweet chocolate, chopped
2 ounces/56 ml Grand Marnier
4 tbsp/56 g butter
4 eggs, separated
2 tbsp/28 g sugar
1 cup/225 ml heavy cream
sprigs of mint, for garnish (optional)

## EQUIPMENT

medium pot
3 mixing bowls
balloon whisk or electric mixer
rubber spatula
serving bowl (or cute, individual parfait glasses)
pastry bag with tip (optional)

**SERVES 6**

### PREP THE CHOCOLATE

In the medium pot, bring a few cups of water to a simmer. Place a mixing bowl over the pot and add the chocolate. Stir gently to help the chocolate melt and prevent it from scorching. Whisk in the Grand Marnier, then whisk in the butter, a tablespoon at a time. Stir in the egg yolks, one at a time, making sure each yolk is incorporated before adding the next.

### LIGHTEN THE MOUSSE

In another mixing bowl, using a whisk or an electric mixer, whip the egg whites until they hold soft peaks, gradually adding the sugar. Whisk one fourth of this mixture into the melted chocolate, then use the rubber spatula to fold in the remaining egg-white mixture. In the third mixing bowl, whip half the cream until it holds soft peaks. Fold the whipped cream into the chocolate mixture. Gently transfer the mousse to the serving bowl (or spoon or pipe it into glasses), cover, and refrigerate for at least 2 hours.

### GARNISH AND SERVE

Don't even *think* about using Cool Whip or Reddi Wip. I'll know. And I'll find you.

Just before serving, whip the remaining cream until it holds stiff peaks. Serve the whipped cream alongside the mousse, or pipe it through a pastry bag onto the top. Garnish with sprigs of mint, if you like.

# chocolate hazelnut tart

## INGREDIENTS

8 ounces/225 g dark chocolate,
  chopped
3 ounces/75 g butter
2 cups/450 ml heavy cream
2 egg yolks
5 ounces/140 g hazelnuts

1 prebaked 10-inch/25.5-cm tart shell
  (see basic tart dough, page 250)

## EQUIPMENT

medium stainless-steel mixing bowl
small pot
tart pan

**SERVES 8**

Place the chopped chocolate in the mixing bowl and add the butter.

In the small pot, bring the cream to a boil. Remove the pot from the heat and pour the boiling cream over the chocolate and butter. Let sit for 5 minutes, then add the yolks and mix well. Stir the hazelnuts into the chocolate mixture. Pour the mixture into the tart shell.

Refrigerate for 2 hours before serving.

# charlotte de marrons

## INGREDIENTS
2 cups/450 ml water
2 cups/450 g *plus* 1 tbsp/14 g sugar
4 ounces/110 ml dark rum
16 ounces/450 g chestnut purée
  (see Suppliers)
1 cup/225 ml heavy cream
26 ladyfinger cookies

## EQUIPMENT
small pot
3 medium mixing bowls
spoon
whisk or electric mixer
rubber spatula
rectangular terrine mold
plastic wrap
serving platter

**SERVES 8**

### MAKE THE SIMPLE SYRUP
In the small pot, combine the water and the 2 cups/450 g of sugar and bring it to a boil. Let it boil for 5 minutes, then remove from the heat and stir in the rum. Transfer to a mixing bowl and set aside.

### THE FILLING
Place the chestnut purée in another mixing bowl and soften gently with fingertips and a spoon. In the third bowl, beat the cream to soft peaks with the whisk or electric mixer. Add the tablespoon/14 g of sugar and continue to mix until it holds its soft peaks. Using the rubber spatula, fold the whipped cream into the chestnut purée.

### ASSEMBLE
Line the rectangular terrine mold with plastic wrap, using enough extra so that the top of the charlotte can also be covered. Soak the ladyfingers, one at a time, in the simple syrup until they are soft but still firm enough to handle. Place the soaked ladyfingers in the bottom of the terrine in a single layer and line the sides of the terrine in the same fashion. Spread half the chestnut filling evenly over the ladyfingers until the terrine is half full. Top that with another layer of soaked ladyfingers and that layer with more chestnut filling. Fold plastic wrap over the terrine and store refrigerated for at least 4 hours. Unmold the terrine just before serving, and serve in thin slices.

# clafoutis

## INGREDIENTS
1¹/₂ lb/675 g cherries, pitted
3 ounces/75 ml kirsch
1 tbsp/14 g butter
4 ounces/112 g sugar
6 eggs
4 ounces/112 g flour
1 tsp/5 ml vanilla extract
1 tbsp/14 g confectioners' sugar

## EQUIPMENT
small bowl
9-inch/22.5-cm baking dish
large mixing bowl
whisk
rubber spatula
testing skewer
small sifter or strainer

**SERVES 6 TO 8**

**Very nice with cherry vanilla or vanilla ice cream.**

### PREP
Place the cherries in the small bowl and toss with the kirsch. Let macerate for 1 hour.

### ASSEMBLE AND BAKE
Preheat the oven to 450°F/230°C. Grease the baking dish with the butter and coat with a pinch or two of the sugar. Place the pan in the refrigerator.

In the large mixing bowl, beat the eggs with a whisk, then add the sugar and beat well to fully incorporate. Mix in the flour and the vanilla extract, stirring enough so that all the ingredients are homogenous but without overworking the flour. Using the rubber spatula, fold the cherries and their accumulated juice into the flour and egg mixture, then pull your prepared baking pan out of the fridge and turn the mixture into it. Bake in the oven for 40 minutes, or until a golden brown crust has formed on top. The skewer inserted into the center should come out clean—*not* wet. Using the small strainer or sifter, dust the top with confectioners' sugar, and serve.

# poached pears in red wine

## INGREDIENTS
1 bottle/1 liter of red wine
1 cup/225 g sugar
4 pears, any variety,
  peeled and cut in half lengthwise
1 tsp/5 g black peppercorns
1 cinnamon stick
3 pieces of star anise
1 bay leaf
1 tsp/5 g juniper berries

## EQUIPMENT
large pot with lid
paring knife
serving bowl

**SERVES 4**

In the large pot, combine the wine and sugar and bring to a boil. Cook at a boil for 5 minutes, then add the pears and the spices. Reduce the heat to a simmer, cover the pot, and cook the pears for 30 minutes, or until they are very tender and easily pierced with the tip of the paring knife. Remove from the heat, remove the lid, and let the pears cool in the syrup. Once they are somewhat cool, transfer the pears to the serving bowl with the spices and some of the syrup, and serve.

# lemon tart

## INGREDIENTS
$^1/_2$ **cup/110 ml lemon juice**
$^1/_2$ **cup/112 g sugar**
**4 large eggs**
**1 cup/225 ml cream**
**1 10-inch/25.5-cm prebaked piecrust**
  (see basic pie dough, page 248)

## EQUIPMENT
mixing bowl
whisk

**SERVES 6**

### PREP
In the mixing bowl, combine the lemon juice and sugar and whisk until well blended. Add the eggs and whisk well until the eggs are incorporated, then whisk in the cream.

### COOK
Preheat the oven to 325°F/170°C. Pour the mixture into the piecrust and bake for 25 minutes, or until the custard is set. Remove from the oven and let cool before slicing. Serve with whipped cream, lightly sweetened (2 tablespoons/28 g sugar mixed with 1 cup/225 ml cream).

# blueberries with lime sugar

**INGREDIENTS**
3 tbsp/75 g sugar
juice of 2 limes
1¹/₂ pints/840 g blueberries
1 sprig of mint, leaves cut into
  a chiffonnade (ultra-thin slice)
confit zest of 2 limes
  (see citrus zest confit, page 263)
¹/₂ cup/112 g crème fraîche
  (or sour cream)

**EQUIPMENT**
large bowl

**SERVES 4**

In a large bowl, combine the sugar and lime juice and stir to dissolve the sugar. Add the blueberries and toss well, coating all the berries. Add the mint and lime zest confit and toss well again. Serve with the crème fraîche on the side.

# glossary

**In all cases, I give the modern, used-in-American-kitchens meanings, as opposed to the classic, archaic, or literal ones. Not all terms below are used in the text, but I hope they will prove helpful.**

**BAIN-MARIE (ALSO CALLED "BAIN" AND OFTEN PRONOUNCED "BAYNE"):** Specifically, a double boiler, usually a stainless-steel bowl nestled over a saucepan of simmering water. In modern kitchens it has also come to mean any stainless-steel crock or container used or usable in a steam table (even when used for storage), as in: "Gimme a bayne fulla potatoes."

**BATONNET:** A large, sticklike cut, about finger-sized. Like a jumbo julienne. The carrot sticks at the office Christmas party? Probably a clumsy, indifferently cut batonnet. (From the word *baton*.)

**BAVETTE:** Flank steak.

**BEURRE ROUGE:** Exactly like beurre blanc (see recipe on page 258), except that it's made with red wine rather than white.

**BISQUE:** Yet another term that has been so totally corrupted over time as to become unrecognizable. Originally, bisque was thought to be the original soup: usually shellfish, pounded with rocks or primitive mortar and pestle by our apelike forebears until soupy. Classically, a bisque is a soup of lobster or crab in which the pulverized shells are an element or thickening agent. These days, however, it seems to mean any damn soup you throw in a blender until a rough purée is achieved, e.g., tomato bisque. A pretentious creamed or puréed soup.

**BISTRO:** A small mom-and-pop–style restaurant or café, usually serving regional specialties. A relatively limited menu with daily specials is implied.

**BLOOD CAKE:** A "cake" formed of thickened blood of pork or chicken. Usable as a garnish or as a thickening agent.

**BOUI-BOUI:** A greasy spoon. A dive.

**BOULE:** A ball. Used here to describe a round, domed loaf of country bread, as opposed to the more common (but actually less "French") baguette.

**BOUQUET GARNI:** 1 sprig of flat parsley, 2 sprigs of fresh thyme, and 1 bay leaf, tied together with string and used for flavoring (usually in stews or sauces). Tying the bundle in cheesecloth makes it easier to retrieve from the pot.

**BRAISE:** Sear and then stew.

**BRASSERIE:** A big place that serves beer or cider. An Alsatian brew pub. The French version of the Greek diner (with a similarly large, standardized menu and continuous service). One of the few good things the Germans have done for France.

**BRUNOISE:** A tiny uniform dice.

**CALVADOS:** Expensive apple brandy from France, specifically Normandy.

**CHARCUTERIE:** Sausages, pâtés, terrines, and various cured or cold meat preparations.

**CHARCUTIER:** Someone who makes any of the above products.

**CHARTREUSE:** A dinosaur-era dish usually referring to game bird and cabbage cooked and shaped in a mold. Like "napoleon," however, it can now imply any dish cooked or shaped to resemble the original. (Also the name of a liqueur.)

**CHEESECLOTH:** Gauze used for advanced straining of "fine" sauces.

**CHIFFONNADE:** An ultrathin cut that produces shredded basil, parsley, cabbage, or other greens.

**CIVET:** A dark stew of furred game, usually with red wine, bacon, and pearl onions. Classically thickened with blood.

**CLARIFIED BUTTER:** Butter that has been melted down, from which solids have been removed—so as to raise the smoking point (burns at a higher temperature). At one time, this stuff was the ubiquitous sauté medium in restaurant kitchens. Now fallen into disfavor. Its principal use these days is for hollandaise and béarnaise sauce—and for dipping lobster in at fish houses.

**CLARIFY:** As in "clarify" a consommé. The process of removing impurities from a stock or sauce (or butter). Egg whites, chopped vegetables, and lean meat (or fish) are introduced while the liquid is cold, then agitated with a whisk and slowly brought to a gentle simmer. If done right, the egg whites and other ingredients rise to the top and form a "raft," bringing along any specks, scum, and impurities with them. The "raft" is then delicately removed before the liquid is strained, leaving behind a flawlessly clear, clean product. If you haven't done this before, and are trying it for the first time, all I can say is good fucking luck.

**CONFIT:** (Usually) game bird or duck or goose, cooked (and stored) in its own fat. Once relied on as a method of preserving or conserving without refrigeration.

**CORNICHON:** That tiny, sweet-sour pickle that is inevitably sitting next to your pâté.

**COURT BOUILLON:** Flavored poaching liquid (usually water, mirepoix, maybe a few leeks, and a bouquet garni).

**CRACKLIN'S:** Crispy fried skin (most often duck or pork).

**CREME FRAICHE:** Expensive French sour cream.

**DAUBE:** A cut of meat braised in red wine. Usually neck or shoulder of beef or lamb.

**DÉBROUILLARD:** Every professional kitchen needs one. A Sergeant Bilko–like "extricator," a scrounger who can get you out of any catastrophic situation with a few smooth (if often sleazy) improvisations. Often, the *débrouillard* is a practitioner of the fabled System D (see below).

**DEGLAZE (FROM THE FRENCH DÉGLACER):** To add liquid (usually booze, or stock) to a hot pan after searing, roasting, or sautéing to loosen and incorporate the *fond*—all those crispy brown bits of pure flavor stuck to the bottom of the pan.

**DEMI-GLACE:** Once referred to a mix of reduced veal stock and *sauce espagnole* (an old-school brown sauce). Now it implies a dark, thick, greatly reduced veal or even chicken stock.

**EN SOUVIDE:** One of many dirty little secrets of the three-stars. Vacuum-sealed in plastic. God, the French love their vacuum sealers. Some very famous French restaurants—if you were to look in their refrigerators—look like the Birds Eye warehouse these days. Good for portion control, for preservation—and increasingly good to cook in. You can sear a duck breast stuffed with foie gras, for instance, put it *en souvide* in plastic, and slowly poach it like that. The plastic helps it cook gently and evenly, without the foie squirting out into a pan.

**FATBACK:** Lovely, white, uncured, unrendered pork fat.

**FOIE GRAS:** The fattened liver of a goose or duck. Unfortunately, an endangered menu item with the advent of angry, twisted, humorless anticruelty activists who've never had any kind of good sex or laughed heartily at a joke in their whole miserable lives and who are currently threatening and terrorizing chefs and their families to get the stuff banned. Likely to disappear from tables outside of France in our lifetimes.

**FOND:** The tasty brown stuff that clings to the surface of the pan after searing or sautéing or roasting. You deglaze the pan to get the *fond* into your sauce.

**FUMET:** Pretty much means fish stock.

**GARDE-MANGER:** The cold station. In pre-refrigeration days, this was where all the food was kept cool on or near ice. Now usually refers to the salad station or salad and cold appetizer person. Also refers to the art of preparing cold display platters, usually for buffets.

**HACHÉ OR HACHIS:** On a menu this word means "chopped." Steak *haché,* for instance, would be a hamburger. *Hachis* is minced meat.

**JARRET:** Shank

**JULIENNE:** A terribly misused term. Should mean a precise, matchstick-thin cut.

**LARDONS:** Thick, oblong chunks of country bacon.

**LIAISON:** The result of tempering a cold liquid with a hot one by slowly incorporating some of the hot into the cold—aside from the main body—so as to avoid breaking a sauce or substance (as with pastry cream).

**LYONNAISE POTATOES (POMMES LYONNAISE):** French home fries. Sautéed spuds with onions.

**MADEIRA:** A fortified wine, presumably made from grapes from the island of Madeira.

**MIGNON:** A little piece; usually implies from the tenderloin, as in filet mignon.

**MIREPOIX:** Standard vegetable mixture used in the beginning stages of stock making: 50 percent chopped onion, 25 percent chopped celery, and 25 percent chopped carrot. Can also refer to same as ingredient in stews or other dishes. As in: "You need more mirepoix in that stock" or "Cut me a nice mirepoix to garnish that stew!"

**MISE EN PLACE (ALSO "MEEZ"):** In French it means "put in place." This is your setup, your state of readiness, all the ingredients and utensils you will need during the service period. A way of life, the mania, the religion of all good cooks.

**MONTER AU BEURRE (FRENCH FOR "MOUNT WITH BUTTER"):** To finish a sauce with a nice wad of softened butter to give it that mellow, rounded taste and professional consistency. Usually accomplished by spooning and swirling directly into the sauce while off the heat (or on reduced heat) to emulsify and to avoid breaking the butter into its constituent elements.

**ONGLET:** Hanger steak. Also known as the "butcher's tenderloin," or the hanging tender.

**PAILLARD:** Basically a fatter cutlet.

**PALERON:** A noble, flavorful, and relatively tender cut from the shoulder of beef or veal, inexplicably called the "chicken steak" by American meat-cutters.

**PAVÉ:** A lean, fairly tender cut of beef from the center of the top butt (leg), used at Les Halles for steak au poivre (pepper steak).

**POITRINE:** Here refers to pork belly, either fresh, cured, or semicured. And a wonderful piece of meat it is. Currently in vogue at better restaurants.

**POUDRE ("POWDER"):** What more and more French three-stars are using instead of stock.

**QUENELLE:** A means for old-school French chefs to unload every scrap of nasty-ass leftovers, fish left on the bone after the fillets are gone, old poultry. It's basically extruded protein, whipped or pulverized, formed, and then poached like a gnocchi or a dumpling and usually heavily sauced. A Chicken McNugget, unbattered and then poached, might qualify as a quenelle.

**RAMEKIN:** That tiny, soufflé-mold-like thing they sometimes serve butter or jelly in at brunch.

**RILLETTES:** Boneless pork or duck or goose (most often) cooked in its own fat until it falls apart into a glorious, emulsified mush. You can eat it like a dip.

**ROUX:** The dino-era thickening agent, made from cooking flour and butter together. Looked down on these days by just about everyone.

**RUMSTECK** ("rumpsteak"): The humble cut of beef from the leg or "round" section traditionally used for steak *frites.*

**SAUTÉ:** To make jump around in the pan.

**SCALOPPINE:** Technically, a very thin cutlet made from the tenderloin or loin of veal. These days it refers to any thin slice of pounded veal or meat. (Has anyone yet seen "scaloppine of monkfish"? It's coming.)

**SEAR:** To brown all surfaces of a piece of fish or meat, either to "seal in" the juices or to add flavor, color, and texture.

**SIMPLOT CLASSIC:** The ubiquitous crap frozen French fry that just about everybody who doesn't bother to make their own fries uses these days. Sadly, the industry standard. A distant relative of the potato.

**SYSTEM D:** What MacGyver (and cooks in extremis) uses to "get out of the weeds"—meaning, any corner-cutting improvisation, shortcut, substitution, or sleazy abrogation of policy to attain one's ends. Classic French bistros, with their tiny kitchen spaces, are a breeding ground for every variety of System D trickery. A classic (and unforgivable) System D move would be to sear a duck breast stone raw, slice it, then "color" it, or finish it under the broiler or salamander. Or squeeze a medium-rare filet with one's total body weight to make it "medium." Or use a microwave for anything.

**TERRINE:** These days it pretty much means a pâté mold, typically ceramic. Or anything (usually chopped) that is cooked in a pâté mold.

**TOURNEDOS:** Used to mean the filet of beef, trimmed of all fat and the "chain," but now often refers to any fatless, boneless piece of tenderloin from any animal. One even sees "tournedos" of fish on menus, usually referring to a piece of fish cut into medallion shapes. Unless used in conjunction with "Rossini," it's often a license to steal, meaning a way to sell scraps or odd bits by giving them a fancy name.

**TROTTERS:** What the Brits call pig's feet.

**TUREEN:** A big bowl with a lid for serving soup or stew or broth.

# suppliers

**BAVARIA SAUSAGE, INC.**
**Beef and pork products, sauerkraut, sausages**

**RETAIL**
6317 Nesbitt Road
Madison, WI 53719
Tel: 608 271 1295 or 800 733 6695
Fax: 608 845 9963
www.bavariasausage.com

**CHEFSHOP**
**Beans, duck products, pink salt, spices,**
**truffle products**

**RETAIL**
305 9th Avenue North
Seattle, WA 98109
Tel: 206 286 9988 (retail store)
    877 337 2491 (orders)
Fax: 206 267 2205
www.chefshop.com

**D'ARTAGNAN**
**Cured meats, duck products, foie gras, mushrooms,**
**poultry and game birds, sausages, spices, Tarbais**
**beans, truffles, and truffle products**

**(NOT A RETAIL LOCATION)**
280 Wilson Avenue
Newark, NJ 07105
Tel: 800 327 8246 ext 0
Fax: 973 465 1870
orders@dartagnan.com
www.dartagnan.com

**DEAN & DELUCA**
**Charcuterie, cheese, foie gras, mushrooms, meat,**
**pantry items, *quatre-épices*, seafood, truffle products**

**RETAIL**
560 Broadway
New York, NY 10012
Tel: 212 226 6800

**RETAIL**
697 South St. Helena Highway
St. Helena, CA 94574
Tel: 707 967 9980

Tel orders: 800 221 7714
www.deandeluca.com

## FOSSIL FARMS

Duck, foie gras, foie gras sausages, quail, pheasant, rabbit, wild boar, and other wild game

**WAREHOUSE (OPEN TO THE PUBLIC)**

294 West Oakland Avenue
Oakland, NJ 07436
Tel: 201 651 1190
Fax: 201 651 1191
fossilfarms@aol.com
www.fossilfarms.com

## LEVILLAGE.COM

*Boudin blanc* and *boudin noir,* charcuterie, cheese, duck and duck products, foie gras, game birds and poultry, snails, truffles, and truffle products

**MAILING ADDRESS (NOT A RETAIL LOCATION)**

United Gourmets, Inc.
LeVillage
211 South Hill Drive
Brisbane, CA 94005–1255
Tel orders: 888 873 7194
Fax orders: 415 562 1137
www.levillage.com

## OTTOMANELLI

Cheese, demi-glace, duck and duck products, foie gras, game and poultry, meat, seafood, and truffle products

**RETAIL**

285 Bleecker Street
New York, NY 10014
Tel: 212 675 4217

**MAILING ADDRESS**

567 West Street
New York, NY 10014
Tel orders: 800 370 6073
ottomanelli@worldnet.att.net
www.ottomanelli.com

## SCHALLER AND WEBER

Specialty hams, sausages, smoked pork loin, slab bacon, *boudin blanc,* goose fat, real sauerkraut

1654 Second Avenue
New York, NY 10025
Tel: 212 879 3047
Fax: 212 879 9260
retail@schallerweber.com

# further reading

**The authors referred to the following books for information and inspiration while preparing this one:**

## SOURCE MATERIAL:

**LE MEILLEUR ET LE PLUS SIMPLE DE LA FRANCE**
—Joël Robuchon (Lafont)

**LA CUISINE DU MARCHE—Paul Bocuse (Flammarion)**

**THE BEST RECIPE-COOKS ILLUSTRATED**
—(Boston Common Press)

**LA CUISINE DE TERROIRS**
—Robert Jean Courtine (La Renaissance du Livre)

**LA CUISINE DES VIANDES, VOLAILLES ET GIBIERS**
—Dominique and Martine Lizambard (Solar)

## INDISPENSABLE REFERENCE:

**ON FOOD AND COOKING—Harold McGee (Fireside)**
All questions about why food behaves the way it does—when it does—answered and explained, by the ultimate food wonk/authority on such things.

**JACQUES PEPIN'S COMPLETE TECHNIQUES**
—Jacques Pépin (Black Dog and Leventhal)
Pépin is Big Daddy, the Zelig of modern French culinary history in America—and this book the Bible of basic French techniques. In a perfect world, everyone would be required to read this book before being allowed to purchase a French knife.

**THE FOOD OF FRANCE—Waverly Root (Vintage)**
Where—exactly—did this dish come from? Why? What's it like? Now you'll know.

**LAROUSSE GASTRONOMIQUE**
—Prosper Montagne (Clarkson Potter)
The argument-ender. If you ever find yourself in a

drunken brawl with a bunch of chefs or food nerds over questions of historical culinary minutiae, or "correct" ingredients, this mammoth, irreplaceable work should settle the matter. Endlessly useful. I have neatly avoided fisticuffs on many occasions by quickly producing a copy.

**THE PROFESSIONAL CHEF, 7TH EDITION**
—The Culinary Institute of America (Clarkson Potter)
The standard text from my excellent alma mater. Have I mentioned that it's the best professional culinary school in the country?

**LE REPERTOIRE DE LA CUISINE**
—Louis Saulmier (Barons Educational Series)
Don't worry. It's in English. When you can't flash the heavier *Larousse* in time, this is a lighter, more concise reference manual. It explains quickly the classic garnishes, implied ingredients, classic references.

## AND TO PUT YOU IN THE MOOD:

The following are simply timeless and wonderful reads which should put you in exactly the right frame of mind to cook and eat French Old School.

**AS THEY WERE—M.F.K. Fisher (Vintage)**

**THE APPRENTICE: MY LIFE IN THE KITCHEN**
—Jacques Pépin (Houghton Mifflin)

**THE BELLY OF PARIS—Emile Zola (Sun and Moon)**

**BETWEEN MEALS—A. J. Liebling (North Point)**

**AND LET US NEVER FORGET: JULIA CHILD. Everything started—everything changed—with her.**

# acknowledgments

First and foremost to Laurie Woolever, who translated and scaled down the recipes from their original garbled, inscrutable, food-stained form; acted as intermediary between two difficult, distracted, and very busy authors; personally wrangled all the ingredients; tested all the recipes; and in every way behaved like the lone professional in a monkey house. The book could never have been done without her.

José de Meirelles and Philippe Lajaunie were insane enough to conceive and create a restaurant specializing in raw and bleeding meat at a time when that seemed suicidal madness. They were also crazy enough—in 1998—to give me a job. To whatever unholy forces threw these characters together, I am eternally grateful. Thanks to chef de cuisine Gwenael Le Pape, who really runs the day-to-day in the kitchen at Les Halles and who deserves all the credit for its continued wonderfulness. And to the heavy lifters: butcher-*charcutier* Hubert Marie; *mis carnales,* sous-chefs Carlos Llaguno García and Omar García Rodriguez; *grillardins* Antonio Hernandez and José Bautista; "saladero" Rigoberto Pérez; plongeur Ramón López; butcher number two Ismael Martinez; and manager David Costa.

I want to thank my mom, for feeding me adventurously as a child, always cooking well and determinedly showing me (early, often, and frequently against my will) the greatness of French regional cuisine.

I couldn't do anything without Karen Rinaldi, Kim Witherspoon, David Forrer, Rose Marie Morse, Katy Keiffer, Sylvie Rabineau, Beth "Grill Bitch" Aretsky, Panio Gianopoulos, Lydia Tenaglia, Chris Collins, Diane Schutz, and Susan Burns.

Thanks to Ethan Trask and Joshua Liberson at Helicopter for their inspired, carnivore-friendly design.

Robert Discalfani took the pictures, managing to make Les Halles' food look as good and as real as it is. He spent hours in the submarine-size space of the restaurant's kitchen without pissing anybody off. In fact the cooks really like him. He recognized right away what I've always found most compelling about both food and cooks in our kitchen—and captured both as they are. No food stylist came anywhere near this project. Every plate of food you see in a photo was eaten.

I want to thank the cooks—all of them who've cooked for me in restaurants, food stalls, homes, farms, markets, and roadside stands around the world. In fact, I want to thank anybody who stands behind a stove or in front of a flame anywhere. There is no nobler toil, nor is there a better profession.

And Joel Rose started it all.

# index

# A

aïoli, 257

aïoli garnish, 209

ANCHOVIES:

    *salade niçoise,* 58–59

    *veau viennoise,* 148–49

APPETIZERS:

    *brandade de morue,* 70–71

    celery *rémoulade,* 68

    *escargots,* 72–73

    *escargots aux noix,* 74–75

    *foie gras aux pruneaux,* 88–89

    *moules,* 77

    *moules à la basquaise,* 82–83

    *moules à la grecque,* 84

    *moules à la portugaise,* 79

    *moules marinières,* 80

    *moules normande,* 78

    *oeufs périgourdins,* 69

    *pâté de campagne,* 90–92

    *pâté de lapin,* 94–95

    *petatou,* 96–97

    *rillettes,* 86–87

    *tartiflette,* 85

apples, blood sausages with, 228–29

asparagus and haricots verts salad, 62

# B

BACON:

    *frisée aux lardons,* 61

    *pommes sautées au lard,* 245

    *tartiflette,* 85

    basil oil, 261

    *bavette* (flank steak), 121

BEANS:

    asparagus and haricots verts salad, 62

    *blanquette de homard,* 109–11

    *cassoulet,* 212–14

    *salade niçoise,* 58–59

    *soupe au pistou,* 42–43

    tripes "Les Halles," 223–25

*béarnaise* sauce, 252–53

*béchamel,* sauce, 254

BEEF:

    about, 119–21

    *boeuf à la ficelle,* 122

    *boeuf bourguignon,* 202–3

    *côte de boeuf,* 120–21, 134–35

    cuts, 120–21

    *faux-filet au beurre rouge,* 129

    filet, sauce porto with roasted shallots, 136–37

    *onglet gascon,* 127–28

    *pot-au-feu,* 204–5

    *salade d'onglet,* 123–25

    steak *au poivre,* 130–31

    steak *tartare,* 133

    *tournedos rossini,* 218–19

beer, *palette de porc à la bière,* 174–75

*beurre blanc,* 258

*beurre rouge,* 129

bisque, lobster, 54–55

*blanquette de homard,* 109–11

blanquette de veau, 142–43

BLOOD AND GUTS:

    about, 222

    adding blood slowly, 208

    *boudin noir aux pommes,* 228–29

    *coeur de porc à l'Armagnac,* 227

# a note on the authors

**ANTHONY BOURDAIN** is the author of the bestselling *Kitchen Confidential,* the urban historical *Typhoid Mary,* and *A Cook's Tour,* which was turned into a successful series by the same name for the Food Network. His novels include *The Bobby Gold Stories, Bone in the Throat,* and *Gone Bamboo.* He is the executive chef at Brasserie Les Halles in New York City.

**PHILIPPE LAJAUNIE** was born in Bordeaux, France, and moved to the United States in 1984. He worked as a busboy, waiter, manager, and general manager until, in 1985, he and a partner transformed an old Italian coffee shop into a French bistro. Manhattan Bistro was an immediate success, and the following year Philippe opened Park Bistro. In 1989, he partnered with chef Jean-Michel Diot, leading to three-star reviews in the *New York Times*. By 1990, he was pursuing the idea of a simple brasserie with grilled cuts as a specialty, offering good hearty food for everyone at all hours of the day and night: Les Halles.

Born in Oporto, Portugal, **JOSÉ DE MEIRELLES** graduated from Lisbon Business School and came to the United States in 1983. He graduated from the French Culinary Institute in 1987, apprenticed at La Réserve restaurant in New York, and after a job at the Hotel Maxim's (now the Peninsula New York), he moved with chef Jean-Michel Diot to Park Bistro in 1989. Two years later, he opened Les Halles as chef partner. With Philippe Lajaunie, Meirelles also opened Les Halles in Washington, D.C., Atlanta, and Miami, and Le Marais (a French *glatt* kosher brasserie) in Times Square. He lives in New York with his wife and two children.